ANDROS ODYSSEY: LIBERATION

(1900-1940)

Stavros Boinodiris
PHD

iUniverse, Inc.
New York   Bloomington

ANDROS ODYSSEY: LIBERATION
(1900-1940)

iUniverse books may be ordered through booksellers or by contacting:

iUniverse
1663 Liberty Drive
Bloomington, IN 47403
www.iuniverse.com
1-800-Authors (1-800-288-4677)

Because of the dynamic nature of the Internet, any Web addresses or links contained in this book may have changed since publication and may no longer be valid.

ISBN: 978-1-4401-9381-1 (sc)
ISBN: 978-1-4401-9382-8 (dj)
ISBN: 978-1-4401-9385-9 (ebk)

Printed in the United States of America

iUniverse rev. date: 12/23/2009

CONTENTS

FIGURES

INTRODUCTION

WORD-OF-MOUTH TRADITION

My father Anthony was a man that had the gift of a good memory. He also liked the excitement of a good story. He talked a lot, narrating stories of what he knew, what he heard and what he read. He had a booming voice and his whole face became part of the story. Most of the people around him would characterize him a religious man with high moral standards. He would always be chanting church hymns as he did manual labor. He also had a meager education – he had not completed elementary school education- but he loved to read. Although his education was meager by his standards, elementary school education in those years was at a different standard than today's schools. Along with Greek and Turkish, the children of his school had to learn French and Arabic.

Those that knew my father up close would characterize him as a highly energetic person, to the point of hyperactivity. At times, he would start dancing, because he felt like doing so. He also was highly emotional; he would be the first to start crying in a sad situation. He was a rather impatient individual and often got in trouble by making impulsively hurried decisions. He had the great fortune though, to marry my mother, also born at the birthplace of my father, a diplomatic woman that I can characterize as the Gibraltar of my family. My mother had the capacity to remain cool and decisive, even in the most adverse situations; in such situations, she would bring balance to my father's impulsiveness, thus saving the day.

When my father reached his sixty-second birthday, he retired as a grocery store owner. He became a gardener, growing produce until his seventieth birthday. Yet, his mental energy was at the fullest, always entertaining his guests with his stories. It was then, that I decided to channel this energy, by asking him to start writing his memoirs. By the time of his death, my father had written ten, hand-written notebooks.

It took me several years before I started reading them. I was surprised with the style of his writing. Although disorganized in the order of events, his memory-derived dates and sources of information were very accurate. In comparison to him, my memory of dates and events is very poor at best. I have to rely on notes, encyclopedias, computers and other means to remember historical events, medical appointments and other daily schedules. My father could remember the names of Turks he met in Mersina seventy years earlier, people that he had not seen since then. Some entries, which I had heard before in his stories during my youth, were especially surprising this time, after I paid the proper attention to what he was saying. The excerpt below is from a translation from the fourth book of my father:

"In this notebook I am recalling what I have been told and what I remember from my childhood. I am recalling political and religious events, from the time that I started remembering events until now. My name is Anthony Boinodiris and I was born in the Old Kalivarion, or Karvali *or Gelveri as the Turks called it then, located in Nigde of Akserai in Cappadocia of Asia Minor. The name of the village today is Guzelyurt.*

Based on a word-of-mouth tradition, transferred to us by our grandparents, our origins are from the island of Andros. Our suspicions are that there is a relationship somehow between the names of our village to Kalivarion of Andros, a small community of the northwestern part of that island, but I have no concrete proof for that. Our ancestors told us that we immigrated to Cappadocia under some unknown circumstances, at an unknown time, lost in the memories of people that preceded us. Our ancestors also told us that other immigrants from islands near Andros ended in locations near ours. They identified that the people of Haskoy, a village to the northwest of Guzelyurt came from Naxos; and that the people from

Kalecik, a village to the north of Guzelyurt came from Lemnos.[1] I was told that our immigration is linked, but I was not told how."[2]

It was a challenge for me to shed some light between my father's biographical data of the 20th century to that of the historical past. I had to find out what events in history were hiding behind the Andros migration to Cappadocia. When and how did all that happen?

GOING BACK IN TIME: RETURN TO ANDROS (EAST COAST OF ATTICA, JULY, 1997)

It was a hot day in July of 1997. My wife Despina and I arrived at Andros on the ferryboat from Rafina. The trip was about two hours and very pleasant. A number of tourists were chatting loudly on the deck. A band of Greek Americans from the Chicago area were speaking in English and arguing whether the United States could use wind power, as in the Greek islands. Several windmills were visible on the top of the mountains of Evia. The tourists were looking forward to a good time at Myconos.

The ferry landed at the small port of Gavrio and started unloading cars and trucks, including my car, a 1967 Toyota Corolla. I drove this venerable car up to an almost deserted mountainside, which according to my father may once have been the stomping ground of his earlier ancestors. What struck me was the architecture of the numerous slate houses, most of them deserted, or used to house animals.

At the village called Kalivarion, there is a church, a cemetery and a handful of populated houses. The cemetery is full of Venetian-sounding names, a reminder of who populated the region after many of the Greeks departed. The place is ideal for "kalives," or sheds, used by shepherds herding animals. Thus, the name remained as "Kalivarion."

We boarded our old Toyota Corolla and drove to the city of Andros. Some of the people of Andros have distinct characteristics that are recognizable in the Kalivarion, or Karvali clans that now live in New Karvali, near Kavala, Greece; men are rather short, stocky, with rough faces, and heavy eyebrows. Cartoonists used these same heavy eyebrows in depicting the ex-Prime Minister of Greece, Constantine Karamanlis; his name also suggests that his ancestors may have come

---

1   Andros, Naxos and Lemnos are Aegean Islands.
2   A. Boinodiris, Book 4, Cover Entry.

from Cappadocia. Women are well rounded. The people are frank, direct and shrewd.

A woman, sitting in front of her house, near the ruins of the Venetian castle (Kato Kastro) of Chora, told me about its recent history during World War II: "When the Italians declared war against the Germans, they mounted a small —as she described it ironically- 'fart-cannon' on the fort, to defend the city. The Germans sent a boat over and they blew the Italian garrison to smithereens, but also causing a great deal of destruction to our homes. We had to rebuild many of the houses in town. So, what you see of that fort is what was left after the Germans were done with it."

"My father believes that our ancestors come from Andros," I said.

"Really?" she responded. "The Andrians now have three roots; the old Andrian, Italian roots and Albanian roots." She paused. "Which roots do you come from?"

Despina looked at her and smiled.

"Stavros thinks that he may have come from the old Andrian people that left this island many centuries ago, before the Italians or Albanians arrived. He is still trying to find out when and how."

She looked at me with a puzzled look and smiled. We got directions from her to the public library, but unfortunately, it had closed for the day. We left Andros and planned another trip. A year later, we entered the library. "Can I help you?" the librarian asked.

"I would like to see Mr. Dimitris Polemis please," I replied. Dimitris Polemis is a known historian from Andros and the supervisor of the local library. The librarian led me to the library office. She pointed to a man sitting behind the office.

"I am Stavros Boinodiris. I called you yesterday."

"Yes. Have a seat. How can I help you?" I told him about my father and his notes.

"My father claims that the original people of Gelveri in Cappadocia came from Andros. They specifically name Kalivarion as the source. There is also a connecting heritage for some locations in Asia Minor, which have links to Lemnos and Naxos."

"This is interesting. I happen to know Gelveri in Cappadocia. Have you been there?"

"No."

"You must go. I did." He looked at me intensely. "I have no historical evidence that Kalivarion existed before the Albanian migration here. The only known ancient place nearby is that of Amolochos. Even then, this island is quite a distance from Cappadocia. It does not look likely that people from here would simply travel to Cappadocia. Do you have any other historical evidence?"

"No. That is why I came to you. One possible source may be that of Theophanes the Confessor, dealing with the period of Kosmas."[3]

"I studied Theophanes. There is not much there about Kosmas. Theophanes does not talk much of Andros."

"Are there any other possible sources?" I asked.

"I suggest you read some of the literature of other immigrants from that area. There is a Center of Asia Minor Studies in Athens. They published a book, titled: 'Religious Life in the Region of Akserai –Gelveri.' I believe we have a copy here." He walked out, towards the bookshelves, as I followed. "Here it is."

I thanked him after he handed me the book, got a copy of the front page and started scanning through it. It covered the recent century with details of religious life in Cappadocia. My mind started wondering. *"Is it possible that the stories propagated from generation to generation on the journey of these Andrians are true?"*

I signed the library visitor's book and departed. My mind was still spinning, as I boarded the ferry, going back to the Greek mainland at Rafina. *"Suppose that these people were trying to tell us their story starting from their beginnings in this island. Why is there no record of this? There are three possibilities: either it did not occur, or it occurred and the information was lost, or someone had tried to suppress this information from the historians of that time. "*

My research had just begun.

It was summer of 1998, when I sat at my computer at Schinias, a coastal resort area near Athens. I was wondering how to explain the ten, handwritten notebooks that my father Anthony left to me. He scribbled the books in Greek on regular notebooks, jumping from fact to hearsay, from one war to another and from one disaster to another. My father had facts describing his own experience, or the experience of

---

3   The first section of this book covered the "Kosmas revolt," an event of 725 AD.

people he talked to on occasion. Many times, he repeated his story. Yet, he was consistent. He always explained how and when he experienced what he wrote. In every instance, where his information was hearsay, he reported how he received it and from whom.

I had two choices, regarding the content of his work:

Write only the facts experienced by my father and others, and scrapping any unsubstantiated stories. This would be a purist approach, loved by historians, like Mr. Polemis.

Write about the facts experienced by Anthony and others, but include the stories passed down to us. To avoid offending purists, I felt that I had to warn the reader when I was presenting information based on word-of-mouth tradition.

I chose the second option. In addition to my father's data, I added my own memories and those of my mother's. To distinguish facts from fiction, I used some different text formatting as follows:

All **fictional characters**, added to build up the story I present in bold text, as shown in this sentence. I ask the reader to treat such sections with such bold entries as fiction.

These books are an attempt to connect the real experience of a few families, burdened with an unwritten tradition, passed on from generation to generation. It is a testament to the human endeavor to survive and create their own way of life in the face of forced migration, wars, hunger, oppression and violence. It takes place over a period of 1300 years and on four continents.

The purpose of this book is threefold. First, to shed some light on this mystery of the Greeks of Kalivarion, or Gelveri; second, to shed some light into this not so well-known time and place of human history; and third, by viewing a story in terms of a very long period, in relationship to world events, to experience how slowly humans have evolved. It shows how many of the issues that our ancestors dealt with are still with us. As Dr. K. Wright said, "… it is depressing to see how slow our progress has been. Youngsters reading this book must be very frustrated, as they have a gleam in their eye in improving the world. Human behavior is changing, not in terms of months or years, but in terms of centuries, over many generations of youngsters, with the same gleam in their eyes."

Human progress has been slow, if someone does not look at history with the right lens. During the four million years –give or take a million years- of human existence, we have come a long way and should be proud of it. Humans, like most other species cannot evolve faster than evolution permits. We need time to alter our primitive instincts and tendencies to violence through rational thought. The 1300 years covered in this series, is just an instance in the evolutionary timescale and it should not depress us. We simply cannot experience human progress in a single lifetime. Human progress can occur only through long term planning, involving multiple generations. We can see this, only by looking at history with the macro-lens, used in the Andros Odyssey series. We must see how our ancestors worked out multi-generational planning. To achieve this goal, "ignorance of our past is by no means bliss." Unless we know how we dealt with our problems in our own historical past, we and our youngsters cannot plan correctly. Our "success in surviving as a species as long as possible," must be widely supported and be a patient, multi-generational process.

This definition of success may seem simplistic, but that is what our own human history and our accumulated knowledge of our environment tell us. We know that no matter how much effort we place in our survival and progress, all we can achieve is a minute step forward, as this step compares with the bigger picture of human survival. Besides that, we are one of many living organisms on this earth, most of which became extinct trying to survive. The mighty dinosaurs that ruled the earth for millions of years vanished in this inhospitable environment. According to the best scientists, our own earth and our solar system have limited life span. Our own universe is doomed to oblivion. Yet, no human, from birth to death thinks of doing anything else but be part of the Human Odyssey, because some strange evolutionary laws drive us.

What evolutionary drive makes us be who we are?

Are we driven by survival and pleasure of life, over which we have no control? Are we driven by curiosity on the mystery of life (thirst of knowledge on how things turn out, no matter what the outcome)? Are we ignoring the long-term demise of our species with the hope that somehow a miracle would save us? Are we driven by a belief that somewhere there is a Supreme Being with a reason for all this and that there is another dimension of life, after our departure from this world?

No matter, what your beliefs are, be patient. You are part of a Human Odyssey. Enjoy every minute of it. You are programmed to do that by evolutionary instincts. The way we can best observe these evolutionary instincts is to pay attention to children. Children think neither of their past, nor of their future. They concentrate on things that grownups seldom do: enjoying the present.

Andros Odyssey is a tiny part of my Human Odyssey. Whether you know it or not, there is a good chance that your Odyssey probably relates to mine, even in the not so distant past. Chances are that some of your ancestors are part of the millions of Byzantines, mostly Greeks who, between 1200 AD and the 1900s made their way throughout the globe.

The evidence of Byzantine Greek influence is all around you. The Greek roots in the English language, or other European languages are by no means an accident. Neither is the way of Western thinking, as it compares with the thinking of other civilizations. People can learn a lot, by simply observing and questioning some common occurrences around them.

DEDICATION AND ACKNOWLEDGMENTS

These books would not exist without the heritage passed to me by my parents. My father worked on his notes for twenty years, until he could not write any more.

Thanks to all of my friends and relatives in North Carolina and in Greece for their encouragement and help. Special thanks are due to my wife and my niece, Dr. Kathryn Wright, both of whom contributed to the enrichment of the book.

This book is a heritage to my children Phaedra and Ismini, and grandchildren Athena, Sebastian and Persephone passed in a manner similar to that exercised by my ancestors throughout the millennia. I am proud to be part of that tradition.

Stavros Boinodiris
February 2007

PROLOGUE

SUMMARY OF ANDROS ODYSSEY: BYZANTINE KALIVARION

During the evolutionary years of Christianity, as the religion was embracing a multitude of nationalities with idolatrous backgrounds, Byzantium struggled to unify and defend its people from the Islamic onslaught. Several ethnic and religious rebellions forced Byzantine emperors to take drastic measures.

One of the many religious rebellions involved "icon worship" in the Greek Islands. After a rebellion by Kosmas, a leader from the Greek islands, Emperor Leo the Isaurian, himself an immigrant from a region of northern Syria, decided to put a stop to all this by secretly dispersing all the icon worshiping rebels, who demanded freedom of artistic expression, from the islands of Andros, Lemnos and Naxos. The forced exile was secret, to avoid further internal rebellions by the other followers of icon worship. In this manner, this event went unnoticed by historians of that period. With an imperial edict for a forced exile, the Psellus family was shipped to Cappadocia, together with many other inhabitants of Andros.

The exiles from Andros established Kalivarion, a Cappadocian colony, naming it after their own home village in Andros. They built a community in caves, utilizing techniques used previously by the local population there, but by adding their own architecture, known from the islands. The people of Lemnos and Naxos formed similar colonies near-by, with the exception that they were established in open, fertile plains and unprotected from invaders. The exile split the Psellus family into two branches, one in Cappadocia and the remaining in Andros.

Both branches of the Psellus family survive four centuries (700-1100 AD) of Byzantine turmoil and struggle. The Cappadocian branch of the Psellus family married into a family from Amorium. When the Arabs destroyed Amorium, part of the Cappadocian Psellus family ended up in Constantinople, working around the Palace. As cooks, instructors, servants and officials they experienced the struggle between Christianity and idolatry and between faith and superstition that took place during that period. They also experienced the ambition, intrigue, treachery and murder plots machinated by the people running the Byzantine Empire.

The Andrian branch of the Psellus family became well known because of Michael Psellus the Elder (780 AD-862 AD), a famous scholar and teacher of the Andros Academy. After repeated attacks by Saracen pirates on Andros, the Psellus family migrated to Constantinople, where they also found work near the Palace. Eventually, in the 9th century, the families reunited.

One of the Psellus family members from Andros participated in the expedition by Emperor Nikiforos Focas to liberate Crete, in 960 AD. Among the liberated Saracen slaves was an illegitimate son of a Greek slave girl. He was adopted by another slave, who took his name, namely **Stravolemis**. The **Stravolemis** family was established when this slave boy, after a profitable raid into Syria built up his wealth as an Arabian horse trainer and dealer. He married into the Cappadocian Psellus family and settled in Kalivarion, where he took over some of the family property.

The Psellus family went through its brightest and darkest period between 970 and 1070 AD. They were now closely involved with the Palace, during the reign of John Tsimiskis, Basil Bulgaroctonus, Basil's brother Constantine VIII and the destruction that followed, after the battle of Manzikert, when in 1071 AD the Seljuk Turks defeated the Byzantine Army.[4] The one that came closest to running the political machine of Byzantium was Constantine Psellus. Young Constantine and a number of his friends collaborated with each other.

---

4   Manzikert is today's Malazgirt, Turkey, north of Lake Van in Asia Minor.

Constantine Psellus became Consul of Philosophers. Because of him and his friends, Emperor Constantine Monomachos endowed the Chairs of Philosophy and Law at the University at Magnaura. The University opened the door to many in a renaissance of learning, because education at the University was now free and available to all who had the ability. Constantine Psellus soon entered the Imperial service where his quick intellect and profound scholarship promoted him to high posts. Constantine Monomachos and many other emperors admired his eloquence. He became a Secretary of State, Grand Chamberlain and Prime Minister. He led the delegates to present the throne to Isaac Comnenus, a task that required extremely high diplomacy. He composed the accusation against the haughty Cerularius, who as Patriarch had rebuffed a Pope and brought the final blow to the schism between the Churches of Constantinople and Rome.

Suddenly, everything fell apart for Constantine Psellus- also known as Michael Psellus. He joined the monastic life and changed his name to Michael Psellus. Yet, he still carried the burden of his obsession to be faithful to his friends in the government, no matter where that was leading him. He secured the deposition of Romanus Diogenes and made sure that his friend Michael Ducas took his place on the throne, betraying Romanus and causing the disaster at Manzikert. Then, all his friends gave up on him. Even Michael Ducas sought his demotion. After his seclusion, Michael Psellus ended up writing the history of those trying times. As a historian, he wrote events, which he not only experienced, but also frequently helped to shape and control. In his historical works, he was so extremely observant in detail, that he could bring a character to life with a few words.

After the disaster at Manzikert, most people saw Michael Psellus, not as a distinguished historian and politician, but as a person, who led the Empire to ruin. As a result, the whole family changed their name to **Megas,** to avoid humiliation.

SUMMARY OF ANDROS ODYSSEY: BYZANTIUM UNDER SIEGE

The saga of the **Megas** and **Stravolemis** families continues as the families faced the insanity and destructive forces of the Crusades. The holy wars of Islam, which expanded through war and forced conversions led to the Crusades, after the Normans appeared in Italy.

Early Muslim expansion was always by the power of the sword, but the Byzantines held. Then the Normans, a new expansionist force from the West appears, with eyes to the riches of the East. After relentless attacks on Byzantium from the West, the Muslims in the East weaken the Byzantines to the point that they cannot hold the attacks. They ask from some help and they get the invasion of the Crusades.

This invasion was initially a series of holy wars to counter Islam. The Byzantium-based families from Andros suffer during the crusader attacks. In one raid, the son of the crusader ruler violates a local girl, before they capture him and kill him. News of the girl's bastard son reaches Thoros, the brother of the rapist. He helps the boy by giving him his father's name (**Leonides** or Leo's offspring) and opportunity to expand a trade business in Cilicia.

The **Megas** families of Constantinople survived the crusader occupation between 1203 and 1261 AD and some of their members participated in counter-attacks against the crusaders under the leadership of the epileptic Emperors of Nicaea. By the time Constantinople was liberated, the Byzantine state was in ruins. In spite of the situation, the Byzantines, now primarily consisting of Hellenic background counter-attacked in the Aegean and regained control of some territories. The Cappadocian families are living in their caves in a defensive posture against Turks, Mongols and crusaders alike. Many other Greeks from the Pontic Mountains find refuge there, after repeated Mongol attacks, which subjugated the Seljuk Turks. The only ones that were thriving were the **Leonides** family in Cilicia, doing business, which had extended its borders and trade into Cappadocia under Mongol protection. The **Leonides** family soon finds itself trading and helping their relatives in Kalivarion. They are soon involved in trade with the Lusignan and the Ibelin families of Cyprus. In their trade business and because of their links to the King Hetoum of Cilicia who was a Mongol ally, they become knowledgeable of Eastern caravan routes to China and meet with Venetian traders like the Polos, who use their valuable knowledge. In an attempt to stop western aggression, the Byzantines were by now actively seeking the reunification of Churches. Facing the Turkish invasion, the **Leonides** family retreated from Cilicia into the caves of Cappadocia. After the Turkish occupation of Cappadocia, the **Leonides** family were renamed the **Aslanoglou** family and the **Stravolemis** were renamed the **Boyun-egri-oglou** family.

As the Turks reoccupied Asia Minor, Constantinople became a battleground between Genoese and Venetian business interests. In spite of repeated pleas to the West for help and a humiliating submission of the Byzantine Emperor to the Catholic Church, help from the West came too little, too late. Even after the Mongol intervention by Tamerland, which resulted in a temporary defeat of the Turks, the West refused to help Byzantium, resulting in the fall of Constantinople to the Turks. Several male members of Megas families in Constantinople were involved in the defense of the City, after sending their families to the Princess Islands in the Sea of Marmara. Some of these men fought and died with their City under the rumble of a new, terrible weapon: the cannon. As the Greek, Genoese and Venetian galleys retreated, the survivors became a source of spirited search for freedom and determined source of resistance against the Turks. One Greek-Genoese family from Chios, the Colon family (later to become Columbus), became raiders against Turkish ships and advanced their knowledge and skills in navigation to the art of exploration. Among the retreating men of the **Megas** families, there were two, whose families survived in the Princess Islands as fishermen. Under the Turkish occupation, the families of these men had to change their names to the **Magioglou** and the **Meroglou** families.

The families in these islands and in Cappadocia survived under a very repressive Ottoman occupation. Almost everything was stacked against them in trying to retain their identities, all but their Hellenic culture and their insatiable thirst for knowledge.

SUMMARY OF ANDROS ODYSSEY: UNDER OTTOMAN RULE

The families, after the fall of Constantinople are experiencing the Ottoman oppression, while the Turks, as conquerors treat them as their slaves and forcing their children to convert and become Janissaries (converted soldiers) through well-established methods of abduction and conversion. Millions of Greeks from Byzantium continue to escape abroad, dispersing into Europe and from there to other continents, spreading their knowledge, expertise and solidifying the effects of Western European renaissance. As the effects of mass exodus were felt, the alarmed Sultans become smarter in dealing with minorities, by trying to stop the mass exodus of Christians, by curtailing slavery and corruption and by trying to reverse it. The only success in the reversal of the population loss came through the enticement of other suppressed minorities abroad, like the oppressed Jews of Europe and the rich rewards of government-sponsored piracy to entice men of fortune to become Barbary pirates.

Meanwhile, through continuous Islamic pressure for conversion, a significant portion of the remaining Greeks converts to Islam, whether willingly, or by coercion and they, together with other minorities become a major contributor to the power that drives the Ottoman Empire to expand its borders from Venice, to Persia and from Africa to Austria.

The remaining Greeks within the Ottoman Empire endure a very patient waiting game using education as their only weapon. While they wait, they use their skills to make themselves indispensable for the Operation of the Empire as interpreters, functionaries, educators, political analysts, bankers and sea merchants. They also drive the legal reorganization of the Ottoman Empire. They attempt to convert it from the religious Koran-based Shariah law to the secular, Byzantine-based cannon law. These skills place them in positions where they are aware of all the intricacies within the Ottoman system of government. Through small, but calculated moves they prepare secret alliances of the Greek minority within the Ottoman Empire with external powers. These powers include the Pope, Venice, Austria, England, the Dutch Protestants and finally Russia.

External powers offered some means of pressure on the uncontrollable mistreatment of Christian populations by the Ottoman Sultans. One power that played a major role was Venice, who occupied major portions of Greece at various times. Their struggle to hold their power helped the Greeks to maintain their identity.

The stark difference between the mistreated Christians who were de facto slaves by conquest and the invited Jewish minorities remained for centuries. Their competition was utilized by the Ottomans to divide these minorities within the Empire and to check any tendencies for rebellion. Educated Sephardic Jews competed for the same posts as Greeks. Some of them, like Joseph Nasi, the Duke of Naxos, established the first autonomous Jewish ruling authority in Tiberias, Palestine for many centuries. Christians saw with jealousy the Jewish alliance with the Ottomans, causing a further rift between Christian and Jewish Ottoman minorities.

In spite of their internal controls, the rebellion against absolute and corrupt rulers came from abroad, after the American and French Revolutions. Greek sailors and students abroad brought in new ideas on how to achieve independence. In spite of the suppression of Patriarchal authority a network of monasteries and secret schools started operating under a new national movement. Through a low key, coordinated effort the naval skills of the Greeks are transferred to Russia. After a long struggle and in spite of English opposition, Russia manages to emerge as a major naval power in the Mediterranean. The Russians get support from the West, including that from John Paul Jones of the American Navy. Finally, Russia becomes a de facto protector of all Orthodox Christian minorities of the Ottoman Empire.

Meanwhile, the rest of the world, including the Americans, fed up with the Sultan's state-supported policy of piracy within the Mediterranean, are now embarking on an all out attack on the Barbary Coast. The first Americans that die on foreign soil die in the Middle East, fighting pirates, supported by the Ottomans.

Under the Russian protection and the indispensable position gained within the Ottoman Empire, the enslaved Greeks emerge as opportunist merchants who broke through naval blockades, pirated enemy vessels and competed effectively with some of the best navies of that time. With every year that passed, progress was rapid. Greek seafarers made a lot of money but they also gained further knowledge and experience and they sought to advance and refine their ships and their men in warfare against the pirates, as they had no navy to protect them. Their new, revitalized spirit made the Greek seamen feel free; the growth of their merchant fleet gave them confidence; their success in fighting off pirates and others to reach their destinations with loaded ships made them feel more independent. Through that spirit of independence and after several failures, they prepared themselves to gain independence, while at the same time they undermined the Ottoman Empire.

The Greek struggle for independence began in 1821 and lasted seven years. Besides sacrificing all they had, they borrowed 2.3 million pounds, expecting that the entire Hellenic nation of about seven million to become responsible and pay off the loan under a solid government of their own. From that, less than one million pounds reached the Greeks. In desperation, they negotiated the loan as "a hopeless affair" at the exorbitant rate of fifty-nine and fifty-five-percent. They spent this sum immediately in the purchase of materials for carrying on the war. When the war ended, a little more than one-fifth of the people who had looked for freedom received it and a little more than a third of the territory fought for was freed, and less than a million people found themselves responsible for the payment of a debt which had been contracted assuming several millions. This raw deal was compounded by the fact that Greece was excluded from the money markets of Europe and had a difficult task to be self sufficient, under the disadvantages of a small territory and sparse population. About a fourth of the population lived by agricultural pursuits on a very small, mountainous and ravaged land. Her merchant marine was engaged in the trade with ports of the Aegean, which Turkey taxed and controlled. The poverty of her people, the feeble resources, the influences of old customs and habits failed to fulfill the unreasonable expectations of enthusiastic Philhellenes.

The liberation on the small piece of land below Thessaly did not mean prosperity for the remaining, much larger Christian population under the Sultan. These people were now under very strict scrutiny, sometimes looked upon as spies and enemy supporters by the Turks. Initially, as the war of independence raged on, fanatic Turkish elements attempted to exterminate them, a village at a time, so that they would be inconspicuous in the eyes of the protecting Russian Czar. Other Turkish elements, sensing a weakened Sultan, began to plan the formation of their own independent states, like Ali Pasha of Albania. Many Christians took to the mountains and became bandits, to escape persecution from the chaos, which characterized the Ottoman Empire of the 19th century. In Constantinople, the prosperous Magioglou family is now out of a job. They can no longer be trusted to serve the Porte as interpreters and advisors. The people of Kalivarion of Cappadocia are under attack from rogue Ottoman generals who hate Greeks. What saves them is their location, their skill to negotiate at the highest level and sheer luck.

In spite of the difficulties, within thirty-five or forty years of freedom, Greece doubled her population and increased her revenues five hundred per cent. They founded eleven new cities on deserted sites. They rebuilt more than forty towns, reduced to ruins by the war. Some roads have replaced the foot and saddle paths that were the sole avenues of communication under the Turks, and telegraphic communication were extended over the kingdom. Eight or ten ports have been cleared, deepened and opened to communication. Meanwhile, the Russians defeat the Turks and the Treaty of Saint Stefano of 1878 begins to bring added pressure on the Sultan by liberating more Balkan nations.

As Greece was recovering, the first modern Olympics gets kicked off, bringing in international focus on this small part of the world and helping the people of Crete and some islands achieve independence. As the Sultan turns his attention away from Greece and towards his numerous problems at the East and with Russia, one member of the Magioglou family of Constantinople is involved in the modernization of the Ottoman transportation system, using railroads. Eager to regain trust and fame within the Ottoman circles, John Magioglou puts himself to work on the railroad, even at the cost of family and heritage. This causes internal family problems, which will continue into the Magioglou saga of the 20th century.

The families, starting from even before 1800, are now real, documented people, with biographical excerpts, covered by the written material of the author's father. Thus, the latter part of this book is no longer a historical novel, but a historical biography of a group of people who lived and left their mark, as the world was about to enter the 20th century.

EARLY MEMORIES

DRAMA UNDER OTTOMAN RULE (DRAMA, MACEDONIA, 1900)[5]

Drama is a small town in Macedonia, 15 kilometers NW of Philippi, and known from Apostle Paul's letters to their citizens. During Roman times, the city was an important stop on the road network within the extensive colony known as Dravescos. From the large number of Gods in the Greco-Roman pantheon, worshiped in the area, it is Dionysus who stood out. The worship of the god of the vine and wine continued until later Roman years, identified with the Roman deity "Liber Pater" in votive dedications, which have been found in the wider area of Drama.

During the early Christian period (4th -7th century AD), Drama was a small, fortified town, which occupied roughly the same area as the settlement from the classical period. Being the most important settlement in the fertile valley of Philippi, it was, in administrative terms, part of the Roman colony of Philippi. This colony was founded following the battle of Philippi in 42 AD, which was decisive for the course of Roman history.

The colony became universally known with the passage of the Apostle Paul and his retinue through Philippi in the winter of 49 AD and the establishment of the first Christian church. The Christian community in

---

5   The story was taken from A. Boinodiris' notes. He in turn heard it from Angelos Mavrides, an old-timer, born in the 1870s in Drama. He was repeating this story as it was passed from his ancestry and as he experienced it.

Philippi developed gradually into a strong center of the new religion with many bishops. The fortified town of Drama fell within this diocese, the size of the town approaching that of the area protected by the Byzantine walls whose ruins we can still see today. During the mid Byzantine period (9th -13th century AD) Drama developed into a strong-castled garrison town with strategic importance and a vibrant commercial life.

The town was a fortified plateau enclosed by walls occupying roughly 40,000 square meters with a population of 1,500- 2,000 and home of a military governor charged with monitoring the surrounding area. Written sources from the end of this period, which survived, give the names "Darma" (1172) and "Dramme" (1206) for the Castle, which has links with the probable ancient name, but also with its present day name.

During the first half of the 14th century there were disturbances and conflict as part of the Byzantine civil wars between Andronicus II and III Paleologos (1321-1328) and later between Ioannis Kantakouzinos and members of the Paleologos dynasty (1341-1347). During these years Drama was home to Empress Irene, wife of Andronicus II, who later died and was buried in the castle around the first twenty years of the 14th century.

Drama first appeared as an archdiocese, independent of the control of Philippi, during the reign of Michael VIII Paleologos (1258-1282). It is thought that during this time that it developed into an important ecclesiastical and military center. During the years 1344-1345 the Serb prince Stefan Dousan conquered it. Retaken in 1371 by Manuel Paleologos, it remained in the hands of the Byzantine Empire until its capture by the Ottomans in 1383.

Following the capture of the city of Drama by the Ottomans in 1383, it continued to be a small castle in the vast territory of the Sultan, cut off from Constantinople until the fall of the city in 1453 and from Thessaloniki until its conquest in 1430. Gradually, the Christians who made up 80% of the population even during the 15th century began to decrease in numbers due to flight abroad and into the mountains. The number of Christians there in the 16th century was around 40% with the Muslim population constantly increasing and taking over a large area within the otherwise Christian castle.

Heavy taxes, poor administration of resources and frequent robbery attacks caused the residents of the city to feel insecure, effectively slowing down the development of the agricultural economy until the beginning of the 18th century. However, according to the Ottoman traveler Tselembi the city began to expand outside the limits of the old Byzantine walls or the "Varosi" as they were known, creating new Muslim neighborhoods.

By the 17th century a market has been created between the Christian and the Muslim areas around the drainage gulch, which crossed the center of the city. Today, part of the stream has been paved over and it is a roadway.

During the 18th century, the increased agricultural production combined with the operation of small workshops and industries in the city gave the place a new breath of life in terms of commerce. Based on data for other areas in Macedonia, it is safe to assume that the population in Drama increased at this time, mainly among the Muslims, while the Muslim neighborhoods both inside and outside the walls increased in size.

Nonetheless, poor administration and taxation of the residents by powerful landowners did not permit the real economic growth of the city. Even though Drama was the capital of a large region during the 19th century with administrative authorities, courts and the army it could not compete with the port of Kavala as a transit center for the wider area. Major changes took place in the city following 1879 when the production and trade in tobacco brought about an increase in population and strengthened commerce. The arrival of the railway in 1895 and the improvement of the roads to the port of Kavala connected Drama to the large centers of the empire and the commercial sea routes. Large tobacco-trading firms established branches in Drama, tobacco storehouses were built, banks opened offices here, and in England there was even a vice consulate representing the city.

Soon new neighborhoods were created around the waters of Aghia Barbara, and to the West of the walled area in order to meet the needs of a population which now reached 6,000- 7,000. The new residents, Muslims, Christians and Jews, formed separate residential areas in accordance with the practice widespread in the Ottoman Empire. The Christians, whose numbers were constantly being added to by families from Western Macedonia and from Epirus in particular, numbered at least 200 in 1880 and they lived within the old walls and south of the Aghia Barbara area.

The Muslims were concentrated to the west of the market and the Jews settled in the area around the waters of Aghia Barbara. The new public buildings and private residences erected at this time reflect economic prosperity and the influences of European trends. The Greek community during the period 1870 to liberation was marked by its economic development, the formation of educational societies, the construction of schools, and by its charitable bodies.

Since the 15th century, when the Turks invaded the town of Drama, there was a Byzantine church called Aghia Sophia. The Turks turned it into a Mosque, which was named Hissar Tzami (Mosque of the Fort) since it was close to Drama's ancient Byzantine walls.

Centuries later the Christians were allowed to build churches, but not allowed to have bells. The church of Aghia Sophia, which was taken by force from the Greeks, was still used as a Mosque.[6]

After the Treaty of San Stefano (1878) that granted Russia their demands against Turkey, the Christians from Drama sent a letter to the Sultan requesting that the church be returned to them. The Sultan did nothing.

The letter then was copied to the Russian, Italian and French Embassies, which were at the time residing in Kavala. They pressed the matter to the Turkish courts which finally gave them back Aghia Sophia but rejected the request from the Greeks to be able to install a bell tower in their churches. Yet, they allowed the Catholic Church to have a small, flat piece of iron, hanging from a tree, used as a bell. The Catholic Church was used by a small contingent of French and Italian families of engineers who came over to help manage the newly constructed railroads.

In 1900, the Sultan assigned a regional governor in Drama, namely Hamid. The Christians of Drama took the case of bell towers to him since he seemed to be more progressive than anyone before. The Turks at that time had eight mosques, while the Greeks had four churches. While the Moslems had the right to call upon the faithful from the minaret, the Christians could not use a bell.

---

6   This is from narration of actual Drama resident of the 1900s. His name was Angelos Mavroudis. He and other men of Drama were involved in the Macedonian Wars (1904-1910) against the Bulgarians, under Paul Melas. Bishops at that time were Agathangelos and Chrysostomos.

Hamid set up a meeting with the Christians where Agathangelos, the bishop of Drama, and the Church leaders presented their case. They were all worried about the reaction of the Moslem population in building the bell tower, and upon hearing the bell. Hamid gave a permit to build the bell tower with the stipulation that all preparations are done in secret. The Christians had made the bell and they were ready. Then Hamid, along with the chief of police, made his appearance on Sunday to inaugurate the installation of the bell.

When the Turks heard it, they were surprised. When they realized what it was, they became furious and a mob marched to the church, ready to tear it up and to lynch anyone that brought resistance. What they saw were two Turks, the governor and the chief of police ringing the bell in front of a whole detachment of police force. Stunned from their surprise, they became silent and eventually left. Gradually, over a period of six months, more bell towers were installed, one in each church.

The Turkish leaders immediately sent petitions to the Sultan, requesting that he removes Hamid as a governor. Their wish was granted. Hamid was out within six months, but the bells stayed.

Figure 1 Aghia Sophia, as it Stands Today in Drama.

THE BOYFRIEND (MAGIOGLOU HOUSEHOLD, CONSTANTINOPLE, FEBRUARY, 1905)

"What is wrong with you?" asked Pandelis, his eyes bulging. He was quite a rebellious eleven-year old, who in this case could not stand to see his sister be like him. "What did you find in that Cappadocian peasant? I cannot stand seeing mother in tears because of you." He paused and looked at his sister with a rude, determined look.

Pandelis Magioglou[7] was the son of a relatively elite Greek family in Constantinople. His father, Haji John (1847-1920) Magioglou was closely related to the Magioglou family of Kalivarion and he was a director of a large railroad construction project for the Ottoman Empire. His mother was Makrina Suzanoglou,[8] a rather rebellious woman at that time. Pandelis' grandfather, Uzun George Magioglou was the person that became the best man in the wedding of an adopted Cappadocian man, Paul Boyun-egri-oglou; he later introduced Dimitris Tsolakoglou, a wealthy merchant, to his bride Katina, Paul's daughter.

Pandelis' childhood encounter with George Boyun-egri-oglou, Paul's son ended up in a dispute, which Pandelis expressed in his utter dislike of George. George's sister Orsia, now in Constantinople, managed to talk to Dimitris Tsolakoglou to bring her young brother near her, to be trained in his business. In 1903, the twenty-two-year old George arrived in Constantinople and started working as an errand boy. His goal was to collect enough money to escape the Turkish Army by fleeing to Russia, using his brother in law's connections. George was a handsome young man. He was stocky in stature, of average height and weight, and had the strength of a weightlifter. He was quite religious and superstitious and had no major visible vices, except one:

---

7   Pandelis Magioglou, also know as Pandel Mayo was born on the 15 Aug 1893 in Constantinople and died in October 1984 at Pompano Beach, Florida, USA.

8   As, Anthony Boinodiris writes, "My grandmother Makrina was one of three Suzanoglou sisters. One of her sisters was Kyriaki Suzanoglou, who was a midwife. She had a grandson who later lived in Nea Karvali and was named George Galaktides. The other sister was Susanna, who had two grandsons. One grandson later lived in Drama, named Anestis Karakoulahis. The other, Basil Kiourtzoglou came to Metamorphosis, Athens ." A. Boinodiris, Book 1, p. 296.

he liked women. He simply could not do without the company of a girl, especially in the evenings. Being in Constantinople for the first time was quite a temptation. Very soon, he started courting secretly the fifteen-year-old Evanthia, Pandelis' sister, who saw him as a breath of fresh air from her dysfunctional family, and a possible escape from them.

"Oh! Shut up!" yelled Evanthia. "This has nothing to do with you." It was obvious to most her friends that Evanthia did not like her family very much, and especially her bully brother. Evanthia's father acquired the name Haji because he had gone to Jerusalem on a pilgrimage, but he actually went there because of his work. As a result, the family became dysfunctional when her workaholic father decided to prioritize his work over his family life. Her father became a powerful, rich and strong-minded individual who served the Ottoman government faithfully. He also expected to run his home like a railroad. He was very autocratic, requiring his wife and children to follow his rules on time and to the letter. He spent little time at home, forcing his wife to dedicate herself to her children. After repeated home arguments and fights with his rebellious wife, she decided to get back at him by turning his son, his pride and joy, against him. The bond between mother and son became so strong, that marginalized Evanthia. Her mother over indulged her brother from babyhood.

Evanthia simply could not stand living in that household any longer. She wanted to get away from her family, her father and her spoiled brat brother. She found a way out, by sneaking off, often to Orsia Tsolakoglou's home where she spent many hours secretly with her lover George. None from her family seemed to care about her other than her bully brother. One day, Pandelis saw Evanthia exiting the Tsolakoglou home with George and told her mother. She immediately placed her under curfew, prohibiting her to see George again. That did not stop Evanthia.

The previous summer, she had left to go to a girlfriend's, but instead, she spent several weekends with George in one of their secret hideouts. Soon, the results of those blissful encounters showed up in morning sickness. Amazingly enough, none noticed her condition for quite awhile. She had to tell her mother that she was expecting a baby. Within minutes, the whole family knew about it. Immediately, Haji-

John called all the family members in a meeting at the kitchen table. After yelling at his daughter and his weeping wife for almost two hours, blaming them for what happened, he set up the rules. Evanthia does not step outside her home until further orders.

Pandelis could not control his anger. "If I see him, I will straighten him out!" he yelled.

It was time for his father to step in. "You are grounded also," he yelled to his son. "I do not want any of this to reach anyone's ears, until I have a meeting with your grandfather." He rose up from the family table and exited the house, quite upset, slamming the door behind him. He could not afford a scandal. He had a rebellious pregnant daughter, a wife whose methods he did not approve, and a son who turned up becoming a brat and a bully. On top of that, he had to go and meet with the German military adviser on railroads in Constantinople, someone named Auler Pasha, to secure additional funds for his projects on the railroad. He waved to the first horse carriage he saw and headed for his father's home.

Minutes later he was talking to his father, who was not sympathetic with him at all. "You caused all this," said George Magioglou. "If you paid a little more attention to your family and less to your toy trains, this would not have happened. I know the Boyun-egri-oglou family. They are not refined, but they are honest, hard working peasants. How do you expect me to go and badmouth them to Dimitris, when I introduced the family to him? I was the matchmaker and best man for his wedding."

"I wish we never met them," said his son, looking at the floor. He did not accept the blame that his father laid on him. In fact, he thought of his father as a fool with a sentimental old-timer mentality. "Now what are we going to do?"

"We will do what we must," said George Magioglou. "We will marry my granddaughter to this young man as soon as possible." He got up. "Get your coat! We are going to see Dimitris and settle this now."

A few minutes later, father and son were riding on a coach to the Tsolakoglou home. It was the custom that Dimitris Tsolakoglou, the oldest available relative of the young man, be also a representative and a spokesman for all the members of both the Boyun-egri-oglou and Tsolakoglou clan.

THE RUSSIAN CONNECTION (CONSTANTINOPLE, FEBRUARY, 1905)

The Tsolakoglou home was a typical home of a rather well to do family. As Haji John paid his coachman, his father was knocking at the door. "I want to talk to Dimitris," George Magioglou said to Katina, when she opened the door. "Is he in?"

"Come on in effendi," replied Katina. "Yes, he is."

Haji John followed his father in as he looked at Katina with a disagreeable look between disgust and pity. Katina became frightened. Haji John saw in her and her family a bunch of peasants that were invading Constantinople from Cappadocia and messing up their good life. The only truth about his feelings was that in the past years, the Greeks of Cappadocia were leaving in drones. These people for years had felt that they were trapped isolated in the middle of Asia Minor since the time of the Seljuk Turks, but they also felt safe there. They were in the twentieth century now, but still living like the Byzantines of the 14th century. The Ottomans had made some changes in Asia Minor, but in the caves of Cappadocia, that change was not felt until recently since information was so scarce. Now, information became available. Roads opened up, rail and telegraph brought news of a world that they had missed altogether. Some of their own kind had migrated abroad and others had created a country of their own. New inventions, like newspapers and magazines started appearing with amazing information about other places and people. The Greek teachers, assigned there by the Patriarchal Office were very keen in the teaching of new languages, geography and mathematics. This information made it to the households, who followed what their children learned at school with both amazement and concern. Their concern was on how long their children will remain by their side before jumping on the first train to go and experience these new worlds.

In spite of the rich soil and healthy environment, the people of Kalivarion, or Karvali were also leaving in droves. The primary reason was that it was in the middle of nowhere, without major transportation and communication routes around it. By the start of the twentieth century, half of the residents of Karvali were living in Constantinople, Adana, Tarsus, Mersina, Selefkia, Ikonium and Smyrna. Later, some moved to Ankara. Karvali was known in the past for good pottery makers, like Paul Boyun-egri-oglou.[9] Many of those had left for Beirut of Lebanon, Constanza of Romania or Alexandria of Egypt. A number of them left for Odessa. Among the people that migrated to Odessa was the Tsolakoglou family.[10]

George Tsolakoglou made a lot of money during the Russo-Japanese War of 1904-05.[11] During that period, he served as mayor of Odessa. He had a large family, but only one son, Thomas. One of the nephews was Dimitris Tsolakoglou, who was running part of one factory. His nephew, Dimitris was a graduate of the military academy

---

9   This is strictly a biography, written by A. Boinodiris, Book 1, and p. 149.

10   As mentioned before, George Tsolakoglou was a wealthy Greek from Karvali, whose great grandfather was a member of Filiki Eteria, a revolutionary organization in Russia that financed the Greek revolution against the Turks of 1821. The Tsolakoglou family came to Odessa from Karvali many years before the Greek revolution. Tsolakoglou's factories processed sesame products: halva, tahini, sesame oil, pasteli (sesame candy), animal food by-products, etc., which were popular at that time.

11   This was a conflict between Russia and Japan over territorial expansion in E. Asia. After Russia leased the strategically important Port Arthur (now Lushun, China) and expanded into Manchuria, it faced the increasing power of Japan. When Russia reneged on its agreement with Japan to withdraw troops from Manchuria, the Japanese fleet attacked the Russia naval squadron at Port Arthur and began a siege of the city in February 1904. Japanese land forces cut the Russian army off from coming to aid Port Arthur and pushed it back to Mukden (now Shenyang). The reinforced Russian army took the offensive in October, but poor military leadership blunted its effectiveness. After the long Japanese siege of Port Arthur, in January 1905 the corrupt Russian commander surrendered the garrison without consulting his officers, despite adequate stores and ammunition for its continued defense. Heavy fighting around Mukden ended in March 1905 with the withdrawal of Russian troops under A. Kuropatkin. The decisive naval Battle of Tsushima gave the Japanese the upper hand and brought Russia to the peace table. With the signing of the Treaty of Portsmouth, Russia abandoned its expansionist policy in E Asia and Japan gained effective control of Korea and much of Manchuria.

in St. Petersburg and served as a Russian officer during the Russo-Japanese War. His home was actually in Odessa, but now he had a base in Constantinople from where he conducted his business. Although the Tsolakoglou clan had their base in Odessa for more than a century, they often traveled to Constantinople and went on a pilgrimage to Karvali. They were major contributors to the church of St. Gregory of Nazianzos. Among other deeds, George Tsolakoglou helped maintain the church of St. Gregory from Nazianzos in Karvali. He donated the one-ton bronze bell, which was hanging on a tower, next to the church.[12] The bell sat on top of a steel tower, positioned over a stone tower, to a total height of 70 meters. It was connected to a box, which moved by pulling a steel chain. The box moved first, before swinging the bell to the point of hearing it. The sound of the bell could be heard all over the area.

George Tsolakoglou modified his factory to supply the Russian army with sweets in addition to his sesame-based line and capable of supplying valuable and durable winter nutrition to troops in distant Siberia. He was processing fruit from Crimea to make jams and jellies. His factories grew now to 5000 workers. His wealth helped him become a benefactor to his community and helped many immigrants when they needed help. The Odessa people were very grateful that this person's family came to their shores. He was recognized for his compassion, charity and his open mindedness in dealing with his workers.[13]

Dimitris Tsolakoglou was napping when the Magioglou men arrived. Katina woke him up and after he was told of his visitors, he washed his face in the basin and joined them in the parlor. George Magioglou opened up the conversation, and with the political tact of a diplomat explained the situation. His granddaughter became pregnant, after having an affair with Dimitris' brother-in-law. Dimitris became extremely angry at first. He threatened to deal with his brother-in-law at a later time, when he comes home from work.

---

12 That same bell was among the relics brought over to Nea Karvali, near Kavala, where the new colony was established. Before the residents could afford a new bell tower, they hung it on a branch of a huge plane tree. The one-ton bell forced the branch progressively lower every year, until one day, vibrations cracked the bell.

13 A. Boinodiris, Book 1, p. 149.

Then, Dimitris asked: "What do you suggest that we do now, Mr. Magioglou?"

"There is only one thing we can do," said George Magioglou. "We must marry them and let them lie on the bed that they both chose for the rest of their lives. They get no dowry from my son. What they get is a wedding."

Dimitris turned to Haji John, who remained silent up to that time. Then, with pressed lips, full of anger Haji John mumbled: "a very secret wedding."

"On behalf of our family, I agree," said Dimitris after some thought. He had no choice, but to accept the offer. He was so angry with his brother-in-law for his utter stupidity that he considered the Magioglou offer to be quite generous. How could this man embarrass him so by impregnating the daughter of his best man and friend? How could he forget what he came to Constantinople for? Did he forget about the Turkish Army?

"I will make arrangements to have the wedding in this house."

SECRET WEDDING (CONSTANTINOPLE, MARCH 1905)

The wedding ceremony between George and Evanthia was very short and without much fanfare. It was done inside the Tsolakoglou home and the only ones present at that wedding from the side of the groom were George's sisters Orsia and Katina. The bride wore a large dress, to hide the bulge in her abdomen. Upon insistence of Haji-John Magioglou, the wedding was kept as secret as possible. Even the priest was brought in from a remote location of the suburbs, registering it to the church records there. None was to find out that his daughter was already pregnant, when she was married.

"How are you going to keep this a secret, especially after your daughter gives birth to a baby within five months of her wedding?" asked his wife.

"I want them out of Constantinople," said Haji-John in a booming voice. "It is embarrassing to our family. I will pay their fare to go and live in Kalivarion, where that peasant comes from. Let my daughter have her child there, away from my eyes. I don't want to see them near me."

A month later, the couple moved to Kalivarion. In secret, George Magioglou passed the deeds of his vineyards to the couple. The Magioglou family had many holdings in Kalivarion, not only from George Magioglou who served as a judge there, but also from the family of his distant uncle Anargyros and his descendants who also now had judicial duties in Cappadocia. He felt sorry for his granddaughter and since he was getting old, he decided to pass that property to her before he passed away.

Life would be very hard for Evanthia. She had lived up to now in a big city with her education and the servants looking after her. Now, running away from her dysfunctional home into a virtual wilderness, the only thing that would give her strength was her freedom from her past. From the minute she appeared in Kalivarion, friends of the family were curious about the sudden wedding. Everyone knew of her famous, rich family.[14] To anyone asking about her wedding, the answer was that she was married in 1904 and not in 1905, so as to hide the shame associated with a pre-marital child conception.

NEWBORN (KALIVARION, SEPTEMBER, 1905)

Evanthia held the baby boy in her arms, as she looked around the church of St. Gregory of Nazianzos. A little more than a month earlier she had just given birth to a son. Her life in Kalivarion in the past few months represented an excruciating pain, yet she did not complain. She had nobody to complain to. All her husband's relatives were people she did not know very well. They tried to help her in her pregnancy, but to a brand new mother, nothing they did brought comfort. The midwife of the village came often, tested her and advised her on what to do until the time came for her delivery. Like most midwives, she liked to talk a lot. Listening to her talk could make a woman forget her labor pains and divert her mind on other, trivial things. She talked about the

---

14 The Magioglou and the Sarafis families were often in contention as to who is richer. One story has it that two men argued about this in a café, to the point that they ended up hurting each other pretty badly.

graffiti she saw on the walls of a monastery.[15] She also discussed how in the old times people did not paint icons, but designs, like the Turks.[16]

"It is shameful," said the midwife. "These monasteries were built with a great deal of pain and represent a place of worship. Why do our young boys and girls go there and desecrate the icons by writing their names over them?"

Evanthia knew all about the graffiti. When she was young, visiting Cappadocia with her family, all the young girls talked about these places, where boys and girls were going on dates and making out. What a better place to vow an eternal love to someone than a holy place like this?

"In the old times," continued the midwife, "there were numerous monks taking care of the monasteries. About one hundred years ago though, the Turks started taxing them heavily and the monks could not survive. That is why they left, leaving these places unguarded and to the mercy of the people who live in the villages around them. All the monasteries around the Goreme Valley are suffering from graffiti drawn by Greek youngsters from all over, but especially from visitors from Constantinople who somehow have no respect for our monuments."

She had delivered her baby, as she was working in a field in a location called Gofoul, near Kalivarion. The midwife had to rush to the field and with the help of two of Evanthia's relatives delivered the baby under a tree. The two relatives were her mother-in-law Katina and her sister-in-law Irene. A few days earlier, Evanthia wrote a letter to her father about the boy's birth. She told him that the baptism would be at the end of February and asked her family to come and visit her. She eagerly waited to see how her family would react.

---

15   See similar graffiti in Figure 1.
16   An example of iconoclastic designs of early churches is shown in Figure 260.

Figure 2 Graffiti Defacing Icons of a Goreme Valley Cave Monastery

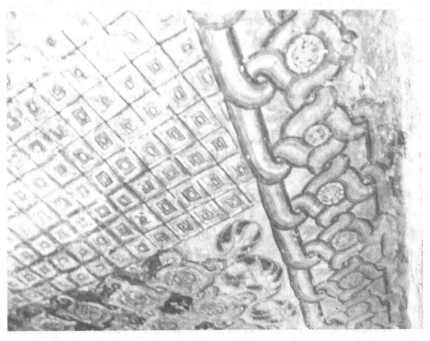

Figure 3 Iconoclastic Period Icons of a Cappadocian Monastery

Arrogant Men (Kalivarion, April, 1906)

Evanthia could not understand her father. She had written almost eight months ago and received no response. Also, none appeared at the boy's baptism. She named the boy Anthony.

In Constantinople, when the letter arrived, Haji John tore it to shreds. His wife kept on asking about her daughter's condition. She wanted to go and visit her, but her husband would not allow her to do any such thing. His anger towards his daughter was so big, that in revenge, he wanted her to feel the "pain" of her decisions. He was also plagued by his trouble with the Ottoman bureaucracy, while trying to complete the Hejaz railway project. Finally, after an argument with his wife, he told her about his daughter's letter. She had already found out about it from other travelers.

Haji John was not unique in his fatherly arrogance. During those times, a father was considered the leader of a family and he exercised all means at hand to squash any rebellion within the ranks of his family. His word had to be obeyed, or severe consequences would ensue. The only weapon available to his wife and his children was continuous complaining and nagging. For someone on the outside it may be hard to believe that a Greek servant of the Sultan would turn out to be a tyrant in his own home, but that is how some oppressed humans react to subordinates.

Such behavior has been the scourge of humanity since several million years ago, when we started differentiating ourselves from other animals and came down from trees. We saw ourselves as superior beings, and even created gods to our image. Although we were still developing at evolutionary slow speeds, we decided to speed things up, by eliminating those amongst us that we found undesirable. We called this "war." We invented new concepts, methods and machines, inventions that made our dreams of a grand existence come true, forgetting that humans are still nothing more than an evolving living organism on a planet of the universe. Our arrogance raised our status to the level of god-like, "intelligent beings," even though we were burdened with an immense number of shortcomings and primeval behavioral instincts. It takes only a reminder about the kind of creatures we really are, to bring some sense in us. Often, we are reminded of our shortcomings when failure, severe illness, or imminent death reduces our arrogance to reality. Meanwhile, most of us feel superior to those that are different, subordinate, less fortunate, or under our care. Most of our kind of living organisms, as ridiculous as it may seem, act in demeaning, vengeful and arrogant manner against other such organisms that they consider of "lower status" when they decide to act differently.

Due to this inherent human arrogance of Haji John, the Magioglou couple continued their daily squabbling, which tore up any civility between husband and wife. The youngster Pandelis had to grow up amidst father's explosive anger, added to mother's passive aggressive rebellion.[17] As a result, Haji John and his wife would not see his daughter and grandchild for almost five years.

Meanwhile, anxiety was harassing George Boyun-egri-oglou. George was upset, because he did not expect this as the final outcome. He had left Cappadocia for Constantinople to escape from the Turkish Army and go to Russia. The Turks up to now talked about enlisting non-Turkish minorities into their army, but they had implemented it only on a volunteer basis. In case of war though, all minorities would end up as bashi bazouks.

George came to Constantinople hoping to move to Odessa. There, he met a beautiful, rich girl of the famous Magioglou family, and like Odysseus he became distracted from his destination by another Circe.[18] Initially, Evanthia satisfied his weakness for a female companion. Then, after finding out that the girl was pregnant, he rationalized his actions by seeing the rich girl as a possible ticket to a better life. This backfired on him when after his short-lived affair, he was married and tossed back into Cappadocia where he came from with a wife and a child and absolutely no dowry to compensate him for his trouble. Like many arrogant men of his time, George started blaming everyone else, except himself.

---

17 This would have a devastating effect in shaping Pandelis' character as an adult. He would become a very strict and domineering person, especially towards his own family members.

18 Circe was an ancient Greek goddess (or sometimes called a nymph, witch, enchantress or sorceress). Circe's father was Helios, the god of the sun and the owner of the land where Odysseus' men ate cattle. Circe transformed her enemies, or those who offended her, into animals through the use of magical potions.

Anthony Boyun-egri-oglu (Karvali, 1909)[19]

I, Anthony, was born in Kalivarion, shortened by the Greeks as Karvali (now the Turks call it Guzelyurt) of the county of Ikonium (Konya) of Cappadocia and sub-region of Nigde, in a field called Gofoul. My father's name was George Boyun-egri-oglu (Stravolemis) and my mother's Evanthia, of the Magioglou family. I was the first born in my family. The county where Karvali lay was under the regional government of Akserai.[20]

My godfather was Paul Uzunoglou (son of the tall man). He baptized me on February 26 1906, as it is documented in the archives of Nea Karvali, a small community near Kavala in Greece. It is an officially recognized document as part of the Greek Government records.[21] Paul was a steelworker. Most of his work was making and fixing agricultural tools, like plows. I do not know my exact birth date, but baptisms of that time were typically done when the baby was about six months old. Therefore, I am guessing that my birth date might have been in September of 1905 AD.[22]

My father's father was named Paul Boyun-egri-oglu. He was born in 1849 (he was 75 when we came to Greece in 1924). My father's mother was named Katherine, from the family of Makisoglou. My mother's father was Haji-John Magioglou. My mother's mother was Makrina, from the family of Suzanoglou. My father was born in 1882 and my mother in 1888. My younger sister Irene was born later, in 1913.[23]

I started writing this notebook with the encouragement of my son Stavros on my 74th birthday, in 1979. I must ask for the forgiveness for my bad writing, spelling, grammar and especially my order and organization. I ask you Stavros, my son to improve on all of these as you transcribe them in a proper form. I am writing from memory, which sometimes fails me due to my age. The only way I can excuse

---

19 These entries by A. Boinodiris were written in 1979.
20 A. Boinodiris, Book 1, p. 230 and Book 4, p. 1 and Book 2, p.1.
21 A. Boinodiris, Book 1, p. 230 and Book 4, p. 1.
22 A. Boinodiris, Book 1, p. 230 and Book 4, p. 1.
23 A. Boinodiris, Book 4, p. 1.

myself is that I had very little education due to continuous wars and the dire need for the survival of our family.[24]

ROOTS OF THE KALIVARION PEOPLE

In this notebook, I am recalling what I have been told and what I remember from my childhood. I am recalling political and religious events, from the time that I started remembering events until now.

Based on a word-of-mouth tradition transferred to us by our grandparents, our origins are from the island of Andros. Our suspicions are that the name of our town is related somehow to a place called Kalivarion of Andros, but I have no concrete proof for that. Up to now, the time that I am writing these words, I have not been at the island of Andros, but I believe that a small community named Kalivarion must exist on the northwestern part of that island. Our ancestors told us that we immigrated to Cappadocia from there under some unknown circumstances, at an unknown time, lost in the memories of people that preceded us. We were also told that other immigrants from islands near Andros ended in locations near ours. Our ancestors identified that the people of Haskoy, a village to the northwest of Guzelyurt came from Naxos; and the people from Kalecik, a village to the north of Guzelyurt[25]came from Lemnos.[26] I was told that our immigration is linked, but I was not told how.[27] These two places, until a few generations ago were referred to by both, the Turkish name and the name of the Greek island.

Even though we came from Cyclades, I was told that we were relatively newcomers. Greeks populated Cappadocia since the time of the Hittite and Persian Empire many centuries before Christ. Hittite structures can be found and sometimes copied by the locals.[28] For millennia, these Greeks intermarried with other nations that came in

24 A. Boinodiris, Book 1, p. 230.
25 A. Boinodiris, Book 2, p. 127.
26 Andros, Naxos and Lemnos are Aegean Islands.
27 A. Boinodiris, Book 4, Cover Entry.
28 Hittites developed a corbel arch technique (similar to the Mycenaean corbel arch), a way to built subterranean passages by using the arching-vaulting strength of stones, a precursor to the Roman arch. A corbel arch is constructed by offsetting successive courses of stone at the spring-line of the walls so that they project towards the archway's center from each supporting

contact and prospered in Cappadocia under the Byzantine Empire. When our people came, they had to build their own establishment, naming it Kalivarion, next to other Cappadocian villages, near the Church of St. Gregory of Nazianzos. Many of the existing villages were formed by excavating caves. The local people had excavated the hills, making underground hiding residences to escape attacks from raiders. Survival instinct was very strong in the minds of all residents in that region. In spite of the excavated hills though, the area has quite a few isolated fertile plains with lots of water near these refuges.

Figure 4 Church of St. Gregory of Nazianzos, used as a Mosque today at Kalivarion, Karvali, or Gelveri

side, until the courses meet at the apex of the archway (often capped with flat stones).

Figure 5 Houses Built by Greeks at Karvali (Recent Photo)

KALIVARION, KARVALI, OR GELVERI DESCRIPTION IN THE EARLY 20TH CENTURY

Kalivarion, or Karvali, or Gelveri is today's Guzelyurt, meaning in Turkish "beautiful homeland." Its inhabitants called it Gelvery until 1923.[29]

In spite of the rich agricultural production of the region, Karvali was suffering economically. Their products, in spite of their quality were not able to reach other markets to be sold.

Youth was fleeing, not only because of wars but because they were desperate for exchange cash. They went to large metropolitan areas. Half of them left for Constantinople. Many others left for Adana, Mersina, Selefkia, Ikonium, Smyrna and Ankara. The ones that were in high demand were the pottery makers. They left for Beirut (Lebanon), Alexandria (Egypt), Constanza (Rumania) and Odessa

---

29   This segment was derived from the Argeus Tourism and Travel of Cappadocia, on Guzelyurt.

(Russia). In Odessa, they found a benefactor from Karvali called George Tsolakoglou.[30]

Akserai was a short distance to the northwest, but was plagued by mosquitoes and malaria, since it was very near the Lake Tata. All the wealthy Turks from that town, including governing officials had a summer home in Karvali. They used to send their children and their wives first, joining them when they could. One of the reasons that Karvali survived the massacres that Turks had in store for the Greeks of Asia Minor was that the governing Turks knew all the Greeks of Karvali intimately. Among the most powerful Greeks that had a great deal of influence in the Turkish government were the Magioglou,[31] Sarafis and Loukides family. They and their children could save a man's life (Greek or Turk) from hanging during those days. These people had homes in which Turkish officials spent their vacations free of charge.

Karvali is in a region 18 hours walk from the Salt Lake Tata. When I state hours, I mean the time it takes to travel using a strong, well-traveled horse or mule, or a well-fed donkey.[32] It is located 12 hours walk SW from Nev Sehir (Neapolis). It is located 7-8 hours SE walk from Akserai. The town of Bor[33] (the birthplace of Athanasiades-Bodosakis)[34] is to the SE;[35] it is also located west of the Melentir (now Melentiz) mountain range. This range connects with the Anti-Taurus

30 A. Boinodiris, Book 1, p. 148.
31 These families have been traced to long roots from Andros in all the previous books. The Magioglou family came from the Mega-oglu (son of Megas), which was Megas before the Turks. The Megas family changed the name themselves from the original name of Psellus in the eleventh century.
32 A. Boinodiris, Book 2, p.1.
33 Bor is the ancient city of Tyana.
34 Prodromos Athanasiades-Bodosakis was born in Bohr, Cappadocia. After the exchange of populations he became a Greek industrialist who in 1934 took over Pyrkal, an armament company and one of the oldest defense industries. He became one of the most important figures in 20th century Greek industrial history. Pyrkal eventually became part of a huge industrial empire, involved in mining operations (several companies, holding dominant position in the country), textiles, chemicals and fertilizers, glass manufacturing, engineering and constructions, as well as services (shipping, insurances etc.). Prodromos became a target and was assassinated by the leftist November 17 terrorist group on March 1, 1988.
35 A. Boinodiris, Book 1, p. 142.

(Hassan Dag) range. On the foothills of Anti-Taurus are the ruins of an ancient Greek town, named Achelais. Akserai is a town with a good size river crossing it on its way to Lake Tata. The river springs are located on hills surrounding Karvali and flow on both sides of the village to connect and form the river that crosses Akserai.[36] Nigde is to the SE of Karvali, at a distance of about 12 hours, almost the same distance as Nev Sehir, which is to the NE of Karvali.[37]

Cappadocia had numerous Greek villages, spread all around Mount Argeus, near Caesaria. Mt. Argeus, with elevation of 3950 meters is the tallest mountain of Asia Minor, after Mt. Ararat. Since ancient times it was a volcano, which spewed lava and ash throughout the region at a distance of 70-80 kilometers. It was this ash, that when it fell it formed pyramidal mounds, which the residents found to be very useful in terms of making homes and barns in them, by excavating them within these mounds. The ash was easy to carve in the interior of the mound. It solidified into a hard concrete surface after it was exposed to air. Over time, people had built a network of caves and tunnels that were used as catacombs, shelters and fortifications to protect themselves against foreign invaders.[38]

Karvali was built on a defensive location. It is positioned on top of rocky formations, forming high cliffs, overlooking three riverbeds. The springs that feed those riverbeds have high quality clean water. Like other Cappadocian towns, the rocks are naturally shaped like pyramids resembling Meteora in Greece. The rocks are made out of the soft ash material which when wet can be carved easily by a cutting tool like a knife, but when dried by air it becomes very hard. This allowed humans to carve into the mountain spaces of their own design. At various times these spaces served various needs and occupants. Some were used as residences, others as storage warehouses, water cisterns, animal shelters, chapels, churches, etc. The hewn rock kept the space at a relatively stable temperature, warm in the freezing winters and cool in the hot summers. The ash tends to keep the interior very dry and provides natural insulation.[39] Some of the structures built around Karvali also

---

36 A. Boinodiris, Book 1, p. 143.
37 A. Boinodiris, Book 2, p.1.
38 A. Boinodiris, Book 2, p.1-2.
39 A. Boinodiris, Book 2, p. 2.

resemble those that the initial settlers from Andros used in their islands centuries earlier.[40]

Karvali had a low mountain to the northeast. Small hills were towards the southwest. To the west lay a plain, behind some hills; in fact, the village was surrounded by hills full of vineyards and orchards. The hills to the northeast were called the Tunkuru. The southeast hills were called Iskalka. Further to the south, the area was called Old Vineyards (Eski Paglar). To the northeast, the hills were called Kertiz and Tavzani. To the north were the St. Spyridon hills. Residents of Karvali cultivated all these hills and tended them extremely well. Whenever you visited the fields, you would find no weeds and no footsteps, until harvest time.[41]

Figure 6 Karvali Area Barn- (Architecture Copies the Andros-style Houses)

---

40 Amazingly, the author found that the structure he photographed and shown in Fig. 6 is very similar to the structure displayed at the museum of Andros; this structure was used for several millennia before Christ and is still abundantly present throughout the island.

41 A. Boinodiris, Book 1, p. 147.

LIFE IN KALIVARION

Some of the residences were defensive in nature, allowing multiple entrances through cliff-hewn steps and blocking the narrow entrances with rolled millstones, each with an opening at the center to shoot arrows or guns. There were lots of customs and folklore left over from past eras, all the way back to the Persian occupation.

There were also houses, not built inside hills. These were built with flat stones forming door openings with large, overhead stones, shaped as a bridge upon which the stonework continued. The roofs were also built with large beams supporting lighter flat stones. The roof was then sealed with clay-like dirt which, when dry, does not allow any moisture from the rain to seep below. At the roof edges of each house they had gutters made out of ceramic feeding onto lion-head spouts. When it snowed, people went on top of the roof and with wooden shovels cleaned it up so that the clay-like sealer did not become too soggy. Most winters we had snow up to one meter.

One of the caves was specifically built for wild pigeons to roost. Smart people who knew what they were doing toiled and built these special caves. These caves were on the face of rocks, 100 to 150 meters high. The openings on the rocks were small enough for pigeons to fit. Yet, the caves had large interiors with human-size corridors that led all the way to an accessible entrance from Karvali. A door blocked each corridor. The pigeons were fed with leftover food, thrown in the cave by humans. Such food was made out of grape seeds, grape skins, etc. All of these leftovers were from grape processing. Grapes were used to make such products as wine, ouzo, petmezi and retseli. The pigeons roosted there, not only from the heavy winters, but also to find food. The cave had nests where the pigeons laid eggs and multiplied with new hatchlings. During the winter, we would unlock the wooden door to the entrance and using a candle, we would find our way to the main chamber. In the dark, we would grab male pigeons which we would slaughter and fill a basket. We used their meat for numerous dishes.

In addition to the meat, the pigeon manure was used as a fertilizer. Just before Easter time we would clean the chambers of manure, load it into bags and use the fertilizer in vineyards and gardens. This fertilizer was very potent in nitrates. It would kill even a large tree if one used it as it came naturally. It requires dilution with other dirt and it must be dispersed thinly during fall, when the rains are plentiful. When used in this manner, the quality and yield of vineyards and gardens explodes.

During winters, men would go frequently to hunt quail. The birds could not find food in the snow, so they were forced to come close to populated areas, foraging on rooftops and yards. Some kids would manage to capture a few alive, roosting under bushes or buried in snow.[42]

All clothing in Karvali was made out of wool. We did not have any cotton. Clothes, blankets, mattresses and rugs were all woolen. All the people had sheep and goats. The poorest of the poor had at least ten heads. Many had cattle. Karvali must have had 20,000 goats and sheep and about 2,000 heads of cattle.[43]

Snow was present in shady areas of the hills until March 1. After March 13, everyone was out in the fields. The roots of vines were cleaned and irrigation ditches were dug next to the roots. Pruning, weeding and tilling followed. We never used pesticides or insecticides, yet, for some reason[44] we had very few pests or diseases. The only thing that would hurt the crop was an occasional hail fall.[45] A location, called "Rocks with bird drops" (Puklutza Kagia) was not protected from cold winds blowing from Mount Argeus. Mount Argeus was also called the St. Basil's mountain. In that location, grapes would ripen very late in the season. Therefore, people planted mulberry trees, used for the cultivation of silk.

One of the best quality wheat I have ever known grew in Karvali. It had long storage life and the bread made from it was very tasty, with a distinct aroma. It tasted and smelled as if it had walnuts, filberts and almonds in it. I never knew that bread could taste so different from one place to another, until I came to Greece. The cakes made out of flour from Cappadocian wheat were delicious. Bread was baked in ovens made out of two stones that formed a chamber like clamshells. The top one had a hole in it. The chamber could hold up to 200 kilos of bread. Under the stones was the fire chamber, which was lit and made the stones white-hot. The stone chamber is wiped with a wet cloth tied on

42 A. Boinodiris, Book 1, p. 143-145
43 A. Boinodiris, Book 1, p. 326.
44 The reason for this may be attributed to the high altitude of Cappadocia and the low humidity of the landscape.
45 A. Boinodiris, Book 1, p. 148.

a pole and the dough is placed in it. In one hour, you have 200 kilos of fresh bread.

The orchards around Karvali blossomed late in the spring, because the winters were consistently cold and their cycle was not disturbed by mid-winter false summers. Weeks before harvest, the trees had to be supported, because they were overloaded with fruit. The apricots were so sweet and plentiful that we had to dry them in the sun, in drying racks.[46]

Healthy food, exercise and clean water helped keep the people of Karvali healthy. The only sick people were those that returned home from other places.[47]

During Sultan Hamid's reign, the Ottoman Government sent a doctor of Greek origin to Karvali. He stayed one year, having no patients at all. He and his family had a fine vacation. He then decided this was not such a good idea, since he needed practice. If he kept on like this, he would forget everything he knew and he had to pay loans for his studies. Therefore, he applied for a transfer to a less healthy location. In his application he wrote:

"I respectfully request that you send me to an unhealthy place, where I can practice my skills. I spent a great deal of money to become a doctor. This place is so healthy, that I can lose my skills in no time. I cannot afford that."

Soon after his application was sent, he received his transfer papers.

A medical practitioner called Jordan met most of our medical needs. He went to medical school but left before he could finish, due to illness. He found Karvali the proper place for him and his illness. Most of his cases were related to winter sniffles. A few cases of colds, pneumonia, and rabies developed once in awhile.

The area around Karvali was considered a vacation place for people from Akserai and other locations.[48] Greeks often sent their children in the summer there; the houses of relatives became summer camps, where the children's became their custodians. In these summer camps, children played together and when they became teenagers, they met, and secretly dated in the cave monasteries. Since their older relatives,

---

46   A. Boinodiris, Book 1, p. 147.
47   A. Boinodiris, Book 1, p. 338.
48   A. Boinodiris, Book 1, p. 146.

like aunts or uncles kept a strict eye on them, the monasteries were their favorite secret dating place. Many Greek marriages were the result of a first dating encounter at those monasteries. Naturally, they had to eventually go through the formal process of marriage by arrangement, but before they found someone to "arrange" the wedding, there was lots of hanky-panky. In later years of their lives they would come there in a pilgrimage to their first secret encounter with love.

KALIVARION UNDER ABD AL-HAMID II (1876-1909)

Our situation, as Greek minorities worsened during the first twenty years from my birth. It was around 1909 when the Turks had a civil war, trying to overthrow their monarchy.

The Sultan at that time was Abd al-Hamid II (1842-1918). He was an Ottoman Sultan of Turkey between 1876 and 1909. He was son of Abdul Mejid (1839-1861). He succeeded his brother Murad V, who had been declared insane. In reprisal against Turkish misrule in the Balkans, Russia declared war against Turkey in the second year of Abd al-Hamid's reign. He suffered disastrous military reverses and, by the terms of the Treaty of San Stefano in 1878, was deprived of most of his European territorial possessions. There were also massacres of Armenians in Turkey during 1895 and 1896, when Abd al-Hamid refused to intervene, despite international protests.

The Sultan was very good to the Greeks of Cappadocia. He encouraged agriculture and commerce and allowed minorities to practice their religion freely, as long as they did not impede the Turkish government. They let them have private schools, opened up commerce and brought into government positions many educated people from the non-Moslem minorities. Non-Moslems had to pay additional tax per person, called head-tax, to qualify for all benefits of a Turkish citizen, without having to serve in the Armed Forces. As a whole though, Moslems saw his policies differently. Internal dissatisfaction with his despotic rule led to the development of the powerful revolutionary organization known as the Young Turks.

The Young Turks were military officers, who were educated primarily in Germany. General Paul Von Hindenburg of Kaiser Wilhelm II (1859-1941), emperor of Germany and King of Prussia (1888-1918), whose policies helped bring about World War I (1914-1918) helped in the organization of the revolt. The leaders were three officers, Emver, Niazi and Talaat, who deposed Abd al-Hamid II. The Young Turks managed to raise the dissatisfaction of the minorities by using propaganda. This propaganda included Armenians and Greeks, using the Armenian massacre (1895-1896) as an example of Hamid's oppression. All this was forgotten later, when the same Young Turks turned and massacred the Armenians in the second Armenian massacre. Many Christians were fooled and joined them. They had little problem raising the Turkish population against the Sultan. The average male Turk had to serve five years in compulsory military service. After this, most of them became professional soldiers, laborers, farmers and very few public servants. The military service virtually destroyed them economically. The Armenians specialized in crafts. The Greeks specialized in arts and crafts, commerce and shipping.

The Young Turks' revolution succeeded very fast and with relatively little bloodshed. They came in secret to Thessaloniki and there organized the Turkish divisions in secret. The minorities were promised "a change to a better, modern Turkey." The Greek sailors and boat owners of Thessaloniki helped them to be transported to Thrace, unsuspecting that they would be betrayed soon, by being double-crossed into a compulsory suicidal draft, or deportation. They suddenly appeared in Constantinople, finding little resistance and they captured the Sultan in Dolma Bachtse. When he figured out what happened and the crucial involvement of the Greek sailors, with an angry and emotional voice he said:

"It is pitiful that even you, the Greeks took arms against me, helping these anarchists. They have plans to destroy you. You will regret your actions. These anarchists hate non-Turks. They do not understand that you cannot have beauty in nature with a single flower. You need diversity to prosper. Every flower blooms in its month and contributes to the beauty and aroma of this world. Every bee and butterfly helps make the world livable. We will lose these flowers and bees that make our country diverse and prosperous."[49]

49   A. Boinodiris, Book 5, p. 1-4. This statement seems to be contradictory to the history books that blame Sultan Hamid for "hate crimes" against non-Turks of that period. In fact, historians that recorded the event attributed the first Armenian massacre to him. Was he an evil Sultan that had last regrets for his actions? Was there someone else responsible for

When the Young Turks deposed and exiled Abd al-Hamid, they put in his place his brother Resat, with a new constitution of their own. The Sultan and his family were brought to Thessaloniki on April of 1909, where they were placed under guard in a meat factory, called Alatini. He had to be educated in Greek, since most people there spoke Greek. The Turks of Thessaloniki ridiculed him and spit on him during his outings. "Why don't you bathe with milk now effendi?" people said to him. This was a common yell, noting the Sultan's custom to have hot bath in ass's milk, which was supposed to soften the skin.

The sultan was silent and took all that was being dished to him.[50]

After 1909, when Abd al-Hamid II was deposed and exiled, the Young Turks abolished the head-tax and took all the privileges from the minorities; everyone had to serve in the military, including all minorities. At that time, minorities comprised most of the financial strength of the Ottoman Empire. Such a change put pressure on them, to serve or to leave the country. They would soon discover that serving in the Ottoman Empire as a Christian soldier was suicidal, since fanatic Moslem officers made sure that Christian soldiers did not survive long. In the pending wars, Christian soldiers that fought in the Ottoman Army never came back. They were mistreated, deprived of food, beaten and placed on continuous hard labor. The Christian population knew this, even though the Turkish propaganda kept on refuting this to this day.[51] As a result, their only alternative was to leave the country.

REVOLUTION (KALIVARION, JUNE 5, 1909)

Some of the early things I remember happened on June 6, 1909, on that Saturday morning in which we celebrate the day of the Holy

what happened and the Sultan simply lost control of the situation? The ex-sultan lived under captivity in Thessaloniki until 1912. Then, when the Greek forces attacked the city, he was taken to Constantinople where he spent his final days studying, carpentering and writing his memoirs in custody at Beylerbeyi Palace. He died on February 10, 1918, just a few months before his brother.

50 A. Boinodiris, Book 5, p. 4-5.
51 A. Boinodiris, Book 5, p. 1-5.

Ascension.[52] There is a monastery dedicated to the Holy Ascension, carved in a typical Cappadocian cave.

In preparation for the celebration, during the previous day, young men hitched horses and mules onto carts. Everybody put on his or her Sunday clothes and the whole neighborhood started traveling to the monastery of Holy Ascension. My father saddled two horses, one for himself and one for my mother. I was small enough to be held in their arms.

The youth, Greeks and Turks gathered at the caves near the monastery and started playing musical instruments and dancing. In the caves, they were cooking several traditional dishes, delicacies made out of boiled eggs, pastourma and other goodies. They drank wine and ouzo. My mother was busy making certain dishes. I, a playful four-year old youngster was running around the caves, dancing with the music and slowly getting more daring with the environment.

As I was wandering around, I fell into a dry well, yelled and after hitting my head I fainted. The people rushed to find me and pull me up with a rope. After they threw cold water on my bloody head, I came to my senses. I remember that my father chastised my mother for not watching over me. Then Father Cosmas came over, bringing some very potent ouzo and washed my wound on my head. They also placed some medicinal paste on my wound. I later found out that that paste was made out of baby mice, dissolved in olive oil over a long time. After a week, my head swelling went down and I was well.

In that picnic, my father was dancing and singing with all the rest to a very popular Turkish song of the period:

"Yasasin Houriet (long live liberty), Yasasin Atalet (long live rest), Yasasin Mousavat (long live equality), Yasasin Ortu (long live blanket).

Yasasin Houriet Yasasin Atalet, Yasasin Osmanli Toplanti ana korouyucu (long live the assembly of Ottoman defender mothers) vatan (of the motherland) yavrou siouyouz silahtan korkmayiz (chicks

---

52   Carikli Kilise (The Church of the Sandal) is a church with a cruciform nave, two columns, three apses and four domes (one central dome and three cupolas). Its frescos date from the 13C. The name of the church derives from a footprint below the Ascension fresco. The entrance to the church is from the north and the apse is directed to the east.

fearless of firearms) kouruyusountan kasmakiz pis (defending against foul oppression) vatan kartasiyiz (as friends of motherland)."

It was a revolutionary song against the Ottoman Sultan Abdul-Hamid II. Turk and Greek youths sang it alike. My father, George was one of these young men that sang it. I did not realize it then that he would soon regret it.

At night, the Greek grandfathers of the village (my grandfather Paul and Father Kalinikos, his priest brother) were upset with the young men for their brainwashed actions.

"Why are you singing these songs?" they chastised the youth. "You should know that these revolutionaries would be worse than the Sultan ever was. They want you to take their side, only to turn around later and take away all privileges that the Sultan gave you, in order to annihilate you. You expect equality, but what may hit you is harder Turkish nationalism and Islamic intolerance."[53]

---

53 A. Boinodiris, Book 4, p. 147-152.

Figure 7 Recent Photo of the Carikli Kilise, known as the Church of Holy Ascension to the Greeks[54]

---

54 One of the dry wells is shown above the tree.

ARMENIAN ADANA HOLOCAUST (1909)

The fears of the elders of Karvali were not unfounded. The Greek and Armenian hopes for equality were quickly dashed in 1909 when armed military units rose up against the Turkish Government. The counterrevolution began on April 13, 1909 and was largely supported by Muslim theological students who wished to steer the country to Islamic rule. Riots and fighting soon broke out between the units and the government until the government was able to put down the uprisings and a court martial was established to try its leaders.

In late March, rumors had spread to the Armenian populated region of Adana on the Mediterranean Sea that a counterrevolution had succeeded in pushing the new government out. Seizing upon this notion, many Muslims who had opposed the overthrow of the Sultan in 1908 struck out against Adana's Armenian population, who had supported the revolution. Turks in Adana resented the Armenians since the Turks were poor and the Armenians were the richest and most prosperous class in the region. In Adana, Armenians had attained a high standard of living. In every field, they were ahead of the Turks. They further resented the fact that Armenians were being given broader rights; they took advantage of the revolution by massacring Armenians in the towns and cities of the provinces. Mobs armed with sticks, clubs and pistols roved around Adana killing Armenians and many Turkish soldiers took their side or did not help quell to the violence.

After the violence was over, between fifteen to twenty thousand Armenians were murdered in the course of what was called the "Adana Holocaust." Many Armenians who had supported the Young Turk Revolution were thus disillusioned by the level violence that had been exacted against them and felt betrayed by the new regime.

This was by no means the first time that Armenians were slaughtered by Turks. Armenians were always pressuring Sultan Abdul Hamid to sign a new reform package designed to curtail the powers of the Hamidiye, a paramilitary unit made up of Kurdish irregulars who were tasked to "deal with the Armenians as they wished." On October 1, 1895, 2,000 Armenians had assembled in Constantinople to petition for the implementation of the reforms; then, Turkish police units converged towards the rally and violently broke it up. Soon, massacres by Turks and Kurds against Armenians broke out in Constantinople and then engulfed the rest of the Armenian populated provinces of Bitlis, Diyarbakir, Harput, Sivas, Trebizond and Van. Estimates differ on how many Armenians were murdered, but European documentation of the violence, which became known as the Hamidian massacres, placed the figures from anywhere between 100,000 to 300,000 Armenians.

Although Hamid was never directly implicated for ordering the massacres, he was suspected for their tacit approval and for not acting to end them. Frustrated with European indifference to the massacres, Armenians seized the European managed Ottoman Bank on August 26, 1896. This incident brought further sympathy for Armenians in Europe. It was lauded by the European and American press, which vilified Hamid and painted him as the "great assassin" and "bloody Sultan." While the Great Powers vowed to take action and enforce new reforms, these never came into fruition due to conflicting political and economical interests.

After the Adana Holocaust, the Armenian resentment would increase and be the cause of further conflict, leading to a much greater violence against them in 1915.

Figure 8 Photo of 1910 of the Karvali Governing Body of Elders[55]

55 From Top-Left: Magioglou (from the Anargyros Magioglou side), Zopoglou, Averkios Karakoulahis, unknown, unknown, unknown; Bottom

MY GRANDPARENTS' VISIT (MAY, 1910)

Haji John Magioglou was laid off from his post several months before his project ended. After the Young Turks revolted, Turkish nationalism at high levels terminated any high power jobs held by Greeks, Armenians, or even Jews. The railway had started in 1900 at the behest of Sultan Abdul Hamid II and was built largely by the Turkish government using the best expertise available, with German advice and support. Germany had vested interests in the railroad construction. Before the construction, a German military adviser in Istanbul Auler Pasha estimated that the transportation of soldiers from Istanbul to Mecca would be reduced to 120 hours. At the same time, the Berlin to Baghdad Railway was being built. Both railways were interrelated and aimed to deepen the authority of the Empire over Arab provinces. Another intention was to protect Hejaz and other Arab provinces from an English invasion of the Middle East. The railway reached Medina on September 1, 1908, the anniversary of the Sultan's accession.[56] Unfortunately, the Young Turks dismissed the best qualified planners and operators of the railroad (like Haji John Magioglou); because of that, compromises were made to finish in time, with some sections of track being laid on temporary embankments.

Meanwhile, my grandmother Makrina Magioglou would not allow her husband a moment's peace for his behavior towards her daughter. After continuous fighting and attrition from nagging, Haji John Magioglou and Makrina decided to visit their daughter's family in Kalivarion in the spring of 1910 and see their grandson. During his

---

Left: Haji Sarafis Loukides, unknown, unknown, unknown.)

56   The Hejaz railway from Damascus to Medina (820 miles) was completed on September 1, 1908, the anniversary Sultan Hamid's accession. In 1913 a new station, the Hejaz Station, was opened in central Damascus. From its outset, the railway was the target of attacks by local Arab tribes.
The line was repeatedly damaged in fighting during the First World War, particularly at the hands of the guerrilla force led by T. E. Lawrence (Lawrence of Arabia) during the Arab Revolt. Following the break-up of the Ottoman Empire, the railway never re-opened south of the Jordanian-Saudi Arabian border.

visit, Haji John could not sit and rest. He did not want to be in the same room with George, his son in law. He always considered him as an egocentric, opportunistic peasant, who married his daughter for her money. He vowed not to leave any part of his property to her family. This forced George to work very hard to make ends meet. My father was a merchant of sorts, traveling back and forth to Mersina.

To get away from his son-in-law and to show his contempt on him, Haji John left and went fishing to Lake Burdur and Egridir, 150-200 kilometers west of Ikonium. He seemed to like fishing and he had to go that far because our closest lake, Lake Tata (Tuz Golu) was a dead salt lake.

My aunt Katina, wife of Dimitris Tsolakoglou came with my grandfather. Dimitris had to go to Russia for his business in Odessa, leaving his young wife in Constantinople. But the 1909 Turkish Civil war in Turkey prohibited him from returning. So, his wife Katina decided to join her brother in Karvali, enjoying her brother's baby son. Her sister, Orsia was married to Justinian Ioakimides, a Constantinople merchant, and she stayed there. I (Anthony) vaguely remember Katina playing with me. She really loved me a lot. At that time, our family consisted of Grandpa Paul, Grandma Katherine, my uncle Charalambos, Aunt Irene, my father George and his young bride Evanthia, my mother.[57]

THE ESCAPE (CONSTANTINOPLE, AUGUST 1910)

In 1911, Pandelis Magioglou was destined to go to the military academy of Turkey. His father's reputation was on the line, if he did not. Pandelis though had different plans. He was a rebellious young man, especially towards his father. Just like his sister, he wanted to punish him for his abusive behavior towards his mother. It did not take long before Pandelis was expelled from High School. He was a fierce bully, always getting into fights with other kids. His father decided to place him in a private school at Tsotili, to straighten him out. After a short trial period, he rebelled and wanted out.

"What is wrong son?"

---

57   A. Boinodiris, Book 1, p. 150.

"I hate Turkey. We are Christian Greeks; the Turks treat us like dirt; how do you want me to feel? I want to go someplace where people are treated as people, no matter who they are; someplace like Greece, America; anywhere, but here."

"There is no place like that anywhere in the world," said his father with a wry smile; "especially Greece. From what I hear, most of the Greek spirit of self-sacrifice and volunteerism that made Greece great is dead. Most of today's Greeks are uneducated goat thieves and bandits, who know only how to swear a lot, steal, save their own skin and profit from dirty politics and friendships. They are willing to see other people suffer, just to make themselves live one day in comfort, not thinking at all about improving the society for everyone. Find me a country with lots of volunteerism and a good team spirit and I will join you. As for America, forget it! I heard that they shoot people in the streets, just for fun. That may not be totally true, but it does not matter. America is so far away that we might as well consider you dead. Think what it will do to your mother, who will never see you again."

Pandelis would not listen. His parents were very upset. They had property at Fanari, where there was a grocery store with an apartment house on top of it. They set him up in the apartment and urged him to work in that store for the summer. They were hoping that he was good at something, maybe by going into business. After leaving him alone there for the summer, they came to Karvali.

While in Karvali, they received a letter from Pandelis.

"My father, the store at the corner location at Fanari is for sale at a good price. I also have a buyer for our own store, but we need to move fast to get it. It is an opportunity to sell our store and buy the new one. If you want this done, send me a power of attorney."

His father had to give his son a chance. Therefore, he went to Akserai, where the local government resided and got a power of attorney for his son, to sell and buy the stores.

Pandelis sold the store for 250 golden liras. He kept 50 and sent the 200 to his parents with a letter.

"I sold the store. I am keeping 50 golden liras out of 250 from the proceeds. I am going abroad, possibly to Greece, or America. I had enough of Turkey. Do not look for me."[58]

---

58   A. Boinodiris, Book 1, p. 296.

The letter and the money arrived in Karvali during that summer of 1910. That is how they found out that their son took a boat and escaped to an unknown destination. His father sent immediately a message to some of his assistants, to search for him on any ship crossing the Dardanelles. Their search was futile. Pandelis, who knew that his father had the means to stop him, acted accordingly to foil his attempts. Instead of heading to the Dardanelles, he took a ship to Rumania, which much later came through the Bosporus and the Dardanelles into Piraeus. By then, the search for him had been terminated.

MY NEW GRANDMOTHER (KALIVARION, OCTOBER, 1910)

When my grandmother Makrina heard the news, she developed gastrointestinal complications. In spite of being summertime, my grandfather brought snow from the Taurus Mountains to subside the inflammation. In spite of attempts to save her, she died in Karvali. Ironically, Pandelis became the unwilling cause of his mother's death.

After his wife's death, my grandfather, Haji John Magioglou, acted very coldly to us. It was probably because of my mother's rebellion against him. Instead of inviting us to Constantinople to live with him and escape from poverty and rentals, he left us in misery. Forty days after his wife's death, he disappeared to Nev Sehir (New City - Neapolis) where more girls are born than boys. In contrast, Karvali was known for oversupply of boys. He comes back with a new wife, Helena, a twenty-year old girl who was two years younger than my mother. The custom was that when your father remarries, the daughter calls her father's wife mother. My mother refused to call "mother" a girl two years younger. My mother blamed her father, but she also blamed the 20-year old woman that found an opportunity to get rich with a 63-year old man.[59]

After the introductions in which my mother was polite, my grandfather became uneasy. In his mid-60s, he decides to go back to Constantinople alone and work, because he simply was a certifiable workaholic. He opened up a store at Fanari, where he placed some of his money to get a steady income. At that time, people had no social security, so a person had to get a steady income from rents, or business

59 A. Boinodiris, Book 1, p. 295-296.

leases. Most elderly would eat up their savings, or have their savings stolen in no time and be left penniless. Haji John's store started selling salt fish from Lake Burdur and Egridir, the place he liked to fish, 150-200 kilometers west of Ikonium. It seems that Haji John was doing a lot more than go fishing in those lakes. He made smart business deals to sell the catch from the lakes into the Constantinople market. While he was in Constantinople, he left his young bride back at Nev Sehir,[60]even though she had to stay at my grandmother Makrina's house.[61]

By the end of 1909, the Young Turks started forcing young Greeks to serve in the Turkish Army. My father was getting anxious about his status. When my aunt Katina received word from her husband to join him in Odessa, my father urged her to go and see what she can do about bringing him over too. She was sad to leave her 5-year old nephew, but she departed for Odessa, Russia, late in 1910.[62]

Pandelis arrived in Piraeus, Greece, early in the summer of 1910. There, he expected the Greeks to treat him with the respect he was accustomed to, as the rich kid he was. The Greeks in Greece turned out to be very different than what he envisioned. They did not think in the Greek way, that he knew. He soon discovered that, unlike the Greeks of Eastern Thrace and Asia Minor the population of Greece consisted of a mixture of Greeks and other nationalities. Among the most prominent ones were Arvanites. These were people that the Venetians "imported" into Greece in the 16th and 17th century from their colonies in the Adriatic, primarily Albania, when they realized a severe shortage of labor in their occupied lands of Greece, because so many Greeks fled to the West.[63] Some of the Arvanites adapted the Greek culture, but

60   A. Boinodiris, Book 1, p. 297.
61   A. Boinodiris, Book 1, p. 297.
62   Katina returns to Greece after 51 years, in 1961. From all those that she left behind, she would find only three alive: my father, Aunt Orsia and me. A. Boinodiris, Book 1, p.151& 293 and the author's own memory.
63   The number of Byzantine Greeks that left for the West, starting from the period of the crusades is not well known. Some estimates range from 4-6 million souls. This migration was in a period when Western Europe was not very densely populated. Many historians attribute to this migration the Renaissance, the existence of so many Greek-rooted words in Western European languages and the Greek freedom of expression, found in Western cultures. Indication of how fast these Greeks were assimilated in the countries

the majority had their own codes of conduct. The same applied with other minorities that Pandelis got in contact. These were the Vlachs, Bulgarian and Slav-speaking peasants that resided in Greece, roaming Gypsies, Jews and the majority of the population, the poverty-stricken Greeks.

Most of the Greeks that he met were illiterate and very used to surviving by stealing from each other to make ends meet. They immediately surrounded him, smelling rich pickings from a rich boy. After a short, disappointing stay in Piraeus, Pandelis made up his mind that this was not the dream-land he envisioned for himself. Like most of his predecessors, he escaped to the West for a brighter future. So, in September of 1910 the once rich boy boarded a ship for America, now barely been able to pay his boat fare.

IRENE (KALIVARION, NOVEMBER, 1910)

My father George had to travel to Mersina for business during the fall and winter months. One day he came back very sick from the trip, which was an ordeal. He traveled by donkey for one week, each way, in bad weather over mountains.

My Aunt Katina and my mother were trying their best to make my father comfortable and bring his fever down. He was in a coma for eighteen days, with high fever and pneumonia symptoms. I must have been either four or five years old. My aunt Irene grabbed my hand.

"Come Anthony. Let us go to the chapel of Archangel Michael. I must pray for my brother's recovery."

We went in and she knelt in front of the icon of the Archangel.

"Please God. Do not let any harm come to my brother. If you must take a soul, take me instead. He is married with a wife and a baby. "

I looked at her puzzled. She had tears in her eyes. She kept on praying, but I got tired and started roaming around the church. She stayed kneeling for almost three hours. By then, I was climbing the walls. Finally, she got up, wiped her tears and we went home.

My Aunt Katina and my mother were all night trying their best to take care of my father. I was sleeping in the next room with my Aunt Irene. Suddenly I hear my father yell next door.

---

that they migrated can be seen recently, even in the last hundred years, with the Greek immigrants all over the world.

"By Saint George, turn up the oil lamp Katina. Bring me the icon of St. George." The two women brought him the icon. He hugged it crying and kissing it.

"It was not a dream. I saw St. George come smiling. He stepped on me with his foot and told me that I would be well after eighteen days."

Slowly my father recovered and started walking. At the same time, my Aunt Irene became sick. On the third day, my father took his sister to Jordan, the local practical doctor, carrying her on his back. The doctor examined her and took her brother outside.

"I don't understand George. You will lose your sister. She is dying, but I cannot find anything wrong with her. "

Irene died shortly after. To this day, I strongly believe that my Aunt Irene Boyun-egri-oglou[64] sacrificed herself for my father George. What is more important, she died because she believed that she owed the Saint her life.

We buried her at the family cemetery near the church of Holy Mary on our street. I made it a point every holiday to visit her grave and light a candle on the grave of this gentle, loving soul.[65]

In those early years, my uncle, Charalambos Boyun-egri-oglu, was around 18-years old and I ran after him to see what he was doing. He was trying to earn enough money for his train ticket to Constantinople. Like the rest of the young men, he wanted to get out and escape from being drafted in the Turkish Army. He left in 1911 for Constantinople. He worked there to earn enough money for his escape. It would take until 1912 for him to escape to Greece.[66]

AMERICA, AMERICA (ASTORIA, NEW YORK, DECEMBER 1910)

Pandelis, now a 17-year old youngster, lands in New York's Staten Island. He immediately sought employment, washing dishes in Greek diners in Astoria, NY and Greenwich, Connecticut. Disappointed by the low wages paid by restaurant owners, he heard of higher paying jobs in the steel industry. Not knowing English very well, he started working in

---

64   Irene Boyun-egri-oglou lived from 1892 to 1910.
65   A. Boinodiris, Book 1, p. 292-293.
66   A. Boinodiris, Book 1, p. 293.

the steel mills of Pittsburgh, Pennsylvania. Eventually, the steel mills became too hot for him. He returned to Astoria, NY resuming his job at diners and washing more dishes. The winter of 1910-1911 was very cold and he had no money to buy clothes. His later comments were:

"I had never seen so much snow and felt so cold in my life. My shoes had holes at the bottom and the snow was several feet deep. I was very depressed, sleeping with other Greeks in back rooms of restaurants like sardines. Then, someone told me that I could join the American Navy and have my meals, clothing and shelter for much less work and suffering. The next morning I found myself walking into a U.S. Navy office..."

By 1911, Pandelis, now 18, enlists in the American Navy, where food, shelter and clothing were offered to him at no cost.

Figure 9 Karvali (Guzelyurt) and Environs

KIVEN (KALIVARION, JUNE 1911)

One fine morning around June of 1911, I awoke and found nobody at home. I started crying, like all six year olds do, when they cannot find their parents. We were renting a small place, 150 meters away from Grandfather Paul's house. The owner named Sophia walks over and tries to calm me down.

"Don't worry Anthony. Your parents probably went to do some work in the fields. They will be back at night."

She gave me something good to eat and then took me over to my grandpa's house. The two arranged for her to watch over me. My parents were indeed working, collecting a product called "KIVEN." Kiven is a bush, which grows in meadows. It grew only in Cappadocia and was very much in demand for the sticky glue, named "kitre," or "yellow," that came out of processing kiven.

It seems that during those times, strong and versatile adhesives were in high demand and kiven provided one such adhesive for some unknown purpose. In order though for someone to cultivate it, first kiven had to be isolated and protected from animals. It was so tasty, that the animals went after it first. People constructed tall, roofless sheds around it to protect it. They also marked those sheds, indicating sole harvesting rights, by those that staked the bush first.

The bush has protective thorns, like pine needles. Expert workers clean the bark and make three cuts, using a sharp knife. A container is placed under the top cut, from which a white, milky substance runs in it. In a week, the container could collect over two kilos of this kitre substance. If it does not rain, the undiluted kitre sells for one golden lira for two kilos. The middle cut is more yellow but less expensive, selling for half the price. The lower cut, close to the roots is somewhat dark, almost black and sells for one fifth the price.

This milky substance is so tasty to the animals that they go crazy, trying to get to it. Goats were known to have destroyed shacks to get to it, thus wasting all the human effort to collect it.

My mother and father happened to go to the meadows, gathering the product and having a good time. This fun encounter made my mother pregnant, resulting in my having a sister in a few months. A few times, they took me with them. They collected enough money for food and fuel. They also worked in the vineyards, picking grapes, making grape juice and by-products like petmezi and retseli. They used the thorns from the kiven bush as fuel, to boil the grape juice for that process. Kiven was a very oily and flammable plant, so it was ideal for fuel.

THE ITALIAN CONFLICT (FALL 1911)

At this time, the Turks had to deal with the Italians, who had claims over Libya. The claims of Italy over Libya dated back to discussions after the Congress of Berlin in 1878, in which France and Great Britain had agreed to the occupation of Tunisia and Cyprus respectively, both parts of the then declining Ottoman Empire. When Italian diplomats hinted about possible opposition by their government, the French replied that Tripoli would have been a counterpart for Italy. In 1902, Italy and France had signed a secret treaty which accorded freedom of intervention in Tripolitania and Morocco. However, the Italian government did little to realize the opportunity.

The Italian press began a large-scale propaganda in favor of an invasion of Libya at the end of March 1911. It was fancifully depicted as rich in minerals, well-watered, and defended by only 4,000 Ottoman troops. Also, the propaganda claimed that the population was hostile to the Ottoman Empire and friendly to the Italians. The future invasion was described as little more than a "military walk".

An ultimatum was presented to the Ottoman government on the night of 26-27 September 1911. Through Austrian intermediation, the Ottomans replied with the proposal of transferring control of Libya without warring, maintaining a formal Ottoman suzerainty. Giolitti refused however, and war was declared on September 29, 1911. The Italian fleet appeared off Tripoli in the evening of September 28, but only began bombarding the port on October 3. The city was invaded by 1,500 sailors, much to the enthusiasm of the interventionist minority in Italy. Another proposal of a diplomatic settlement was rejected by the Italians, and the Turks became determined to defend the province.

The first disembarkation of troops occurred on October 10. The Italian contingent of 20,000 troops was deemed sufficient to accomplish the conquest. Tobruk, Derna and Homs were easily invaded, but the same was not true for Benghazi. The first true setback for the Italian troops happened on October 23, when poor placement of the troops near Tripoli led them to be almost completely encircled by the more mobile Arab cavalry, backed by some Turkish regular units. The attack was portrayed as a simple revolt by the Italian propaganda, but it nearly annihilated much of the Italian expeditionary corps. The corps was consequently enlarged to 100,000 men who had to face 20,000 Arabs and 8,000 Turks. The war turned into one of position, and even the first use of aviation in a modern war had little effect.

Italian troops landed in Tobruk after a brief bombardment on December 4th, 1911 and occupied the seashore and marched towards the hinterlands facing weak resistance. Few Turkish soldiers and Libyan volunteers were later organized by Captain Mustafa Kemal.[67] The 22 December Battle of Tobruk resulted in Mustafa Kemal's victory. With this achievement, he was assigned to Derna War quarters to coordinate the field on 6 March 1912.

With a decree of November 5, 1911, Italy declared its suzerainty over Libya, although it controlled only some coastal stretches which were almost under siege by the local troops, with the exception of Tripoli. Italian authorities adopted many repressive measures against the rebels, such as public hanging. Italy, however, maintained total naval supremacy and could extend its control to almost all of the 2,000 km of the Libyan coast between April and early August of 1912. Italy began operations against the Turkish possessions in the Aegean Sea with the approval of the other powers that were eager to end a war that was lasting much longer than expected. Italy occupied twelve islands in the sea, the so-called Dodecanese, but this raised the discontent of the Austro-Hungarian Empire who feared that this could fuel the nationalism of nations such as Serbia and Greece, causing unbalance in the already fragile situation in the Balkan area.

In the fall of 1911, my father George left again for Constantinople. I could never understand his reasons, because he knew that my mother was pregnant. My mother kept on telling me that he had to leave, so that the Turks would not send him to be killed.

---

67   Mustafa Kemal (Ataturk), was born Ali Rıza-oglu Mustafa (May 19, 1881 – November 10, 1938) in Thessaloniki, Greece, when that city was part of the Ottoman Empire. He was an army officer, revolutionary statesman, and founder of the Republic of Turkey as well as its first President.

My father started working in Constantinople, collecting some money for his escape. He started a store with a partner named Lazarus Kagiaoglou at Scutari (Uskudar), on the Asiatic side of Bosporus. He avoided seeing his father-in-law by staying mostly on the Asiatic side of Bosporus. We were elated to receive news from him. At that time we were living in the rental house, because it was close to my grandfather's home.

PAYMENT IN BLOOD (CONSTANTINOPLE, SUMMER, 1912)

In the summer of 1912, my father sent me a package from Constantinople. The package had clothing, food and some money.

At that time, living was tough at Constantinople. Cholera had taken its toll. The winds of possible Balkan Wars forced Turkey to delay payments to public workers, in preparation for the War. The economy collapsed. My father and Lazarus Kagiaoglou hired his half brother Charalambos for some help. He was doing grocery deliveries for several households, upon order.

One hot summer day of 1912, he was sent to a Turk public servant's home to collect money for previous deliveries. When Charalambos knocked at the door, his wife appeared at the door and start screaming.

"Help...! This filthy Greek is trying to rape me."

The neighboring Turks and her prepared husband gathered around ready to lynch Charalambos.

"Who does that infidel think he is? Let's hang him, to teach all the infidels a lesson."

Charalambos made a run for his life. He arrived at the store out of breath and gasping, he told Lazarus Kagiaoglou (my father was absent) what happened.

"Are you sure that you did not make any improper gestures?"

The nineteen-year old Charalambos started crying.[68]

"Are you kidding? I am going in a Turkish neighborhood, fearing for my life. What sort of a crazy person do you think I am? I swear on everything Holy, that I did nothing wrong. "

---

68   A. Boinodiris, Book 1, p. 301-302.

Lazarus Kagiaoglou was surprised. He suddenly realized that the
Turk staged the setup, not only to avoid payment, but also to blackmail
him into getting payment instead. He also knew that if this escalated
to a Turkish court, the court would find Charalambos guilty, simply
because he happened to be Greek. This happened so often in those
times that Greeks and Armenians avoided as much as possible any
contact with Turks they did not know.

"I want you to disappear and hide in your uncle's factory. This bully
will come searching for you. He will try to kill you, to save face and to
extort money. He owes us six months worth of food. Now he will come
back and instead of paying, he will demand payment in blood."

The Turk was satisfied that his staged setup worked; yet, in order
to look good to his neighbors, who looked at him as a husband that
would defend the honor of his wife, he picks up his scimitar sword and
rushes to the store, seeking vengeance and satisfaction. He enters the
store, finding only Lazarus Kagiaoglou in it; he started yelling with a
bared scimitar:

"Where is that man you have hired? I am going to slaughter him
like a goat. He violated my wife's honor."

Lazarus Kagiaoglou did not respond, while the Turk searched all
around. Then, Lazarus went to a dark warehouse, as if to pick some
merchandise. The Turk followed him in the dark, thinking that Lazarus
was trying to hide him. As he entered the dark room, Lazarus hit him
on the head with a long piece of hard wood, flattening him on the
ground in a pool of blood. After leaving a note for his partner George,
he picked up all the gold cash he had, locked the store, and calmly
walked to the pier, where a Greek ship was anchored; the ship was
coming from Odessa and heading for Piraeus, Greece.

He walked up the plank and told the captain the whole story. The
captain felt sorry for him and immediately hid him in the boat. In a
few days, he found himself at Piraeus, Greece. There he started his life
anew. He began a business as an egg salesman, which eventually gave
him a prosperous living.[69]

Meanwhile, my father knew nothing of what had happened. He
came back to his store, loaded with new merchandise he had just
purchased from wholesalers, only to find a dead Turk in the warehouse

---

69 A. Boinodiris, Book 1, p. 301-302.

and a note from Lazarus on the cashier's table, telling him of the events. Lazarus included the fact that the Turk owed money and came to the store attacking.

My father immediately managed to send all the new merchandise to stores of other relatives. Then, he called the police:

"I was out. When I came, I found this letter on the table and the dead man in the store."

The Turkish police took him to the police station jail. They also jailed Lazarus's uncle, named Minas Kagiaoglou. Minas was a shop-owner that sold olive oil. Minas said to the interrogator:

"I don't know why you are holding us. If anyone is guilty, it is my nephew Lazarus. George, or I were nowhere near the scene of the crime, and we can prove it. If the government needs to get the guilty party, go find my nephew. We do not know where he is."

They were held for twenty days in jail, where they were tortured by not allowing them to sit, or sleep. They slept standing up. When they saw them sitting on the floor, the guards poured cold water on them every hour, to keep them awake. Finally, a court was held and the Turkish State confiscated half the holdings of Minas' store and let them free.[70]

In the fall of 1912, the Balkan Wars started. My father George was drafted and was taken to a camp. To avoid being taken, in spite of the fact that he was not yet of age, Charalambos decided to hide in the factory of his Uncle Thanasis Kesisoglou. Unfortunately, a young man who was shopping there saw him and he thought he recognized him, but was not sure. To make sure, he decided to pick a fight. Thanasis signaled to Charalambos to avoid the fight, and so he did. He let the Turk throw him to the floor. However, when the Turk went again at the fallen Charalambos, Thanasis grabbed him and beat him. The Turk went straight to the police, stating that at the factory is hiding a Greek, deserter from the army.

The military police moved in and grabbed him. He was immediately dressed in a uniform and the Turks started training him in a boot camp. His training lasted three months. They found him to be a good cavalryman, so they made him a Turkish general's attaché at Uzunkopru, 10 kilometers from the Evros River.

---

70   A. Boinodiris, Book 1, p. 303-304.

GOLDEN HORN CHOLERA (ANTHONY'S MEMOIRS, KALIVARION, CHRISTMAS 1912)

One day, close to Christmas, my mother receives a package from my father and a letter with the news that her father Haji John Magioglou died from a cholera epidemic in Constantinople. My father wrote:

"I am sorry to inform you that your father is dead. I found out that he sold his store for 200 gold liras and a few days later, he died. Do not say anything to your stepmother Helena.

Your father's property was looted and the store sold. It was unknown where the proceeds of the sale went. By the time I heard the news, there was nothing to be had from his property..."

They called this cholera the Golden Horn cholera. It seems that the wells were polluted from a defective sewage system. People were dropping like flies. About 25,000 people were said to have died from that epidemic. The authorities had no time for burials. They simply opened up mass graves and threw bodies in, covering them up with lime.

Among those that died in that epidemic was George Kilitzoglou, the 25-year old husband of my Aunt Magdalene Kilitzoglou, who was getting ready to leave for Odessa. He was the father of Anika Magioglou and Elisabeth Dermentzoglou who lived in Drama later on.

My mother kept her father's death a secret from Helena, but eventually the news of her husband's death reached her from her uncle in Constantinople. Around February or March of 1911, they wrote to her to take the right steps for her inheritance.

She immediately thought of my mother and that if my mother found out she would empty her father's home. She calls her 50-year old father and about 20 women and moved everything that could be moved out of my grandfather's house in Karvali to her house at Nev Sehir. This included furniture, rugs, blankets, comforters, copper pots and pans, including utility vessels for processing grape juice. After doing that, she walked to our rental house on the other end of Karvali and weeping she discloses the "news" of my grandfather's death to my mother. She also told the news to the two sisters of my grandmother Makrina, Kyriaki and Suzanne who also lived in Karvali.

"Ah Evanthia, what was this catastrophe. I was told that Haji John died from cholera. You lost your father; I lost my sweet husband. Please come to our house, so that we can prepare for a memorial tomorrow."

The next day, my mother took my baby sister Irene and me to my grandmother's house. It was then, that we noticed that the house was empty. It was cold and the only heating they had was from a copper pot on a stand, filled with ashes, and live embers. This was called mangali and it was a poor person's heating system. There we meet my mother's aunts Kyriaki and Suzanne, who were lamenting:

"Poor Helena…! She is left a widow so young. Poor Haji John; He died all by his lonesome. Was it necessary for you to get married? You were almost 65-years old? You destroyed the poor young woman."

My mother could not hold her temper. She immediately went on the offensive:

"Alright ladies; my father wanted a woman. What did she want? Didn't she know his age? Didn't she know that sooner or later she would be a widow? Why didn't she marry someone of her own age?"

Helena started crying:

"What will happen to me? Even his daughter is against me. My husband took all the furniture and sold it, leaving me with these worthless items. He even sold my own gold jewelry to get capital for his store."

I, now almost six years old was listening to the two women yell at each other. I sat there and curiously enjoyed the show. There was a big, loud catfight going on between my mother and her stepmother and of course, I was on my mother's side.

My mother knew better. She knew how carefully my grandfather equipped his houses. She knew that the store at Fanari was sold for 200 golden liras and he did not have enough time to spend it before the cholera epidemic hit him. She knew that he was making a great deal of money from selling many fish. She also knew that her father was very meticulous in his letters. She looked around, trying to find a hiding place. Her eyes fell on the icon box, a special cabinet holding icons and bibles. There was typically an oil lamp, named candela hanging in front of it. She set up a chair and climbed up, reaching for the oil lamp.

"What are you doing?" said Helena.

"I will light the oil lamp," responded my mother. "It must be lit to his memory."

She fumbled inside the cabinet, where the wicks were typically stored and found wicks and a book of psalms, which also had all the chants for the dead. Inside it, she discovered a brand new letter from her father, written ten days prior to his death. She pockets it in secrecy and comes down with the book of psalms, wicks and the oil lamp. She went to the sink around the corner and started reading the letter.[71] After reading the letter to herself, she turned and calmly produced it to the rest of the women:

"This is a letter from my father to Helena before he died."

Helena tried to take it away from her, only to be pushed onto a sofa. The aunts also objected.

"It is not right to read a personal letter from a husband to his wife."

"It is right, since what this letter contains is my father's last will and testament," said my mother.

She started reading the letter, in spite of protests from Helena:

"My dear Helena, I am miserable here all alone, without you. I have a good job here, which I enjoy. However, I also have expenses here and there, maintaining two households. I have been sending you money there for your comfort, but mainly for your expenses to come here, but I have not heard from you. I need you badly, to take care of me because I am too busy to take care of myself properly. Please contact the following people to disperse all house items, before you come: My brother Haji Prodromos Magioglou, who was a district attorney at Ikonium and now retired. Also contact Andreas, the son of Suzanne, my sister-in-law. I also want you to contact my daughter Evanthia, to whom you will deliver all furniture and the keys to the house. I want them to be free of rentals and finally return to her father's home. I want you to take all your gold jewelry and sew them in your coat, so that they can travel safely to Constantinople. I want you to tell the coachman to bring you to Ikonium, but before you leave Ikonium, I want you to write to me, so that I can pick you up at Scutari (Uskudar), at the Haidar Pasha Train station. Please hurry. I miss you very much. Love, John Magioglou."

---

71 A. Boinodiris, Book 1, p. 298-299.

The women were dumbfounded. My mother continued:

"Dear Aunts. This letter is an official document. Ten days before he died my father gave specific instructions to be followed, which were not. What do you think will happen when I contact my Uncle Prodromos, the ex-District Attorney? These are grounds for grand theft, bearing severe punishment. For almost a year, this woman stripped this house and lied about it. She did not take care of her husband, as she was asked to do, possibly causing his death. She also lied about her gold jewelry, which was in her possession few days before my father's death. I want all furniture returned; otherwise, Helena will end up in jail."

Helena started crying, now in earnest. She sent word to her father at Nev Sehir about my mother's threat. I still remember the mules from Nev Sehir, loaded with furniture, which were hidden at various houses of their relatives arriving back at my grandfather's home. They were unloading them even through the night. My mother took inventory, requesting all the pieces that were missing. Days later, Haji Prodromos arrived, with Uncle Andreas, who distributed the contents according to Turkish law. Helena was entitled a portion, which she took and left for Nev Sehir. Among her share were two Maltese goats. We inherited the house, which saved us from paying rent.

We contacted Pandelis Magioglou in America. We told him about his share, asking him what he wanted to do with it. He wrote back, instructing us to give his share to Helena, making sure she has no claim on the house. That is exactly what we did and the inheritance issue was resolved.[72]

DESPERATE FLIGHT TO THE UNKNOWN (KARVALI, SPRING, 1913)

Every Greek and Armenian was afraid of the draft. Rumors among Greek and Armenian minorities were running rampant about their family members. The Turkish Army was said to use unarmed Greek and Armenian conscripts as cannon fodder in their front lines. The rumors were not without merit. Jordan Aslanoglou, one of the local young men drafted to the army, was never heard of again.

By year's end of 1912, George Boyun-egri-oglou faced a problem. He could either serve in the Turkish army, facing certain death, or try

72   A. Boinodiris, Book 1, p. 298-301.

to escape. Daringly, George decided to escape from his barracks. He walked straight to the Russian Embassy, where he asked for political asylum. The Russian Embassy was packed with about another 200 asylum seekers, most of them Greeks and Armenians. A Russian ship appeared and the Russian soldiers herded all these deserters under their protection onto it in front of the eyes of Turkish military police. They departed for the port of Odessa, where George found his sister Katina and his brother-in-law Demetrius Tsolakoglou. His sister had been in Odessa since 1910. George found work at the factory of George Tsolakoglou as a distributor's aid, until he mastered the Russian language.[73]

I was only seven years old, when we heard that my father had escaped to Odessa. We heard the news with a heavy heart, not knowing if, and when we would ever see him. My mother now worked in the vineyards of my grandfather, while I was in the second grade of elementary school.

During Easter week of 1913, my uncle Charalambos asked for a leave from the Turkish general he was serving, to celebrate his holiday. The general gave him a few days leave. Charalambos then proceeded to communicate with his father (my grandfather) Paul Boyun-egri-oglu. Paul told his son to get out of the army as fast as possible because he did not like the radical ideas of the Young Turk revolutionaries. Charalambos was late returning to his unit by two days. The general got very upset, because his horse needed tending and as a result, he ordered him to be beaten. He was beaten so hard, that it took several days for him to recover. This beating strengthened his resolve. He immediately started talking to six other Greeks in the Turkish army and organized an "escape band." One spring night of 1913, the seven men, with all their weapons made their way out of the camp with their horses and crossed the Evros River Bridge.

Their escape was remarkable and was noted as a heroic act by those that witnessed it. They managed to silence their horses by wrapping rags on their hoofs. Then at night, they surprised the guards by running through their Turkish border positions and tossing live grenades among the Turkish guard positions. The Turks did not expect an attack from their rear. By the time, they realized what was happening, Bulgarian

---

73   A. Boinodiris, Book 1, p. 150-151 & 303-304.

guards, who were alerted by the grenade explosions, surrounded the escapees.

When the Bulgarians saw the attackers coming from the Turkish border, they were ready to kill them in spite of the fact that these riders were surrendering with their hands high. They thought that the attack could be a feint, to penetrate their positions. They were thrown down from their horses and knives were placed on their bared throats. When someone brought a light and their throats were revealed, they found that all of them had crosses hanging around their necks. An interpreter was called that could speak Turkish.

"We are Christian Greeks and do not want to fight on the side of the Turks," Charalambos told the interpreter. Instead of cutting their throats, the Bulgarians gave them food and transported them to the Greeks, who at that time were their allies. The seven were soon placed in the Greek army, where they later fought with distinction.[74]

THE PLIGHT OF THE BALKAN WARS (1913)

With the fall of the Sultan, the Ottoman Empire started to decline. The Young Turks took the side of Germany, who supported them in their revolt. Some Young Turks started to reconsider whether they did the right thing by taking out Sultan Hamid. In fact, some Turkish correspondents came to Thessaloniki to ask him what should be done to minimize Turkey's losses. His response was: "After all your insults all these years, what do you want from me? It is too late now. You turned all our minorities against us. The reality is that the Ottoman Empire consists of only one fourth of the population being Turks; the rest are minorities. The whole world, including the Greeks is being armed and wages war against us. To keep Greece neutral, you should transfer Crete to the Greeks."

The Balkan states saw in the Turkish revolution of 1908-1909 and the Turko-Italian War of 1911-1912 an opportunity to retaliate against the Turks, their former oppressors. In 1911, the Italians won against Turkey and got the Greek Dodecanese Islands and Libya. Italian diplomats decided to take advantage of the situation to obtain a favorable peace. A treaty was signed at Lausanne on October 18, 1912. It was clear that the main items of the Treaty did not concern Greece.

74   A. Boinodiris, Book 1, p. 304-305.

In the Treaty and in the accompanying agreements, declarations and protocols the following issues were decided:

- Eastern Thrace, the islands of Imbros and Tenedos and the Straits were given definitively to the Turks. The Dodecanese was recognized as belonging to Italy.

- The representatives of the Entente, with Venizelos' agreement, proposed the creation of an International Committee in which Britain, France, Italy and the Balkan countries were to participate in order to administer the "Free Harbor" of Alexandroupolis and the railway line from the Bulgarian borders to the Aegean Sea along the demilitarized bank of the river Evros.

- The Straits were to remain as before demilitarized and open to international traffic, but with the proviso in favor of Turkey that in the event of Turkey being involved in a war she had the right to impede access to the Straits to her enemies. The International Committee of the Straits was to remain in place, but not as an international government with its own policing force.

- The boundary line between Turkey and Syria was redrawn in a manner more favorable to Turkey - in comparison to what had been decided in the Treaty of Sevres in September 1920.

- In respect of the north eastern boundaries of Turkey, the earlier agreement between Turkey and Soviet Russia (Treaty of Alexandropol, 3rd December 1920) was confirmed.

- No mention was made of Armenians or Kurds.

- Turkey fully recognized the ceding of Cyprus to Britain.

- The Capitulations (the immunities and privileges awarded by the Porte) were abolished.

- The question of Mosul which had been occupied by the British since 1922 was referred to the arbitration of the League of Nations which decided in 1926 in favor of the British.

- The Allies waived the issue of the payment of war damages by Turkey and the Kemal delegation agreed to waive a similar demand if Greece in return ceded Karayats to the Turks.

The terms were formally equal to those requested by Istanbul at the beginning of the war and maintained a formal Ottoman suzerainty over Libya, which received only an autonomous status under the judiciary rule of Kadis elected by the Sultan. Meanwhile, Italy looked at Greece defensively, knowing very well that eventually they would want their islands back. So, to torpedo this eventuality they established a policy to support Turkey against Greece.[75]

Meanwhile, Venizelos[76] did his preparatory homework between 1908 and 1912. He secretly met in the office of Patriarch Joachim III in Constantinople with the Balkan representatives of Serbia, Bulgaria and Montenegro, under seemingly religious reasons. He did it secretly, because the British, and especially the head of the foreign office, Kitchener, would oppose such an alliance. To evade the British, the Greek, Bulgarians and Serbs raised the Macedonian issue, a red-herring conflict between these allies to dispel rumors of conspiracy. It was then, that Paul Melas, a Greek military officer started his guerilla warfare, fighting against Bulgarian insurgents in Turkish-held Macedonian

---

75   A. Boinodiris, Book 1 p. 49

76   Venizelos, Eleftherios (1864-1936), was a Greek political leader and diplomat, born in Crete, and educated at the University of Athens. He served in the Cretan assembly, participated in a revolt against Turkish rule, and intermittently headed the government of Crete between 1898 and 1909. In 1910, he became Prime Minister of Greece, and in 1912, he formed the Balkan League. Subsequently he guided his country through the Balkan Wars. During World War I differences with Constantine I, king of Greece, who was pro-German, kept Venizelos out of office. In 1916, however, he formed an opposition government that took control and in 1917 went into the war on the allied side. In the elections of 1920, he was overwhelmingly defeated, and he did not actually return to leadership until 1928, when he began a 4-year term as Prime Minister. He served as a stabilizing force in Greece, which was in constant conflict between royalist and anarchist forces. Having twice again served briefly as Prime Minister, Venizelos led an unsuccessful republican revolt in Crete in 1935, after which he was forced into exile. The International Airport of Athens, Greece bears his name.

territory. When the allies were ready, the guerilla warfare stopped among guerillas and turned against their common enemy.

In March 1912, Serbia arranged a treaty of alliance with Bulgaria. Greece concluded a military convention with Bulgaria the following May. Tension increased steadily in the Balkan Peninsula during the summer of 1912, especially after August 14, when Bulgaria dispatched a note to the Turks demanding that Macedonia, then a Turkish province, be granted autonomy.

The three million Bulgarians, led by King Ferdinand and his sons Boris and Cyril lined up 250,000 fighting soldiers, armed with Russian weapons. The 2.5 million Serbs, led by King Peter Karagiorgevich lined up 150,000 soldiers. The 300,000 people of Montenegro lined up 30,000 soldiers. The Greeks could barely line up 100,000 soldiers; Greece at that time was a small country (about 2.5 million) that had just acquired Thessaly. It was barren and poor, with most of its population dispersed in Russia, Egypt, Rumania and many other countries of the world. Yet, Greece had the only strong Navy of the alliance.

Serbia and Bulgaria had signed treaties to split between them the land of Vardar Macedonia, what is now the part of Macedonia along the Axios River. Greece did not take part in it though. After Greece vetoed the breakout of war several times in the summer, in order to better prepare her navy, the First Balkan War broke out in October 1912 following an impossible ultimatum given to the Porte.

The Balkan states began to mobilize on September 30, and eight days later Montenegro declared war on the Ottoman Empire. On October 18, the Balkan allies entered the war on the side of Montenegro, precipitating the First Balkan War. The Balkan Alliance won a series of decisive victories over the Turks during the next two months, forcing them to relinquish Albania, Macedonia, and practically all their other holdings in southeast Europe. After Montenegro and Serbia declared war, the Turkish correspondents visited the Sultan, asking him to comment. His response was: "These people need their mountainous land to live. Give it to them. Yet, be careful of Greece. If they join in, we are in trouble."

After Greece joined in, he advised: "I suggest you take me away from Thessaloniki, before I fall prisoner to the Greeks. "

His wish was granted. A train took him soon to Bursa. The Greek Navy attacked the Turkish Navy in the North Aegean. The Bulgarian Army advanced to the Aegean, closely watching the outcome with the Greek Navy, ready to bug out, to avoid being encircled by a Turkish landing in Kavala, where there were many Turks. Meanwhile, the Bulgarians captured Alexandroupolis, Komotini, Xanthi, Kavala, Drama and Serres.[77]

Following the troubled period of the struggle for Macedonian liberation and the first Bulgarian occupation, the Greek Army liberated Drama on 1st July 1913 following 530 years of foreign occupation. The Bulgarians recaptured the city and difficult times were endured but following this, the three religious communities in the city (Greeks, Turks and Bulgarians) gradually began to form neighborhoods where members of all three groups lived together, these mainly being in the present day commercial center.

Late in November, the Turks sued for an armistice. An armistice agreement was signed on December 3 by all the Balkan allies except Greece, which continued military operations against the Turks. Later in the month, representatives of the belligerents and the major European powers met in London to decide the Balkan question. The Turks rejected the peace conditions demanded by the Balkan states, and the conference ended in failure on January 6, 1913. On January 23, a successful coup d'état brought an extreme nationalist group to power in the Ottoman Empire, and within a week fighting resumed.

After reaching the Strymon River, the Bulgarians met up with the retreating Turkish army. They chased them to the Peles Mountains, near Lake Doirani, where now the Greek and Serb armies converged. When the Bulgarians realized that the Greeks captured Thessaloniki,

---

77   This narration comes indirectly from a Bulgarian bailiff of the Drama High School, who served in Drama during their occupation of the city during 1941-1945. According to him, he was a private in 1912, anxiously reading news on the battleship Averof of the Greek Navy. If the Greek Navy lost, these troops were ready to run back to the mountains of Bulgaria. The Turks of Kavala rejoiced that the Greek battleship Averof was hit, when the Turkish Army passed false rumors. The news was only partially true. Averof was involved in a battle, was damaged on the smokestack, but the Turkish flagship was sank. Greeks landed on the islands of North Aegean, from Thasos to Ikaria.

they requested from Prince Constantine, son of King George I of Greece to allow them to enter in that city for rest and recreation for a battalion of their army. King Constantine, the commanding general of the Greek army agreed, but without the consent of Venizelos, or his father. The King was a naïve politician, giving the Bulgarians an opportunity to send in 20 brigades into the city, in the middle of a rainy, fall night. Venizelos found out what was happening and realizing that he could lose the city to the Bulgarians forever, he sent King George there with additional reinforcements. Unfortunately, a sniper, called Schinas, shot King George, as he was entering the city. Even though the sniper may have been working for the Bulgarians, Venizelos kept it under wraps and requested that the allies capture Adrianople, to secure their position. Bulgarians surrounded Adrianople in all directions except the south for six months. Venizelos made the point that with the 20 brigades (about 35,000 troops) in Thessaloniki, the Bulgarians could totally surround and capture Adrianople. He offered the Greek transports from Thessaloniki to take the Bulgarian troops to the Bay of Xeros for this operation.

It so happened, with some exceptions. The pressure of Bulgarian occupation from Thessaloniki was taken out; the Bulgarian troops were boarded on Greek ships, only to be taken prisoners to the Cycladic Islands. Some of these troops came back to Macedonia during their occupation of World War II and laughingly told us of their lives in the islands and how much they appreciated the hospitality of their captors. The few Bulgarian troops that remained in Thessaloniki were taken care of by 3,000 Cretan troops with baggy pants who took them by force to the Bulgarian border.

Epirus was still under Turkish hands. 40,000 troops under Eshat Pasha held up in the forts of Bizani. In the subsequent fighting Greece captured Ioannina, Albania and Adrianople (now Edirne, Turkey), which had previously fallen to Bulgaria. The Turks obtained an armistice with Bulgaria, Greece, and Serbia on April 19, 1913. Montenegro accepted the armistice a few days later. Another peace conference, with the major European powers again acting as mediators, met at London on May 20. By the terms of the Treaty of London, concluded on May 30, the Turks ceded the island of Crete to Greece and relinquished all territories in Europe west of a line between the Black Sea port of Midye and Enez, a town on the coast of the Aegean Sea. Boundary questions and the status of Albania and the Aegean Islands were referred to an international commission.

Division of the re-conquered Balkan territories, however, resulted in the Second Balkan War in June and July of 1913, which Bulgaria lost to Serbia, Montenegro, Greece, the Ottoman Empire, and Romania; consequently, Bulgaria lost considerable territory. In the second Balkan War, during the summer of 1913 the Bulgarian Army was barricaded in Kilkis, preparing to capture Thessaloniki, bitter about the double-cross from Venizelos. The French military experts of that time thought that their strength and fortifications were not easily breached. The Greeks, after finishing their operations in Epirus regrouped and before the Bulgarian attack, they mounted a pre-emptive strike against their fortifications. The attack came at night, surrounding their trenches and found them asleep. They routed them from Kilkis to Lahana lost all their holdings all the way to Nestos River. The Treaty of Bucharest settled the Second Balkan War.

DRAMA, A TOWN ON THE MACEDONIAN FRONT (DRAMA, 1913)

At the beginning of the 20th century, the population of Drama reached 14,000, economic growth continued, and sporadic violent episodes began to occur as part of the undeclared war for the liberation of Macedonia. The Bishop of Drama, Chrysostomos, town dignitaries and the people organized the defense of the Greek community.

One of the local men in Drama was involved in the Greek guerilla fighting to aid in liberating Eastern Macedonia from the Turks and the Bulgarians. His name was Gatsoulis, whose trade was fishing. He was the bodyguard of bishop Chrysostomos, who was the underground leader of the fighters. He was often riding his horse with bishop Chrysostomos, visiting all villages of the county of Drama, organizing the Greek resistance. He and Chrysostomos had a few good men with them and had many skirmishes with Bulgarian guerillas, which objected to their presence and were led by their priests. In one skirmish, Gatsoulis was wounded on his right leg by the Bulgarians and has limped ever since then.[78]

The Bulgarian priests and civilians, under the leadership of an officer named Manistas were doing the same, with equally strong interests to liberate the county from the Turks and attach it to Bulgaria. The two groups often fought each other, even though they were still under the Turkish government's authority.[79]

During the Second Balkan war, violent events occurred. As Bulgarian soldiers were fleeing from Kavala, five Greeks from villages around Doxato killed and wounded several members of a Bulgarian group in an ambush. The Bulgarian troopers of that group then entered Doxato and started shooting indiscriminately anyone they found in the streets, in cafes or their houses. Over one thousand dead resulted from that massacre of 1913.

At the same time, Italians and Austrians were instrumental in creating Albania, attaching to it the Northern Epirus that was populated by Greeks. Austria wanted rights in the port of Thessaloniki. The many Jews that lived there, having primarily Austrian nationality and strong ties with the Jews of Vienna, supported them on this. Upon seeing that, the Greeks of Thessaloniki resented the resistance that the Jews of that city presented against the Greeks during its siege. The Jews of that city supported the Turks monetarily and politically to the end. This continued later, throughout the First World War, with their political influence through Austria.[80]

At the end of the Balkan wars, the British Foreign Office accused Venizelos in complicity against Britain's interests in securing the integrity of the Ottoman Empire in Europe. Venizelos responded smiling: "I am

---

78   He was again in trouble during the Second World War with the Bulgarians, when in 1941 they forced him to use his boat for fishing. The Bulgarians got drunk. In his stupor, one of the Bulgarians shot him in the left arm. He became invalid for the rest of his life. Gatsoulis' son became a pediatrician. In fact, he was the author's physician in the 1950s.
79   A. Boinodiris, Book 1, p. 346-347.
80   This resentment would have catastrophic effect on these Jews; the mass rounding up and extermination of Thessaloniki's Jewish population by the Nazis, thirty years later is uniquely identified by a widespread apathy of its population for the fate of their Jewish neighbors, as compared to other Greek cities, where the citizens made strong efforts to save them.

not a merchant, who makes a deal that must be kept. I am a lawyer in defense of my country and not required to disclose to you everything, when such disclosure jeopardizes our interests."

Venizelos failed to inform the British of his intentions. If the British knew of his intentions, they would shore up Turkey to keep status quo in the Balkans.

During the armistice, 70,000 Turkish prisoners were exchanged. Turkey signed a treaty, delivering Crete and the Aegean Islands to Greece.

After the first Balkan War, Charalambos Boyun-egri-oglu had settled in Drama. There, during the continuous border insurgency operations of the second Balkan War, he got into a fight with a Bulgarian-Turk, who was menacing the Greeks of the area. In a hand fight and in self-defense he killed him with a bayonet, still attached to its sheath. He escaped lynching and arrest by the Bulgarians and took the name Pavlides to avoid detection by both, Bulgarians and Turks, who were allied in the subsequent World War I. He decided to escape again to the Greek side over the Strymon River and volunteer into the Greek army.[81]

RUSSIAN ADVENTURE (UKRAINIAN COUNTRYSIDE, AUGUST, 1913)

In Odessa, George had loaded his horse cart full of crates of halva, a small barrel of sesame oil, and a barrel of tahini and proceeded to his destination at Kryvyy Rih, about 200 miles to the north-east of Odessa. He was to deliver these goods, which were paid for by the local merchant and return with a consignment of hides, which was used as barter with the Tsolakoglou Enterprises.

He had taken his time, delivered his goods after four days of traveling and was returning with the hides. He was about sixty miles away from Kryvyy Rih, approaching the town of Bashtanka, of the

---

81 Charalambos Pavlides retired from the Greek Army; married a Thracian woman called Panagiota and had two sons: Paul and Andreas. He died in 1955. Andreas Pavlides lives today in Drama. He has an appliance store and for some time was the president of the local soccer team, called Doxa (meaning "glory," in Greek).

Mykolayiv district; there, he decided to call it a day, rest his animal and go to sleep.

During this month, the farmers reaped their grain and stacked it in huge, almost hemispherical stacks, to dry and then to be loaded and taken to the stone-covered flats, where the seeds are separated from the hay. Then, they place the seeds in sacks and ship it to mills to make flour. The sun was going down and the night started to blanket the Ukrainian plain. As George was looking around for a good place to spend the night, he saw several of these hemispherical stacks of dried wheat stalks in the fields next to the dirt road. He drove his cart to one of those stacks, unhitched his animal and tied it to the wheel of his cart, letting it graze on the dried stacks of wheat. He then grabbed a loaf of bread, some pastourma,[82] and some tahini on bread and thus had his supper, which he washed down with some wine. After that, he opened a hole in the stack, wrapped himself with his wool overcoat and crawled in it, to go to sleep. Even though it was August, nights in Ukraine tend to be rather chilly and the stack of wheat was the perfect shelter for such cool nights. Anyway, he was tired and it did not take long for him to fall asleep.

George was in deep sleep, when suddenly he was awakened by a loud growl, accompanied by horse whining, more growls and a loud snap. Then he heard horse hoofs running away from him. *"Something is attacking my horse,"* he thought, as he peeked through the wheat stack to see what is happening. In the moonlight he could see that his horse was gone and a large grizzly bear had its back at the stack. Around the animal there were a pack of about one dozen wolves, trying to get to his food provisions, which the bear dragged and laid at its feet. Among his provisions he had pastourma, whose beef aroma the bear and the wolves found irresistible. Having been there first, the bear tore through the hides and had probably attacked his supplies first, laying claim and defending its find. As the wolves rounded the bear, the bear used its huge paws against them, tossing them to the side as they yelped in pitched cries; yet, they still came after the food. As the bear defended its food, it rose on its two hind

---

82   Pastourma is a kind of Greek pastrami, which is preserved with fenugreek.

legs, towering over the wolves, with its back always at the stack. As it retreated in this position, the bear started pushing against George, who started getting scared about being crushed by the butt of this monster. Having no other recourse, he decided to act. He curled himself around, positioning both his legs against the back of the bear and with all his strength he kicked the bear forward. The bear fell forward, among the wolves, which started biting her rear legs and chasing her away. Meanwhile, George crawled through the other side of the stack, landed on the ground and started running in the night. The wolves were so occupied with the bear and there was such a big raucous of yelps and growls that no animal came after him. He ran almost until morning, when he reached a near-by village. He knocked at the first door to ask for help.

The family at that house were simple peasants, and very hospitable. After telling them what happened, they let him rest there. George was so shaken, that he could not sleep all night. In the morning, with the first light, they mounted a search party of horse carts and riders and came to the spot that George had left his cart. To their surprise, the cart was still there, but all the hides were strewn all over the field. On top of that, the large semispherical wheat stack next to the cart was no longer there. All the wheat was strewn on the surrounding area. At almost one hundred meters from the stack, they found George's wool coat, shredded into little pieces by bear claws.

"The bear did not appreciate what you did," said the peasant. "The animal came back wanting revenge, tried to find you and you not being there, it took its frustration out on your coat."

"I wonder what happened to my horse," said George.

"Your horse escaped," said the peasant, pointing to a snapped rope, still hanging at the wheel. "It is probably feeding around here someplace. We will help you find it and be on your way. Next time, don't leave food near you, especially pastourma. These animals can smell it all the way to the Urals."

It took almost a whole day for George to round up his hides, find his horse and be on his way. As he drove through the dirt road, he reached onto his neck, where he had an icon of St. George hanging by a string. He looked at it, kissed it and raised his eyes to the sky: *"Thank you Lord for sparing me.*" Then, his mind wandered back to his home in Karvali, wondering whether it was a good choice to end up in this Ukrainian wilderness.

WAR: A DESTRUCTION OF WEALTH[83] (1914)

Even before war is declared the prospect of conflict between the countries, in which serious difficulties have arisen, affects the financial situation. Credit facilities are restricted; monetary circulation is disturbed; production slackens; orders fall off to a marked degree; and an uncertainty prevails, which reacts harmfully on trade.

Then, the declaration of war and mobilization come. The able bodied men are called to the standards; between one day and the next work stops in factories and in the fields. With the cessation of the breadwinners' wage, the basis of the family budget, the wife and children are quickly reduced to starvation, and forced to seek help from their parishes and the State.

The whole of the nation's activities are turned to war. Goods and passenger traffic on the railways come to an end; rolling stock and rails are requisitioned for the rapid concentration of men, artillery, ammunition and provisions at strategic points.

Not only does the country cease to produce, but also it consumes with great expense in the hurry of operations. Its reserves are soon exhausted; taxes are not paid. If it cannot appeal for loans or purchases from abroad, it suffers profoundly.

Then, the fighting begins, with the earth heaped with dead, and the hospitals overflowing with wounded. Thousands of lives are sacrificed; the young, and the strongest people who were yesterday the strength of their country, who were its future of fruitful labor, are laid low by shot and shell. Those who do not die in the dust or mud will survive, after countless sufferings, mutilated, invalid, and no longer to be counted on for the prosperity of the land. And it is not only the population; essential wealth is thus annihilated. In a few hours armies use up, for mutual destruction, great quantities

---

83 This is a summary from the published "Inquiry into the Causes and Conduct of the Balkan Wars, "Carnegie Endowment for International Peace, Washington, D.C., 1914.

of ammunition. Meanwhile, highly expensive supplies of cannon, gun carriages and arms are ruined. There is destructive bombardment of towns, villages in flames, the harvests stamped down or burned, bridges, the most costly items of a railway, blown up. The regions that are traversed by the armies are ravaged. The noncombatants have to suffer the fortune of war with the loss of their goods. Thousands of wretched families sought security at the price of cruel fatigue and the loss of everything, their land and their traditions, acquired by the efforts of many generations.

After the Balkan Wars, each nation was beginning to take stock of its inventory. The armies returned home after demobilization. The soldier again became peasant, workman, merchant; the hour of the settling of accounts, individual and collective, had struck. The government, which had been in the hands of the military during the war, was restored to the civil authorities and the period of regular financial settlement began.

Nevertheless, the traces of the war were still fresh. If the corpses of the victims were not visible their countless graves were everywhere, the mounds not yet invaded by the grass that next summer will hide them away. Visible too were the wounded in the hospitals and the mutilated men in the streets and on the roads; the black flags, hanging outside the doors of the hovels, a dismal sign of the mourning caused by the war and its sad accompaniment, cholera.

You could see towns and villages laid in ashes, the house fronts torn open by shell or stripped of their plaster by riddling shot. There were camps at the city gates where streams of families fleeing before the enemy made a halt. All along the roads you could see their wretched caravans.

An estimate was made of the cost of the double Balkan war. It is too easily carried away by admiration for feats of arms, exalted by historians and poets; one needs to know all the butchery and destruction that go to make a victory; to learn the absurdity of the notion, especially at the present time, that war can enrich a country; to understand how, even from far off, war reacts on all nations to their discomfort and even to their serious injury. The profit and loss of every little tradesman in the corner of his shop, and the wages of every workman toiling in a factory are influenced incessantly by the tremendous pulsation of the universal movement of international exchange. Every war is a destruction of wealth and a step backwards.

First World War
(1914-1918)

The Meat Pie (Karvali, Noon, New Years, 1914)

I heard the following story from both, my aunt Kyriaki Zoumboulidou and my mother Elisabeth, her sister, several times. I believe that the first time I heard it was in Turkish, around 1952, which at the time I understood much better than I do now, as Kyriaki was remembering the event. I later had asked her again in Greek and she gave me more details. Kyriaki was my aunt, but also she was my godmother, because she baptized me. As the author of this book I want to pay tribute to this woman, who treated me like her own son.

Kyriaki recalled vividly a New Years day in Karvali. A light cold wind was blowing from Mt. Argeon, but the sun was out, making the light snow on the ground of Karvali streets shimmer. In spite of the cold, a curious, young, barefooted Turkish boy ventured into the Greek neighborhood of Karvali, to see what is happening there. The child was about five years old, had tattered peasant clothes and looked very hungry.

As he was roaming through the neighborhood, two eyes followed him from a window of a house near the St. Gregory's church.

"He is probably the son of some newcomers that came to work in our farms," said Kyriaki Aslanoglou to her mother, as she watched him intensely from the window.

"Who is?" responded her mother Makrina, who came to the window to watch.

Makrina Aslanoglou[84] was the daughter of Basil Tsekmezoglou (the "sisman" or "fat")."[85] She had married John Aslanoglou[86] at a very young age.

Makrina Aslanoglou had three children, the ten-year-old girl Kyriaki (born in 1904), an eight-year-old boy Michael (1906) and a two-year-old girl Elisabeth (the author's mother, born in 1912). She had at least three other children, but due to conditions of that time, they died young. One was another Elisabeth (1908), who died in less than a year. Infant survival was very limited in those days.

As mother and daughter watched the boy inside the Aslanoglou home, the aroma of a freshly baked meat pie was filling up the air and making the younger children, especially the eight-year old Michael complain, because they all had to wait for their father John to get home from a church meeting for lunch.

Kyriaki loved children, especially her brother and baby sister. She often looked after them, helping her mother. As she watched the boy, she was impressed by his handsome appearance, in spite of his miserable condition.

"Can we give him some of our meat pie mother?" she pleaded. "He looks very hungry."

Her mother smiled and took a plate from the table and filled it with slices of steaming meat pie from the pan that she took out of the

---

84   Makrina was the author's grandmother.
85   Basil Tsekmezoglou was born around 1850 and died around 1920. Tsekmezoglou also means the "son of the unbearable", and because he was fat, he was teased often as "the son of the man who is big enough to break the back of a donkey." The "Unbearable" family can be traced back to Armenian roots, all the way back to Theophylact the Unbearable, who lived in the 9th century, and whose son became Emperor Romanus Lecapenus in 920 AD. (See "ANDROS ODYSSEY, Byzantine Kalivarion"). Makrina's grandfather was Kyriakos Tsekmezoglou (1830-1890) and Kyriakos' father was Stavros Tsekmezoglou (1805-1880). Basil Tsekmezoglou married Maria Zopoglou and had four children, Makrina (1880-1957), Stavros (1875-1915), Calliope (1890-1965) and Kyriakos (1895-1962). The family was still mourning, because Stavros died in Constantinople in the cholera epidemic of 1911.
86   John was the author's grandfather.

still warm oven. "You go and feed him," she said to Kyriaki, with a smile.

Kyriaki immediately put her coat and shoes on and rushed out of the house with the meat pie.

"Please have some," she beckoned to the boy.

"Thank you," said the boy, as he dove into them hungrily.

After eating half the plate without stopping, he paused. "What is your name?"

"Kyriaki," the girl replied, smiling as she stood there, watching him eat.

"I will never forget your name," said the boy, as he wolfed down the rest of the pies smiling.

THE RECOLLECTION (GUZELYURT, NOON, MAY, 2007)

Ninety-three years later, the author, his wife and two friends visited Guzelyurt (the renamed Karvali). We asked the guide, a young lady named Birsen Urcan to see if we could meet with some old timers through the mediation of the Mayor of the town. She did much better than that. She brought us in contact with the District Governor of Gelveri at Akserai, named Ramadan Yildirim and we set up a meeting at the City Hall of Guzelyurt.

Mr. Yildirim promptly arranged a meeting with some locals, one of which was an old man of ninety-eight years old, but in excellent condition. A commemorative photo was taken during the occasion (See Figure 10). The meeting had several observers, local teachers using the internet, and some residents, which included the sons of some Turks that came from Kozani, Greece to Karvali. They commented how much difficulty their parents encountered, especially from locals, who continued until recently to call them infidels. We compared notes, noting the similar prejudice shown on Greeks from Karvali when they arrived in Greece.

The one though that showed the highest excitement was the ninety eight year old man, when I showed him the photo of the Karvali elders, which is shown at the front cover of this book. This photo immediately brought tears in his aged eyes. We all watched with surprise, as we witnessed his excitement. It was with extreme emotion that the prefect translated what the old man was recounting, as Mr. Yildirim was translating into English:

"We lived so peacefully then. What happened to us?"

Then, I heard:

"... and I remember this Greek girl, who brought me this delicious meat pie."

"What was her name?" I asked.

"Her name was Kyriaki. I will never forget it."

Upon hearing that name, I felt that my spine was electrified with such emotion, that if I was not seated I would have collapsed. I immediately recalled the story that I had heard repeatedly from my own aunt and godmother, Kyriaki Aslanoglou (later Zoumboulidou) and due to improbable circumstances of chance, it linked directly with this elder in front of me, ninety three years later.

As the reader will find out, Kyriaki moved to Selefkia, and then to Greece; she later was married in Greece and became Kyriaki Zoumboulidou. She died in Greece on 31 December 1984. The little girl that extended the hand of compassion to this little Turkish boy never stopped doing so throughout her life. Although she loved children, she was barred from having her own due to health problems, detected after she was married. In return, whenever the need arose, she became a proxy mother to all the children of her extended family, from nephews and nieces and to their children, and many outside her family, until her death. This list included me, who fondly remembers the love and dedication Kyriaki extended to me, when I was a five-year old. I lived in her home, scared out of my wits, not daring to go to my own home, after a mortar attack in my neighborhood during the Greek Civil War.[87]

TAURUS CROSSING (MAY, 1914) * 2

"Come Kyriaki! Let's eat. Your father is here!" yelled Makrina to her daughter.

Kyriaki took the empty plate from the little boy and walked in. As they sat on the served table, their father said a prayer and the family started eating. John Aslanoglou seemed nervous.

---

87   (See the next book, "Andros Odyssey: The Return").

"Is anything wrong?" asked Makrina. Makrina, in spite of her several pregnancies was a lively 34-year old woman (born around 1880) with lots of energy.

"Come with me," said John. "You, children stay and eat."

The couple moved into the next room and closed the door behind.

"I formulated the plans for our move," said John, when they were alone.

John was a 39-year old man (born in 1875) and he was among the men that decided to flee for good from Karvali. After consulting with Makrina, instead of fleeing to Greece, or Russia, he decided to go south, to the port of Mersina and from there to Selefkia. In 1908 he went to Selefkia alone, leaving his young wife Makrina and his children back at Karvali.[88] He was from a family with a tradition of being good merchants. His father, Chris Aslanoglou (born around 1855), was a merchant and a church elder of the St. Gregory of Nazianzos Church. They had a general goods store, next to the St. Gregory's Church in Karvali.[89] His house had a walled yard, adjacent to the churchyard. John's grandfather was Haji Prodromos (born around 1830), another elder in his time.

"Did you talk to your folks?" asked Makrina.

"Yes," replied John. "As you know, my father encourages me to make this move, because he has his hands full.[90] But that is of secondary importance. I want my family next to me for your safety. I cannot support you by visiting you in Karvali. You know that the trip back and

---

88   A. Boinodiris, Book 1, p. 139.

89   A. Boinodiris, Book 1, p. 138.

90   John's mother, Kyriaki was born around 1860 in Nev Sehir. Nev Sehir (or New City) is a fertile city, located on a bent of the Alys River. Most of the fields around it are watered from that River, making it quite fertile. Kyriaki died in 1890, five years after having John. The widower, Chris married Elisabeth (born 1860) from Tenegi. Subsequently, Chris had six children with his second wife, three boys and three girls. Being the eldest and from another wife, John was dispensable. After he grew up, his father encouraged the orphaned John to move to Selefkia where he could become independent, so that his father could tend to the rest of his family.

forth is long and dangerous. I can be of no use to anyone, if something happens to me in one of these trips."

Truly, traveling along the route from Karvali to Mersina and Selefkia in those times involved traveling through the Taurus Mountains, which were plagued by bandits, many of them being renegade soldiers. Crime was rampant and many people were killed on that road. Several women were abducted, and their husbands were found with their throats slit. Somehow, the bandits had good information, attacking only those that had something to rob from.

In Selefkia, through his long-term friends, connections and personality he managed to build the biggest import-export warehouse in town, within a reasonably short period. He was dealing with camel caravans that brought goods from the East, exchanging them with manufactured goods that came from Constantinople. As the Ottoman Empire positioned itself to fight against the small Balkan League States of Bulgaria, Greece, Serbia and Montenegro in the First Balkan War, he found himself in a key position to supply the Turkish army, from food, to blankets from the East.[91] He could also see how volatile the Ottoman Empire was becoming and wanted to capitalize on any benefits such volatility offered. In the beginning, John did not know how the war would affect the Greeks of Asia Minor. He was at that stage where he was building up his family.

"When and how do we move?" asked Makrina.

John started explaining his plan. The following week, after finalizing some details of the move, John would send a trusted friend to Karvali. At this time, we shall call this trusted friend Nameless. The mission of the Nameless was to transport his family safely to Selefkia. His friend, a trained Turkish police officer, would arrive in Karvali with extra horses and mules. Then the plan developed into four parts: first, to load the children in large baskets on the mules covered with lamb hides; the two little ones would be in one basket and the older in another, balancing the load of a mule; second, Makrina had to disguise herself as an armed man; third, to cross the Taurus Mountains, like two armed men, carrying hides, a not so lucrative item to rob; fourth, to leave all other types of property behind. The plan was to bring furnishings, utensils,

---

91 Montenegro opened hostilities by declaring war on Turkey on Oct. 8, 1912, and the other members of the league followed suit 10 days later.

etc., at a later time, without jeopardizing the safety of the family. "I suggest that none tells anything to anyone," said John sternly.

Makrina nodded and they both returned to the table and joined their children.

They all prepared in secret until May. Makrina was well known in the whole area for her riding skills. At several times in her youth she had raced against men riders in obstacle course races of the region. She took leather belts and tightened them around her breasts to reduce their size and make herself look like a man. She wore a huge dark outfit of the period, with baggy pants and a hat, hiding her hair inside it. When the guide suggested that she cuts her hair, which was down to her waist, she absolutely refused to do it. She wore two strands of bullets, crisscrossing around her breasts, which helped further to hide them. She was given a rifle, which she did not know how to fire. She loaded the three children in two large baskets on a large mule and covered them with lamb hides.

The Nameless and Makrina left from Karvali one night during the month of May, 1914.[92] The first day they traveled to Eregli, about 50 miles, where they stayed overnight in a relative's house. From Eregli they went to Kayasaray (20 miles). From Kayasaray, they turned west to Kiraman (30 miles). From Kiraman they went east to Atlilar (40 miles), over the biggest part of Taurus Mountains. From Atlilar they traveled to Arlslankoy -village of the Lion (14 miles). From Arlslankoy they went downhill to Mersina (30 miles). From Eregli, it took three days to reach Mersina, where her husband was waiting. The distance to Selefkia was another 60 miles, but it was easy, since now her husband had several horse buggies waiting to take them home.

This Taurus Crossing trek was one of the early memories of Kyriaki. She remembered how Michael who had to share a basket with Elisabeth[93] complained about the stink, every time the little two-year old baby girl went to the bathroom inside the crowded, covered basket.

---

92 This was a timely move, since the Ottoman Empire embarked into World War I in August of the same year.

93 Baby Elisabeth later became the author's mother.

Figure 10 Photo of an Old Turk Recounting his Life with the Greeks of Karvali (May, 2007)[94]

THE MYTH ABOUT GREEKS (KARVALI, CAPPADOCIA, 1914-1915)

"Humility is the sign of a wise man," said my grandfather Paul, as he was loading his donkey with his tools. "We are one of God's creatures, destined to live a very limited time. We believe in life after death, because if we did not, we could not justify what we instinctively do in this life since birth. From the moment we are born, we strive to learn, curious about our world and try to improve our life in it. Our hope for something better and the sheer ignorance of our world tickles our curiosity and motivates us to strive for more. More information, more recognition, more love, more power, and so on. Thank God for that hunger for more. Otherwise we may stop using our mind and revert to being animals with lesser need for a brain, like this donkey here."

---

94 To the left of the old man is Ramadan Yildirim and to his right is the author. The meeting was held at Gelveri City Hall.

Besides being like a father, a philosopher, and my teacher, my grandfather Paul Boyun-egri-oglu (1849-1920) had two occupations; he was a potter and a farmer. As a farmer, he tended to his fields of wheat in a location called Zoful and a number of vineyards. He had an acre of vineyards in Curz and half an acre in Tunkuru, near a brook, with many plum and apple trees. He had two more small vineyards in Yocous Pasi Iskalka, with very good apricot trees. These apricot trees, located next to a Turk's vineyard- his name was Ahmet Agha- were always loaded with very tasty fruit. He had another vineyard in the location of Yasi Koum of a Turkish village, called Ilisou.

During the winter months, my grandfather would sit next to the fire and talk to me about our history. It was then that he told me that our first ancestors came here from Andros. He also knew some Ancient Greek History and philosophized over it.

"Anthony, my boy; do you know what a Greek is? A Greek is someone that follows certain ideals, imparted to him somehow on a way of life, and not necessarily one that had Greek parents. What makes someone Greek is what is in here," he said as he pointed to his brain. "We Greeks never really became a country worth speaking of. Even now, what is called Greece is a minute fraction of where Greeks live and work. Yet, the myth about Greeks makes some people think that all these contributions to humanity came from some large Empire. The truth is that we are spread thin all over the world. Ever since antiquity, all we had were some small city-states. Then, Alexander decided to unite us, and foolishly decided to go and conquer the world. After finding out how big and diverse the world was, his Aristotelian logic took over. 'Why did I do that?' he asked himself. 'Now that I have this patchwork of humanity in my hands, how do I rule it? Even if I conquer these people, I could never change the way they want to live; and, even if I could, I am not sure that I would want to.' He understood that the goal of unification of humanity depended not on military conquest, but on the conquest of human behavior. This was an immensely more difficult task, than conquering the world. I believe that is why he never assigned a successor. He knew that it would be pointless to continue on his original direction. All big empires failed because they sooner or later discovered that human behavior is not something to be conquered, but to be asked politely and be given the freedom of choice. From all attributes of our existence, freedom is the most valuable and if humans are to choose freely, bad habits take time to be erased. For that reason, even small advancements in human civilization take a painstakingly very long time.

What is important about Greeks is that we pass to our children our heritage of thinking logically like Greeks. We also encourage our children to pass our history to the generations that follow, disclosing it as truthfully as we understand it, even if that leads to our destruction. There are people in this world my boy that would alter history, for political gains. A true Greek would rather die than break the tenets, which the fathers of history[95] passed onto us. Always tell the truth, as you know it, no matter how much it may hurt you, your family, or your country. "

Such stories continued until the First World War started in June of 1914. I was then a nine year old and in the third grade. We were fortunate in having some supplies to face the War. We had a can of petroleum, which we used for lighting until 1918. My mother was very thrifty in its use. We saved by using moonlight or candles and fat oils instead of petroleum. At the end, we used petroleum only during Sundays or big holidays, like Christmas, Easter and Holy Mary's days.

When I was about ten years old, I was a student in the fourth grade of the elementary school. We had two hours per week of Turkish, by a Turk teacher. This language was the old Turkish, with the Arabic alphabet. He took us on excursions, and taught us nationalistic Turkish songs. One was about Turkish dreams of regaining Crete, Thessaloniki, Kosovo and Ioannina. It did not sink in to us, Greek children on what was going on, until much later.

From 1912 to 1914, before World War I was declared, my grandfather took care of us very well. He was relatively young (57-59) and capable of doing a lot of work, using his animals to help him. He took care of us like a father and he told us news from my father in Odessa, because he communicated with him regularly.[96]

---

95   By fathers of history he probably meant Herodotus and Thucydides, even though he may not have read any of their writings.
96   A. Boinodiris, Book 1, p. 305.

START OF A WAR (KARVALI, CAPPADOCIA, 1914-1915)

When World War I was declared, Turkey and Bulgaria allied themselves with Germany. Russia allied with Serbia. Russia formally declared war on the Ottomans on November 2, and Britain and France followed suit on November 5. The Ottoman Empire entered the war on October 29, 1914, when Ottoman warships cooperated with German warships in a naval bombardment of Russian Black Sea ports. In December, the Ottomans began an invasion of the Russian Caucasus region.

When Russia declared war against Turkey, all communications with my father in Russia were terminated. The Germans brought their fleet into the Black Sea, and sank three large Russian ships and bombarded Russian ports, including Odessa. Also in 1915, Turkey started losing ground in the land war around Caucasus. Orders came to equip the Turkish infantry with additional animals, in order to beef up the supply lines to the troops of the Turkish army. They were especially targeting Greek and Armenian-owned animals.[97]

The Turkish counter-attack was successful at its inception, but by August 1915, the hold that Ottoman forces had gained had been considerably reduced. Ottoman pressure in the area, however, impelled the Russian government early in 1915 to demand a diversionary attack by Britain on the Ottoman Empire. In response, British naval forces under the command of General Sir Ian Hamilton bombarded Ottoman forts at Hellespont, or Dardanelles in February 1915. The Dardanelles prevented the Russians from being supplied on the Black Sea. In addition, between April and August, two landings of Allied troops took place on the Gallipoli Peninsula, one of British, Australian, and French troops in April, and one of several additional British divisions in August.

The Allied purpose was to take the Dardanelles; however, strong resistance by Ottoman troops and bad generalship on the part of the Allied command resulted in complete failure. The Allied troops were withdrawn in December 1915 and January 1916.

When World War I was declared, the Germans were getting their wheat from Turkey. One mean villager of Karvali betrayed all the

---

97 A. Boinodiris, Book 1, p. 305.

hidden warehouses, inside cave tunnels, warehouses that were extremely difficult to find. As a result, all the hidden deposits of wheat that Karvali had were sent to Germany. Because of this, the price of bread climbed, while the price of meat became cheap. The cattle merchants brought hundreds of large animals, like cows and water buffaloes from nearby meadows to be slaughtered at Karvali. The people of Karvali were processing the skins of these animals for shoes. They were also boiling the meat, making it available at a good price.

At that time, we made a great deal of pastourma slabs, which were the Greek equivalent to the spicy beef jerky. We also made spicy sausages. Since most people were thin and worked hard, beef fat was consumed without fear of cholesterol and in fact was in high demand.

At the beginning of 1916, the elders started talking about the persecution of Armenians. Letters, containing horrid stories of brutality by the Turks from Constantinople and from the East alarmed my grandfather, even though he tried very hard not to scare us. "I hope that what I hear is not true," he said. "God help us all if it is."[98]

1915 ARMENIAN MASSACRE (PUBLISHED IN NEW YORK TIMES, JULY, 1921)

"WHY TALAAT'S ASSASSIN WAS ACQUITTED?"

By George R. Montgomery (Director, Armenia-America Society)

Official Turkish documents produced in Berlin at the trial of the young Armenian, Teilirian, proved beyond question that Talaat Pasha

---

98   During World War I (1914-18), Armenia became a battleground for Russian and Ottoman armies. Between January and August 1916, the Russians conquered the greater part of Ottoman Armenia, but the revolution in 1917 forced their withdrawal, and the Ottomans reoccupied the country. As the war raged on, Ottoman atrocities against Armenians increased, leading the government of the United States to send a formal note of protest to the Ottoman Empire on February 17, 1916. The Ottoman government ordered massive deportations of Armenians from their homelands in Ottoman-held territory mainly to the deserts of present-day Syria. Many Armenians perished from starvation and disease or were killed by Ottoman soldiers during the forced marches.

and other officials had ordered the wholesale extermination of the Armenians.

An Armenian named Teilirian was tried at Berlin of June 2-3, 1921 for the murder of Talaat Pasha, who was chief of the Young Turk Party, and who was, during the latter part of the war a Grand Vizier of the Ottoman Empire. The murder of Talaat of March 15, 1921, drew general attention to the fact that the German Government allowed Talaat to use Berlin as a planning center for his Turkish nationalist objectives. It was expected that the known sympathy of the German Government for the Young Turks would result in the prompt conviction and the execution of the Armenian.

To the surprise of the world, he was acquitted. Teilirian and the Armenian Nation, it appeared, had found a champion in the person of Professor Lepsius, who was bold in bringing out unpleasant, irrefutable truths. The trial of the Armenian developed into the trial of the murdered Talaat Pasha as the greatest of the war criminals. It developed into a case against the German military authorities, which had at least allowed the massacres to continue without protest. Even General Liman von Sanders, who had had charge of the German military forces in Turkey, was called as a witness.

His testimony opened the eyes of the German people, as nothing else had yet done, to the fact of the terrible massacres and to the callousness of the German military authorities to the horrors that happened under their very eyes. Professor Lepsius produced German official reports to show that the total number of Armenians who perished as a result of the so-called deportations was over a million.

Although the technical defense of Teilirian was temporary insanity brought on by a vision of his murdered mother, the real defense was the terrible record of Talaat Pasha. So, that in the eyes of Germany the acquittal of the Armenian of the charge of murder became the condemnation to death of the Turk. That such a trial and such a result occurred in Germany with Germans as jurors is particularly significant.

With respect to the present situation in the Near East, the most important phase of this dramatic trial was the ability of Professor Lepsius to produce Turkish official documents which proved that the heads of the Turkish Government, and particularly Talaat himself to be directly responsible.

Heretofore there have been defenders of the Ottomans who held that the massacres were not a plan of the Government, but were due to the brutality of those who carried out the deportation instructions. At the trial of Teilirian there were placed in evidence facsimiles and translations of signed orders from Talaat -- letters and cipher telegrams that proved that the instructions to massacre originated in Constantinople. As Aleppo was the headquarters of the "Deportations Committee," the capture of Aleppo by the British made possible the securing of these official documents from the archives. This evidence directly linking the murdered Talaat with the inhuman deeds that were covered by the general term "deportation" was irrefutable and overwhelming. The documents established once and for all the fact that the purpose of the Turkish authorities was not deportation, but annihilation.

The object of the present article is to present translations -- with facsimiles -- of some of the

Turkish official documents that created such a sensation when read into the evidence during the trial at Berlin. The first document, although not singed by Talaat, is from the committee of Young Turks of which he was the head, and, inasmuch as its contents are referred to in dispatches signed by him, was valid as evidence. It was written in the spring of 1915, before the massacres had begun, and show the extermination of the Armenians to have been the determined policy of the Government. Jemal, to whom the document is addressed, was the third in the triumvirate of Young Turks -- Talaat, Enver and Jemal. At that time he was Governor of Adana and soon afterward became Governor of Aleppo:

March 25 1915. To Jemal Bey, Delegate at Adana:

It is the duty of all of us to effect on the broadest lines the realization of the noble project of wiping out of existence the well-known elements that have for centuries constituted a barrier to the empire's progress in civilization. For this reason we must take upon ourselves the whole responsibility, saying "come what

may," and appreciating how great is the sacrifice which has enabled the Government to enter the World War, we must work so that the means adopted may lead to the desired end.

As announced in our dispatch dates Feb. 18, the Jemiet [Young Turk Committee] has decided to uproot and annihilate the various forces, which have for centuries been an obstacle in its way, and to this end it is obliged to resort to very bloody methods. Be assured that we ourselves were horrified at the contemplation of these methods, but the Jemiet sees no other way of insuring the stability of its work.

Ali Riza [the committee delegate at Aleppo] criticized us and called upon us to be merciful; such simplicity is nothing short of stupidity. For those who will not co-operate with us we will find a place that will wring their delicate heartstrings.

I again recall to your memory the question of the property left. It is very important. Do not let its distribution escape your vigilance; always examine the accounts and the use made of the proceeds.

Reference to this document is contained in the following order, signed by Talaat and sent to the same Jamal.

This order shows that women and children were to be included in the holocaust:

Sept. 3, 1915
To the Prefecture of Aleppo:
We recommend that you submit the women and children also to the orders which have been previously prescribed as to be allied to the males of the intended persons, and to designate for these functions employs of confidence.

The Minister of the Interior,
TALAAT

Apparently the instructions regarding the women and children called for some reiteration, for on Sept. 16 the following cipher telegram, which showed the instructions as going back to the decision of the Jemiet, or Young Turk Committee, was sent:

Sept. 16
To the Prefecture of Aleppo:
It has been previously communicated to you that the Government, by order of the Jemiet [the Young Turk Committee] has decided to destroy completely all the indicated persons living in Turkey. Those who oppose this order and decision cannot remain on the official staff of the empire. An end must be put to their existence, however tragic the measures taken may be, and no regard must be paid to either age or sex, or to conscientious scruples.

The Minister of the Interior,
TALAAT

Mr. Morgenthau, the American Ambassador at Constantinople, began to exert himself on behalf of the Armenians, and the result was an official order suggesting caution:

Nov. 18, 1915.
To the Prefecture of Aleppo:
From interventions which have recently been made by the American Ambassador at
Constantinople on behalf of his Government, it appears that the American Consul is obtaining information by secret means. In spite of our assurance that the [Armenian] deportations will be accomplished in safety and comfort, they remain unconvinced. Be careful that events attracting attention shall not take place in connection with those [Armenians] who are near the cities and other canters. From the point of view of the present policy, it is most important that foreigners who are in those parts shall be persuaded that the expulsion of the Armenians is in truth only deportation. For this reason it is important that, to save appearances, a show of gentle dealing shall be made for a time, and the usual measures be taken in suitable places. It is recommended as very important that

the people who have given such information shall be arrested and handed over to the military authorities for trial by court-martial.

The Minister of the Interior,
TALAAT

Reference to the effort of the American Consul at Aleppo, Mr. Jackson, to send information to Mr. Morgenthau is contained in the following cipher dispatch:

Dec. 11, 1915.
To the Prefecture of Aleppo:
We learn that some correspondents of Armenian journals are obtaining photographs and letters, which represent tragic events, and are giving them to the American Consul at Aleppo. Have dangerous persons of this kind arrested and suppressed.

The Minister of the Interior,
TALAAT

The need for caution is further indicated in the following telegram:

Dec. 29, 1915.
To the Prefecture of Aleppo:
We learn that foreign officers are encountering along the roads the corpses of the intended persons and are photographing them. I recommend you the importance of having these corpses buried at once and of not allowing them to be left near the roads.
The Minister of the Interior,
TALAAT

The heartlessness of the Turks in regard to the doomed children made a deep impression on the Berlin jury. The following are some of the documents presented on this point:

Nov. 5, 1915
To the Government of Aleppo:

We are informed that the little ones belonging to the indicated persons [Armenians] from
Sivas Mamuret-ul-Aziz, Diyarbakir and Erzeroum are adopted by certain Moslem families and received as servants when they are left alone through the death of their parents. We inform you that you are to collect all such children in your province and send them to the places of deportation, and also to give the necessary orders regarding this to the people.
The Minister of the Interior,
TALAAT

Jan. 15, 1916.
To the Government of Aleppo:
We hear that certain orphanages, which have been opened, received also the children of the Armenians. Whether this is done through ignorance of our real purpose, or through contempt of it, the Government will regard the feeding of such children or any attempt to prolong their lives as an act entirely opposed to its purpose, since it considers the survival of these children as detrimental. I recommend that such children shall not be received into the orphanages, and no attempts are to be made to establish special orphanages for them.
The Minister of the Interior,
TALAAT

The production of the following cipher telegram (No. 830) was particularly telling in its effect on the jury:

From the Ministry of the Interior to the Government of Aleppo:
Collect and keep only those orphans who cannot remember the terrors to which their parents have been subjected. Send the rest away with the caravans.
The Minister of the Interior,
TALAAT

That the Moslem population was not to be held accountable for its share in the massacres was ordered in a telegram dated Oct. 8, 1915:

The reason why the Sanjak of Zor was chosen as a place of deportation is explained in a secret order dated Sept. 2, 1915, No. 1,843. As all the crimes committed along the way by the population against the Armenians serve to affect the ultimate purpose of the Government. There is no need for legal proceedings with regard to these. The necessary instructions have also been sent to the Governments of Zor and Ourfa.

The Minister of the Interior,
TALAAT

All the evidence tends to show, with cumulative effect, that it was the pity awakened in the hearts of some of the local Turkish officials by the miseries of the Armenians, which produced a certain mitigation of the heartless orders that emanated from Constantinople. A small remnant of the race survived. Talaat and his group in the Government were obliged continually to spur some of their tools on to greater severity.

Figure 11 Talaat Pasha, one of the Accused for the Armenian Massacre of 1915

REPLACING ANIMALS WITH HUMANS (KALIVARION, AUGUST, 1916)

"Humans have become animals," said my grandfather in despair. "So, I have to turn into an animal too."

In 1916, a mean Greek villager, who had a grudge against our family, went to the Turkish authorities, telling them that both of my grandfather's children were sent abroad, to avoid being drafted. One was my father George, who was in Odessa and the other was my uncle Charalambos (later to change his name to Pavlides) in Macedonia.

The Turkish Police barged in, asking him:

"Where are you hiding your sons? Why didn't they appear at the draft board?"

The police chief, named Pigik Oglou Botos arrested my grandfather and started beating him, demanding that he produces his sons.

What he produced was two letters from them.

He replied, "Effendi, my children are abroad. Here are their letters," showing them letters from them.

The officials got even madder:

"Gavur, you purposely sent them out, to avoid serving their country." Then they beat him twice with a police baton.

The police officer stopped beating my grandfather and tried to think of a way to punish the old man, and possibly force him to plead to his sons to come back. They were about to depart, when they saw three beautiful animals in my grandfather's fields, a pair of colts and a young mule, 6 months old. They roped and took the two horses, leaving the young mule.

"These go to the Turkish Calvary," they said.

My grandfather was devastated. He was left with an old donkey to pick and shell the wheat, to carry the grapes for his three acres of vineyards and to pick wood for the winter. I was an impressionable boy, barely 10 years old, vividly remembering how much we suffered that year. I remember when my sixty-year-old grandfather looked towards me and said in despair:

"My proud heart, I step down from a horse and use this old, slow donkey, which forces me to walk because of its age. I am tired more of this war, than the walking that is forced upon me. Humans have become animals. So, I have to turn into an animal too."

I felt very sorry for my grandfather and hated the Turks for what they did to us. We were left without strength to plow fields and to transport goods to survive. We only had an old donkey.

How can a person, 60 years old work all these fields with an old donkey?

GROWING UP THE HARD WAY (1916-1918)

After losing our animals, our life changed for the worst. My grandfather Paul, my grandmother Efthimia, my mother Evanthia and I, only 10-11 years old worked in the fields, as a replacement of our animals. We had to walk to these fields, which were at a good distance and do it every day (about 20 miles). They were about 4 hectares (10 acres) at Zoful (near the village Cagil), at the intersection of the road between Nev Sehir and Akserai. We had wheat that needed to be harvested and cleaned. We also had to cut wood and prepare for the heavy winters of 1916-17 and 1917-1918. My mother was young and could stand the hard work, but this heavy work took a toll on my grandfather and grandmother. I was running to help them like a little goat and because they were in desperate need of my assistance, I missed a year's worth of school. I had to work during the days and at night I could not do my homework because we had shortage of kerosene. We started placing a saddle on the young mule, which could not lift much. By the time it grew enough to carry weight, the war was over.[99]

One day in 1916, I loaded wheat on that old donkey to take it to the mill at Ilisos. Karvali had no running water to turn a millstone, because our ancestors, to prevent Turkish migration to Karvali had sabotaged it. They poured mercury onto the spring and it went underground. The only mill available was one powered by a diesel engine, which was shut because of fuel shortage. Thus, I had to travel to Ilisos with 150 kilos of wheat. After the wheat was turned into flour, the mill workers (all friends of my grandfather) told me:

"Careful with this animal; it looks too old; it may fall and die any time on you."

---

99   A. Boinodiris, Book 1, p. 306.

They loaded me up and I left for the long way back home. Half way into my trip, it started drizzling rain. As I tried to cover the flour, the animal fell. There was nobody on the road and the sun started setting down the horizon. I tried to unload the animal, but I was only 11-years old, inexperienced and scared. I was able to only unload the animal and raise it up, but how can I load the heavy sack back on it? I started crying, but nobody heard my wails except the Cappadocian dessert around me. I started praying to our patron Saint Gregory of Nazianzos, crossing myself.

"St. Gregory, please give me strength to load it up."

Then, an idea popped into my head as I saw a bank next to me. I took the animal and tied it to a bush next to it. Then, I dragged the sack on top of the bank, near the animal. All I had to do is lift the sack onto the animal below. I did that, but as I was about to throw the flour on the saddle, the animal moved and the sack fell on the ground. I knew I had to try again. This time I tied the tail of the donkey as well to a rock. After a great deal of struggle, multiple prayers and by crossing myself, I dragged the sack back on the bank. I lifted the sack, which I finally loaded onto the animal. Then, I had to split the sack load on two parts, by pushing flour from one end of the sack to the other. This is extremely difficult for wheat, because it bunches up. I could not manage to balance the load, so I hang a stone on a rope from the side of the sack that was less heavy. With this balancing act, I carefully led the animal home, leading it so that it does not trip in the dark. After some time, I started seeing the lights of Karvali. Then I saw a Turk peasant, named Yagoup Agha riding his horse on the road towards Karvali.

"Which stupid mill person loaded you up son?" he said after seeing the way the animal was loaded with the stone hanging on one side.

I told him what happened.

"My animal fell. That is why it is that way."

Yagoup Agha took another look at me and dismounted. He walked to my donkey, straightened the load and threw the stone away.

"Whose son are you?"

"I am the grandson of Master Paul. From all the animals he had, he was left with only an old donkey, with which we have to do our job."

"Damn these wars." Then as he climbed on his horse, smiled and said: "You must be quite a young man; you have the tenacity needed to survive in these times." He smiled and rode into Karvali.[100]

One day, around January 3 1917 I went to school. It was about one kilometer away from our house. The soles of my shoes had been worn out to the point that even the laces needed replacing. We had no money to put soles on them. I asked my uncle, Father Kalinikos to allow his son George to go caroling with me during the Epiphany to collect money to repair our shoes. My uncle talked to my mother and they agreed to let us go caroling. We did so and I collected 40 Turkish grossia. February came, and during that month there was a lot of sleet. My shoes seeped cold water and I began having abdomen pains. I started wearing wooden slippers. I went to a neighbor shoemaker, named Costas.

"Mr. Costas, can you please fix my shoes?"

"Sure."

"How much will it cost?"

"200 grossia...."

I felt the tears swelling from my eyes. "What? I only have 40 grossia."

"I am sorry son, but the materials are expensive now with the War."

I kept crying, looking at my feet. The shoemaker was moved and started consoling me.

"Come on Anthony. Don't cry."

I looked at him bawling. "I don't know what to do. I don't think that my feet can take it any longer."

"I will make a deal with you. I will fix your shoes for 150 grossia and not take anything for my labor, and when you grow up and make money you pay me up."

I was finally consoled. He fixed my shoes and immediately after I had the money, I paid him back.[101]

School gave me a great deal of pleasure. I was taught in Greek and Turkish. We also were taught French. My favorite lessons were

100 A. Boinodiris, Book 1, p. 307.
101 A. Boinodiris, Book 1, p. 308.

Geography, History and Arithmetic. In Turkish, I had learned a poem about springtime in the fifth grade that I still remember vividly:

Springtime comes with happy nightingales
With the aroma of hyacinths in the air
Youth's love is in the air
With different love songs
Every flower has its nightingale
Moreover, every nightingale has its flower.
Let us give thanks to the Lord
For making the four seasons
No human knows how these are done,
For if they did, nothing would be done,[102]

ANTHONY'S NIGHT ADVENTURE (KALIVARION, SEPTEMBER, 1917)

Before the war, the Turkish government gave us planting seed to plant and collected one eighth of our wheat for taxes and one eighth for seed expenses. After the war, the government collected 50% of all production. That included one-fourth of grain seed and one-fourth for state taxes. This high taxation led to theft from the government by hiding crops from the inspectors. Otherwise, we did not have enough food to survive. We started separating wheat from straw in the middle of the night. With the saved 50% of the produced wheat, we stored it in big, dry holes in the ground, using big sacks. They stayed there, until the inspector went through all production and we delivered the government's portion to the public warehouse.

One night of 1917, I am holding a borrowed mule by the reigns while my grandfather, grandmother and my Aunt Anna were trying to lift one of the buried sacks, so that we could move them to the house, where the wheat can be protected for the fall rainfall. We did all this at night and in silence, so that no police officer, inspector, or traitor knows what we did. My grandmother went on her hands and knees, forming a ladder next to the mule, while my grandfather and aunt lifted the heavy sack.

---

102 A. Boinodiris, Book 4, p. 164.

Suddenly, a night bird that was near us fluttered its wings with a characteristic "purr." This broke the silence of the night and scared the mule. The mule bolted, knocked me over and I fell hitting my head hard on a stone on the ground. I lost consciousness.

When I woke up in pain, it was morning. I was strapped on top of the load, while my grandmother was leading the mule into Karvali. I had fierce pains in the back of my head, so I started crying.

"Please sweetheart, do not cry. Do not let them know what we were doing, or we will be in real trouble. When we reach home, I will fix you some nice medicine to stop the pain."

We arrived at my grandmother's home. She told me that I was lucky. The mule knocked me down, but did not step on me. They had no water to pour on me to recover me from fainting, since they had drank it earlier. My Aunt Anna, a strong, limping woman went and brought some cold water from a place near by. They used it to half-revive me and place me on top of the mule. I was in bed at my grandmother's home until I recovered.

My Aunt Anna's husband was called Black George and he was a good farmer. He had five children, four girls and one boy, named Vlasis. The Turks took Black George in the army and he was killed somewhere, like many other nameless Greeks and Armenians that were used as unarmed targets by the Turks, to flush out the enemy. The children were left orphans and poor Vlasis, who was eight, had to work. In two years, Vlasis was dead from an incurable disease. My grandfather took them all in under his protection, in spite of his own poverty.

Later on, during the boat ride to Greece in 1924, I looked after my cousins, considering them to be part of our own family. Among the girls was Maria, who was married and I helped her on the trip to Greece in 1924. Unfortunately, she died in the quarantine island of St. George, just outside our final destination port of Piraeus. The other girl was Makrina, whom my grandfather had baptized. She died in Nea Karvali soon after. The third girl, named Elisabeth ended up at Ivira of Nigrita, near Serres. We met with her and her family in 1950s, after losing contact with them for many years.[103]

---

103 A. Boinodiris, Book 1, p. 310-311 and Book 4, p. 151-152.

In those days, each one of us had to look after our own survival, but also help out for the survival of others, who happened to fall into hard times. During the years of war, you do not know when you would need your neighbor to help you and your family. This practice of helping out anyone in trouble was a kind of payment for your own life insurance.

U.S.S. Cyclops (Port of Lisbon, March, 1918)

Pandelis bared his arms by rolling up his sleeves. He then washed them with the bar of soap that the sexton of the Catholic Church handed him. He walked to the baptismal and put his hands forward, so that his friend could lay a blanket and a towel over his hands. He took out his "box coat," which he wore with shirt and tie. At that time, the U.S. Navy started issuing their blue dress, which was worn for official ceremonies, inspections and liberty ashore. Not normally visible, blue uniforms were worn with a blue waistcoat with a single row of gilt buttons.

Pandelis and his friend, both Greeks from Constantinople, had taken liberty from their ship, the U.S.S. Cyclops, an oil tanker, for a specific task, which was reluctantly approved by their captain. His friend was married and his wife lived at Mt. Vernon, New York. Pandelis had served in the U.S. Navy since 1911 and was caught in the storm of a World War since it started. While serving in the Atlantic, his friend received a letter that his wife gave birth to a baby boy. The custom was to make sure that the boy is baptized as soon as possible. Communication ensued and after Pandelis agreed to become the godfather, a date was set in March, upon which his friend's wife and the baby would travel with a Greek steamer from New York to Lisbon, where her husband's ship was making frequent runs to refuel American ships. There, the couple would meet and baptize the baby. After quite a bit of planning, wife and baby made it to Lisbon, somewhat late.

The two sailors immediately approached the captain of U.S.S. Cyclops and asked for a day's leave to conduct a baptismal ceremony. The captain knew all about the plan, but the date of the baptism kept on changing with the arrival date of the baby. When he was informed that the baby had arrived, he was reluctant to let his two men have a leave, because he expected any minute his orders to steam off for an unknown destination. Then, the captain gave in, realizing what the two sailors, wife and baby had gone through to set everything up for this baptism.

"I want you to report back here before dark," he ordered.

"Yes, sir," the two sailors responded in unison, with a slight grin and a salute.

The captain must have been a good catholic. He suggested a local Catholic Church in Lisbon that was known to conduct ceremonies to Greek Orthodox men of the Navy. That is because the differences between the two churches are almost trivial. Soon the two sailors had boarded a Portuguese taxi rowboat and headed for the shore.

In the service of Baptism, or Christening three of the seven sacraments are administered to the baby, Baptism, Chrismation and Holy Communion. Baptism is the sacrament in which the baby is thrice immersed in water in the name of the Father and the Son and the Holy Spirit, is cleansed from all sin and is regenerated spiritually. The sacrament itself is divided into two distinct parts. The service, in which the priest reads the various prayers of exorcism, and the baptismal rite in which the baby is thrice immerse in sanctified water in the Name of the Holy trinity.

In the service of the Catechumen, the sponsor (godparent) on behalf of the infant is asked to renounce Satan and everything connected with him. The sponsor then blows and spits three times upon the Devil. This is done facing the west for it is in this direction that the sun descends and was believed by the ancient Greeks to be the direction of the Gates of Hades. Facing to the east, where the sun rises and where Christ began his redeeming ministry, the sponsor is asked if he "unites himself to Christ" and answers in the affirmative.

Then the sponsor recites the "Pistevo," or Creed, which professes the belief of every Greek Orthodox Christian. It is here that the Creed was said in Greek, and the known "Filioque" (and the Son) was omitted, in accordance to the Greek Orthodox Church. Then the sponsor gives the baby a name, as agreed by the parents. This must be a Christian name. The infant is then prepared for immersion three times.

The priest begins the Baptismal Rite with the words: "Blessed is the Kingdom of the Father and of the Son and of the Holy Spirit now and ever unto ages of ages. Amen." Standing before the baptismal that represents the "divine Womb" whence we receive our second birth as children of God, the priest recites the prescribed petitions and prayers necessary for the blessing and purification of the water used to cleanse the infant from the inherited original sin.

Pure olive oil is hallowed and administered to the various members of the infant's body. The priest anoints the face, chest, mouth, nose, ears, legs and feet in dedication to the service of Christ. The sponsor then anoints the entire body of the child symbolical of the Chrismation of kings and in belief that the evils of the devil will slip away. The infant is then immersed three times in the blessed water in the Name if the Father and of the Son and of the Holy Spirit.

The sacrament of Chrismation is then administered to the members of the infant's body by the priest stating the words; "The seal of the gifts of the Holy Spirit. Amen." This sacrament is the completion and perfection of the mystery of baptism in which the neophyte is strengthened and sealed in the gifts of the holy spirit and is dedicated to the service of Christ and his church.

Then the priest cuts the hair of the baby in the form of a cross, in the name of the Holy trinity, for the hair is the symbol of strength. This also represents the very first offering of the newborn Christian to God and his church. It is indicative of dedication, offering and sacrifice. The neophyte is then dressed in white attire signifying the purity of the soul, which has been cleansed from sin. The Godparent is given a white candle symbolizing that Christ is the light of the world and that Christians are to live and die by the light of Christ. The spiritual parent then holds the neophyte in his arms and stands behind the Baptismal font directly opposite the priest who with censer in hand intones; "For as many of you as have been baptized in Christ, have put on Christ. Alleluia." The procession around the Baptismal font takes place three times representative of the Holy Trinity and in remembrance of the early Christians who went to the church following the Baptism on the feast of the resurrection.

After Pandelis finished the procession, he handed the baptized baby to his parents, who proceeded to a corner, where his mother could bare her breasts and feed him. The two sailors paid up the church and the priest.

"Let's go and have lunch before we report back on the boat," said Pandelis' friend. "We have a few hours before dark. Lunch is on me." Pandelis agreed.

Soon, the group of the two sailors, the woman and her baby in her arms walked towards the pier, where a row of restaurants was sited earlier. Instinctively, Pandelis' eyes scanned the horizon, towards his ship, only to realize that it was not there.

"Our ship…" he stammered; "it is gone."

The sailors started running. They found one man at the pier who spoke English.

"The ship steamed off one hour ago," he said.

The sailors were dumbfounded. They went into the first restaurant and there, as they had lunch they decided to report to the American Embassy and make plans to join their ship. At the same time, they could find out about how mother and baby could return to New York.

The American Embassy confirmed that U.S.S. Cyclops had departed because their orders were dispatched during the baptismal ceremony. The Naval Officer at the Embassy ordered the sailors to find local quarters, waiting for another transport ship to arrive in a few days, heading for New York.

"New York?" said Pandelis. "Could the wife of a sailor and his baby go home with this transport?"

The Naval Officer was quite accommodating. After filling several forms and making the sailor sign, he agreed. He even suggested a nearby home, where American sailors bunked in similar situations.

Pandelis and the couple found accommodations in that home. It was an old home, a bed and breakfast place, ran by a widow, who spoke broken English. Her husband, a Portuguese-American sailor from the Boston area had died, and she returned to Portugal, close to her relatives and her father's home, that she had inherited.

After securing accommodations, the sailors, mother and baby went to a near-by restaurant to eat. After a hearty meal with some wine, they went in their rooms and fell asleep. They were tired and that helped them sleep deeply. They slept until after eight. After washing up, they came into the widow's dining room to be served breakfast. To their surprise, they saw a man, already sitting there with his back turned, but wearing a Naval Officer's uniform. As they came close, they recognized the officer from the Embassy. When he saw them, he rose. His solemn look set a tingle of fear in Pandelis' spine. His face turned white.

"I have bad news boys," said the officer. "We received news that U.S.S. Cyclops was hit, presumably by a German torpedo and sunk. None of your friends on the ship survived. I am very sorry." He paused and looked at the shaken sailors.

Pandelis' mind flew over to his shipmates, as he saw their faces in the middle of the Atlantic, facing the inferno of their torpedoed ship, as they were dying in agony amidst the flaming tanker. Most of them were new immigrants, Greeks, Poles, Italians and other nationalities, but after joining the Navy, they were all friends and shipmates. For them, lady luck was cruel. She only smiled for him and his friend.[104] Pandelis felt a weird sense of sadness and guilt; the guilt was there because of some miraculous twist of fate, he was one of the survivors.

TOPAL OSMAN (KALIVARION, AUGUST, 1918)

I was about 13 years old, when the cease-fire was signed with Armenia in the Treaty of Batum.[105] After the treaty, certain fanatic Turks like Topal Osman of Giresun of the Black Sea, with about 500-armed followers started attacking Greek and Armenian settlements. This was in reprisal of the participation of Greece on the allied side. These soldiers were hardened by their losses with the newly formed Democratic Republic of Armenia (DRA) and some of them were instrumental in executing parts of the Armenian massacre in previous years. They wanted to apply the same techniques now on the Greeks, even though he had no such authority from the Turkish government.

---

104 "**March, 1918**: U. S. S. **Cyclops** (fuel ship), gross 19,360 tons; mysteriously disappeared; 309 killed, 236 Navy crew, and passengers: 70 navy, 2 marines, and 1 United States consul." This segment was derived from the archives of **U.S. Merchant Marine, U.S. Maritime Service, Army Transport Service, Military Sea Transportation Service, and Military Sea Lift Command – www.usmm.org.**

105 The Treaty of Batum is a treaty between the Democratic Republic of Armenia and the Ottoman Empire. It was signed in Batum on June 4, 1918. Consisting of 14 articles, it is the first treaty of Armenia. The treaty was signed while the Army of Islam held positions 7 kilometers from Yerevan.

On the 6th of August 1918, on the Day of Ascension, he arrived in Kalivarion. Before he entered the town, he got information on the town from Turkish villages on his path. He was informed that Karvali was an armed fort; the Greeks had houses of stone, with high walls around each courtyard. They would resist, possibly bringing upon him and his men many losses. The Turks of the neighboring villages suggested a peaceful approach, where the Greeks can serve him better by provisioning him with goods and services, like shoeing his horses.

When the band of Topal Osman arrived, he sent a messenger, requesting a meeting with the authorities in Karvali. The Turk head of police, Ali Rizach met with him, while the bells of the town summoned the attention of the population. Ali told him that he is welcomed, but warned him that if there is one incident against any citizen, none will be spared from his band, for he will have guns trained at his group, ready to shoot.

The bluff worked. The band came peacefully, bringing about one hundred horses for shoeing, purchased their goods and the village set up a big table, with the best food and music they could offer. Some of the food served was veal with bulgur (cracked wheat), floating in pure butter, seasonal fruits, ouzo and aged wine. The band, having stacked their rifles in pyramids, ate and drunk amply, supplementing their meal with a dance in the center of the town, where four streets come together. In that dance, the leaders of the town joined in. The bandits were too busy to notice that in the narrow roads behind the main roads, men of Karvali were ready for action, armed with mouser rifles.

When Ali saw all the bandits drunk and their rifles stacked, he consulted with the Greek mayor and his staff. "Do we take their arms and send them to jail in Akserai?"

The head of city council was Anargyros Magioglou. He and others said: "No please. They did not hurt us, so we will not hurt them. When their horses are shoed on the town's expense, we will let them leave in peace. "

On the sixth of August the bandits woke up and after hugging the Karvali leaders with their thanks for the hospitality, they left. These bandits attacked multiple villages in the area of Cappadocia, but left Karvali unharmed. On 20 August, a group came close to the outskirts, to raid some vineyards, but the people saw them and ran into the town, bringing it into a full alert for defense. Fortunately, nothing happened. St. Gregory of Nazianzos, the patron saint of our town protected us. I personally attribute our savior to the use of combining soft language and politics with strong defense against 500 well-armed bandits.

KALINIKOS (KALIVARION, SEPTEMBER, 1918)

Ali Rizach was a very honest Turk police chief. He had high moral standards and became an idol of honesty, not only for Turks, but also for Greeks. Later in my life, I wished that some Greek police officers were half as honest and conscientious as Ali. He had about twenty men, used to chase armed bandits in the surrounding area.

I remember meeting him when his favorite horse became sick. He loved his horse and in those years veterinarians simply did not exist. We did not even have doctors for humans. Not knowing what to do, he asked the hodja (Muslim religious teacher) to help him. The hodja prayed so that his horse can be cured, and Ali gave him a typical reward for his effort. Yet, the horse kept on being ill. Some of the Turks suggested to him to ask a Christian priest, Father Kalinikos to help him out. Father Kalinikos was my grandfather's brother. This priest was well respected as a holy person, by Greeks and Turks alike, so the police commander sent a police officer to tell Father Kalinikos, if he can come and help his horse.

Now about thirteen years old, I heard the conversation by chance and followed the police officer, curious to see what happens, since this had to do with my grandfather's brother. He followed orders and I followed my uncle, Father Kalinikos to see what he did. He picked up Holy Water from the altar, an Easter egg and some other things and walked over to the police station. All of Ali Rizach's men were at the courtyard watching. He asked one of them to bring out the sick horse. He brought out a thin horse, which refused to eat because of some intestinal problem. He ordered all his men to take off their hats in the presence of Father Kalinikos. Father Kalinikos started praying for the sick horse. Then he turned to Ali Rizach.

"Do you believe that God, through prayer can cure this sick horse?"

"Yes, Holy Man," responded the police chief.

"Your faith will cure this animal," said Father Kalinikos. "Please take the blanket off the animal."

The soldiers responded. Father Kalinikos sprayed the whole animal with Holy Water. The horse initially backed off, but then steadied and licked the water. Then, Father Kalinikos faced the horse and cracked the red Easter egg on the forehead of the horse. He peeled the egg and fed it to the horse, which ate it immediately. "Please bring some oats now," said Father Kalinikos.

To the surprise of all, the horse started eating the oats. Father Kalinikos departed. Three days passed and Ali Rizach appears at Father Kalinikos' house.

"My horse is cured Holy Man. It is eating everything in front of it and is gaining weight. I came to pay you what I must."

"I refuse to get paid for something I did not do. It was your faith with God that did it effendi."

Ali Rizach could not believe his eyes. He went straight to the hodja and told him what the Greek priest told him. Then he raised his eyebrows:

"What kind of a holy man are you? Why did you not read God's prayers properly? Were you reading the Koran upside down? I had to go to a Christian priest to do the job right. He did not even want to get paid. You could learn a few lessons from him."[106]

What Ali did not realize was that Father Kalinikos was more than a priest. He knew a few things about curing horses from certain common ailments. If he could use that knowledge to enhance the faith of Greeks and Turks alike, he would not hesitate to go through any ceremony that looks "miraculous," to the ignorant.

ATLANTIC ADVENTURE (OFF THE COAST OF FRANCE, SEPTEMBER, 1918)

Pandelis was fighting off any thought of what had happened to U.S.S. Cyclops six months earlier. He had to think only of how to survive as long as he could now. Huddled under his wetsuit, his clothes soaking wet, his body was numb from the frozen Atlantic waves that were hitting his lifeboat and splashing onto its passengers. More than a dozen sailors, cold and wet, were huddled, staring at each other and the horizon,

---

106 A. Boinodiris, Book 1, p. 286.

hoping that the rescue ship does not come too late. Several hours had passed since the sailors had abandoned ship, many of them by jumping into the cold North Atlantic waters, to be picked up by any lifeboats that managed to survive the torpedo attack on their supply ship. Up to that moment, Pandelis had not seen another lifeboat around.

Fortunately for Pandelis, he happened to be on watch that night. At around three in the morning, he was about to relinquish his watch to a sailor, when the horrible explosion ripped through his supply ship, sailing back from France to New York.

"How did the submarine find us out?" he pondered. *"They probably heard our engines."* Fortunately, they had no ammunition pallets with them. An ammunition explosion would not leave many alive. Unfortunately, they carried some wounded soldiers with them accompanied by the nursing staff. Pandelis had doubts on whether anyone from those wounded would make it.

As the sun rose in the horizon, his mind drifted to New York, after that memorable baptism in Lisbon that saved his life. Soon afterwards, he was assigned to a supply ship, running a route to France. The United States had to supply troops fighting in France with all sorts of provisions. It was a good ship, but now it was in the bottom of the Atlantic. He remembered how he escaped death six months earlier: *"I guess lady luck does not always smile on someone. This time it was my turn to get hit."*

"I see a ship!" yelled a sailor, pointing to the horizon, where a trail of smoke rose from the sea. "Hang on, mates. I believe our ordeal is over."

Soon, the rescue ship came close and lowered a boat with sailors to help the frozen survivors, because their frozen bodies had no strength to pull themselves up, let alone row their lifeboat to the ship.

Several days later, Pandelis was admitted to a Veteran's Hospital in New York, where he would spend several weeks, recuperating. A few months later, after having lost two ships from under him, Pandelis was honorably discharged from the Navy.[107]

107 This information was from the narration of P. Mayo to S. Boinodiris in 1961-1963.

KARVALI AT WAR'S END (CHRISTMAS, 1918)

After the end of the war,[108] many volunteers from Karvali that joined the Greek army came to Constantinople, as part of the allied army detachment. Many of them made the fatal mistake to come to Karvali to get married.[109]

Everyone's ordeal seemed to be at an end. We were all extremely tired, having to carry all supplies on our backs, including our firewood. When we found out about the cease-fire, both, Greeks and Turks celebrated. Greeks were especially happy, since Turkey was defeated and the allied armies and navies entered Constantinople. In addition, we received news of the Greeks from Karvali that fought at the battle of Skra-di Legen on May 16, 1918,[110] including my uncle Charalambos. We all felt that our liberation, after centuries of Turkish occupation, since the time of the Seljuk Turks was finally near.

From what we found out, Charalambos Pavlides (using his new name now) received a medal for his bravery in the battle of Skra. The Allied force in that battle was comprised of three Greek divisions plus one French brigade. The three Greek divisions included the Archipelagos division, the Crete division, and the Serres division. The Bulgarian force comprised one division plus three regiments, which were well defended in well-fortified positions.

Victory of the allied troops was attained by a decisive Greek contribution. In May 1918 Greek military units held a leading part in the battle of Skra di Legen that resulted in the capture of a particularly fortified position, controlled until then by the Central Powers, chiefly Bulgarian troops. The battle of Skra confirmed in the eyes of the allies the fighting readiness of the Greek army that had just been restructured.

In an allied infantry probe in which Charalambos was involved, a large Bulgarian cavalry unit was dispatched to attack them over an open terrain. The Greek officer of the unit ordered retreat and started running for cover, an event that would have led to dismal results in the

---

108 The armistice of World War I was signed on November 11, 1918 at Compiegne, France. As the events unfolded with the Greco-Turkish relations, those men that came to get married at Karvali were trapped and could not leave.

109 A. Boinodiris, Book 1, p. 312.

110 A. Boinodiris, Book 1, p. 311.

open, rolling hills of that area. Charalambos, on his own accord decided to do the opposite. Instead of running, he went forward, grabbing an abandoned machine gun. He laid flat on the ground, firing on the men and horses of the assaulting cavalry. The results of the cavalry assault were less devastating; it was reversed after the Greek unit regrouped and held their positions.[111]

The road to victory was long. In 1917, the allied troops had fought several inconclusive engagements at Monastir, at Lake Prespa and on the Vardar (Axios) River. The Allies initiated an effort to oust the Greek king, Constantine, claiming that his pro-German sympathies and his aid to the Central Powers made it impossible for the Allies to conduct successful operations in the Balkan region. In June, the Allies began an invasion of Greece, and at the same time exerted diplomatic pressure on Constantine to abdicate. He did so on June 12; Venizelos became premier of the government formed under Alexander, the son of Constantine.

In 1917, some Greeks of Russia had left with the Czar's army to join the Greek Army in the Balkans. Among them were some civilians, like my father, George Boyun-egri-oglu, his sister Katina and her husband Dimitris. They came to Thessaloniki, where they worked at the French supply warehouses.

On the Balkan front, the result of the fighting of 1918 was disastrous to the Central Powers. In September, a force of about 700,000 Allied troops, consisting of French, British, Greeks, Serbs, and Italians, began a large-scale offensive against the German, Austrian, and Bulgarian troops in Serbia.

The Allied offensive was so successful that by the end of the month the Bulgarians were thoroughly beaten and concluded an armistice with the Allies. King Ferdinand abdicated in October and was succeeded by his son, Boris III. Bulgaria lost most of what it had gained in the Balkan Wars and all of its conquests from World War I. It was also required to abandon conscription, reduce armaments, and pay large reparations. The German success in Romania was nullified in November when, with the support of allied troops who had advanced into Romania after the Bulgarian capitulation, Romania reentered the war on the Allied side. After the conclusion of the Bulgarian armistice, the Serbian part of the

---

111 A. Boinodiris, Book 1, p. 312.

allied army continued to advance, occupying Belgrade on November 1, while the Italian army invaded and occupied Albania.

It was then that Greece acquired the region between the rivers Nestos and Evros. Venizelos asked the League of Nations for the independence of Pontus and the Kurds. The Italians, upset that they received few gains from Austria objected with this proposal. The supporting power of such a proposal was Russia, but they were in the middle of a civil strife with communism taking its hold in that country. The Russians left Asia Minor and the Greeks of Pontus, Armenians and Kurds of East Asia Minor lost their sponsor. The Russians also left numerous weapons behind, weapons that were to be used soon by the seventh Turkish Army against the Greeks. Then, the Turkish revolution started, led by Mustafa Kemal Ataturk.

GRECO-TURKISH WAR (KALIVARION, ONE MONDAY, JUNE, 1919)

"Who is that kid?" said an old man, staring at a youngster scrubbing the back of a horse, tied to a tree.

"He is Paul's grandson," said another old man who was leading a donkey, loaded to the bazaar.

"I must have a word with him. This kid is taking away all of my business."

The fourteen-year old child was I, Anthony Boyun-egri-oglou. In 1918, when I became 13, I realized that I had to help my family out economically because I had no father to support us and my grandfather and grandmother were getting old. My mother also worked, but she had her hands full with my sister Irene plus an orphan, named Minas, whose mother Sophia had died. Sophia's husband Efthimis was my mother's first cousin. Seeing how much we struggled to make ends meet, I decided to step in and help us survive.[112]

I discovered that Karvali had quite a bazaar every Monday. The area had about 48 small villages around it. Kemal had inducted all the young men into the army, leaving all the work to the old people and to children like me. I wanted to sell merchandise, but I could not find capital. To get capital, I went into service, taking care of animals of those who were coming to the market on Mondays. I was feeding

---

112 A. Boinodiris, Book 1, p. 313.

them, giving them water and cleaning them. I was charging five grossia per animal. The travelers liked me so much, that the local inn started losing business. In two months, I built up a capital of 10 panganotes, or 2.5 gold liras. I could work there, because that year our school had closed. During the previous summer, we had received the news that our school had to be terminated, because schools were used to house war refugees.

War refugees were all around us. First came the Armenians in 1915, Kurds in 1916 and 1917 and now finally the Greeks.[113] After the new war started in May of this year, the Greeks from the western regions of Aydin, Smyrna, Nazili Denizli, Honaz Serai, Egerdir, Bourdur, Sparti and Attalia were trying to escape the war by moving East, to our territories. Like with previous floods of refugees, I had to stop my schooling, on and off, shy of completing elementary school. This time, it seemed that it was to last for some time. Our school accommodated as many refugees as it was possible to stay there, while others stayed elsewhere, wherever possible. I was now in my sixth grade and destined not to finish Elementary School education.[114]

As I said earlier, the second occupation of my grandfather was pottery. Many times, I asked him to teach me this art, so that I can help him. Every time I did, he would refuse, saying: "No grandson of mine should wrestle with mud. It is an extremely unhealthy occupation." He encouraged me instead to go into business, buying and selling goods of every type.

Since I was nine, during holidays, my pastime was wrestling. I believe that I became tough because I walked a lot. Local grownups, expert in the art of Greco-Roman wrestling, oiled their bodies with olive oil and had contests; young men of the same age and weight were matched. I was not the best, but I learned the technique faster than most and was able to hold my own.[115]

The innkeepers were not happy, trying to persuade my relatives to stop me from causing losses to them. I told them that after a small capital to get into business, I was planning to stop. That evening, my grandfather approached me:

---

113 This Greco-Turkish War lasted from May 1919 to October 1922.
114 A. Boinodiris, Book 1, p. 306.
115 A. Boinodiris, Book 1, p. 174.

"Anthony," he said. "I believe it is time for you to give the innkeepers a break. You are undermining their business and they can get nasty. I do not want you to get hurt."

Thus, under protest, I was forced to abandon this business of taking care of animals and with help from my family I became a baker, baking bread for the bazaar. Soon, I had the capital to get an animal and to open a little store. Unfortunately, the shadow of the Turkish Army was over my head,[116] just like it was on all the boys of my age, always wondering whether it was worth investing too much effort in building anything.

THE LITTLE MERCHANT (KALIVARION, SEPTEMBER, 1919)

Sooner or later the Turks would draft me into their army, to fight against my own people. Then, what would I do? I started daydreaming of possible scenarios of my possible escape.

I had no idea what to do towards assuring my future. My grandfather always told me to be alert, not act hastily, but be ready to act, and do the right thing if the opportunity arose. Both, my father and my uncle escaped the draft into the Turkish Army. I was wondering, how I could do the same when my time came. What would happen to my mother and sister? Can my grandfather take care of them?

I started buying and selling tobacco, paper for tobacco, lighters, matches and soap. I was selling it in the market. However, in order to buy this stuff I had to go to Akserai. My grandfather was getting old and had difficulties dealing with the work in the vineyards and fields. He had a temperamental mule that he used in his pottery business. My poor, aging grandmother tried to use this mule, which bolted very easily and it threw her off, as she was returning from Iskalka. My grandmother's leg started swelling and this accident left her incapacitated. My grandfather had to take care of her.[117]

This month, I was traveling to Akserai to get merchandise to sell. Since I had no horse and had to follow a horse caravan for my security, I built up enough stamina to keep up with horses. It required that I had my money, adequate for the purchase hidden in my waist. If I stayed

---

116 A. Boinodiris, Book 1, p. 174.
117 A. Boinodiris, Book 1, p. 313-314.

behind, the Turks could rob me. The caravan always was attached to the armed official mail courier. This courier carried the Turkish flag, indicating official business, protected by law. Any robbers had to face not only guns, but also a countrywide hunt against them, which led to a strict punishment of execution. On the return, I gave my load to someone that I knew was returning, at least until I became 15 years old, when I managed to buy an animal for my business.[118]

MUSTAFA KEMAL (ANKARA, APRIL 23, 1920)

Mustafa Kemal[119] was elated after hearing the news on the voting in the Grand National Assembly. Finally, he was given the leverage to do something about the mess Turkey was in. He began the year by calling for a national protest against the Greek attempt to annex Izmir, and against atrocities in Turkey's southern provinces, as the allegations were leveled against Turkey by the French and the Armenians.

When the Ottoman parliament agreed to a National Pact on 28 January, the occupation forces cracked down on the Turks, arresting and deporting many nationalists and dismissing the Turkish parliament. Constantinople was reoccupied on 16 March. The nationalist government was formed and convened in Ankara. Finally, today, the nationalist's governing council, the Grand National Assembly, met in Ankara and elected Kemal[120] as its leader and the head of its provisional government. Kemal had now the authority to start a War of Independence, starting in Anatolia, where the Greek troops had moved inland from Izmir. He had to rally all the Turks all over Anatolia to fight and die for their survival.

Kemal was born in Salonika (now Thessaloniki, Greece), the son of a minor official who became a timber merchant. When he was 12 years old, he went to military schools in Salonika and Monastir, centers of anti-Turkish Greek and Slavic nationalism. In 1899, he attended the

---

118 A. Boinodiris, Book 1, p. 85.

119 Mustafa Kemal (1881-1938) was a Turkish soldier, nationalist leader, and political leader, who founded the republic of Turkey and was its first president (1923-1938).

120 The name Ataturk (Father Turk) was bestowed upon him in 1934 by the Grand National Assembly as a tribute for his unique service to the Turkish nation.

military academy in Istanbul, graduating as staff captain in January 1905.

Because of his activities in the secret Young Turk movement against the autocratic government of the Ottoman Empire, Kemal was posted to Syria, in virtual exile. There he founded the secret Fatherland and Freedom Society (1906). Transferred to Salonika the following year, he joined the Committee of Union and Progress (CUP) that carried out the Young Turk Revolution in July 1908. He was not, however, in the inner circle of the CUP and therefore played no role in the actual revolution.

Kemal fought in Libya against Italy in 1911 and 1912 and was promoted to major in November 1911. He organized the defense of the Dardanelles during the Balkan Wars (1912-1913) and was military attaché in Bulgaria in October 1913. During World War I, in which Turkey sided with Germany, Kemal made his military reputation in the Gallipoli campaign in 1915, where he played a crucial role in repelling the Allied invasion. He then served in the Caucasus and Syria, where he commanded a special army group just before the armistice was signed in October 1918. When he returned to Constantinople, he watched anxiously as the victorious allied powers prepared to partition Anatolia.

A Greek army occupied Izmir (Smyrna) on May 15, 1919. Kemal, who had been appointed inspector of the Third Army in Anatolia, reached Samson on May 19. After 1919, Kemal's revolutionary army did not recognize the terms signed previously and closed all roads from Constantinople to the East. Ankara became the capital and Kemal managed to get weapons from the Russian army, which was disbanded after the communist revolution started. Finding a vacuum, he recaptured without much loss of life all territories that the Russians had taken from the Turks between 1917 and 1918.[121]

He immediately set about uniting the Turkish national movement and created an army for defense. Although the Turks outnumbered Greeks more than eight-fold, the wars had turned them into a mob. These wars started with the internal civil strife of the Young Turks, followed by the Italian and Balkan Wars, a destructive World War and finally the Greek-Turkish War. Even now, the nationalists continued to

---

121 A. Boinodiris, Book 1, p. 312.

wage war against the Ottoman sultan's regime in Constantinople, which seemed willing to allow the dismemberment of the national territory. Sultan Abdul Hamid II was replaced with Sultan Mehmed V in 1909 before he died in 1918. By 1920, the Constantinople government had been discredited for submitting to the Allied occupation of the capital and signing the Treaty of Sevres, which recognized Greek control over many parts of Anatolia. Kemal, meanwhile, had set up a provisional government in Ankara in April 1920, ready to turn the tables on the Greeks. He knew the Greeks very well, because he lived among them in Salonika. He knew their strengths and weaknesses and was counting on them to make their usual wrong moves.

Figure 12 Mustafa Kemal (1881-1938)

THE VENIZELOS MOVEMENT (SUMMER 1920)

The Greeks are peculiar people. There is a saying that they squabble so much that among five Greeks, you will find ten leaders and no followers. They are such "control freaks," that they rarely trust anyone else to do any thinking for them. They do not know how to follow someone else and be part of a team, like many Western Europeans do. That has positive and negative effects. They invented democracy to overcome this deficit, but even with democracy, their competitive infighting slowed their teamwork to a crawl. They simply could not trust the skills of a selected leader, unless the leader told them exactly what they wanted to hear.

After many years of occupation by the Turks and great many revolts that failed, the few Greeks that remained in the southern Balkan Peninsula rose in 1821, and liberated themselves. With help from their brothers from abroad, they fought as warlords, fighting the Turks, but also fighting each other. Many of their leaders tried to unite them to work with each other as a unit, but most had failed. The supporting powers of Great Britain, France and Russia saw this and started to exert their own influence in the method by which the Greeks should be governed. Each government started supporting a party and the leaders of these parties were eliminated one after the other. Kolokotronis, who was an ex-British officer was captured and placed in jail at Nafplion by other warlords. John Kapodistrias was set as the first Prime Minister of Greece, placed there after serving as a foreign minister in Russia and with support from Russia. The opposing warlords from Mani assassinated him.

After all these internal squabbles, the supporting powers jointly agreed in 1832 to impose a King on Greece, to bring some sort of peace in that land. This was King Otto, from Germany. He came with his queen Amalia and set up a court in a country of rebels, without public support or any semblance of a constitution. They liberated Kolokotronis and tried their best to bring a semblance of normalcy in that land. Finally, the liberated Greeks were to govern themselves, by electing a Prime Minister, while Otto had only the final veto in ratifying the election. Yet, the Greeks were failing miserably in making this system work. By 1843, public dissatisfaction with him had reached crisis proportions and there were demands for a constitution. On September

3, 1843, the Greek infantry assembled in the Square in front of the Palace in Athens. Eventually joined by much of the population of the small capital, the rebellion refused to disperse until the King agreed to grant a constitution, which would require that there be Greeks in his Council and that he convenes a permanent national assembly. King Otto gave in to the pressure and agreed to the demands of the crowd over the objections of his opinionated Queen. This square was renamed Constitution Square to commemorate the events of September 1843. Now for the first time the king had Greeks in his council and the French party, the English Party or the Russian Party (according to which of the Great Powers' culture they most esteemed) vied for rank and power. While on a visit to the Peloponnesos in 1862, a new coup was launched and this time a provisional government was set up and summoned a national convention. Ambassadors of the Great Powers urged King Otto not to resist, and the king and queen took refuge on a British warship and returned to Bavaria the same way they had come to Greece.

Then, new kings were assigned, starting with King George I, originally a Danish prince. He was only 17 years old when the Greek National Assembly, which had deposed the former King Otto, elected him King. His nomination was both suggested and supported by the Great Powers, but the results were the same. Then, in 1915, his son, King Constantine I became the son-in-law of Kaiser. He was in the difficult personal position of deciding to which side to support during World War I due to family ties and emotional attachments. Despite his blood relationship to the British royal family, Constantine's personal sentiments and attachments lay with the German Empire. He had studied at the Prussian Army Staff College in Berlin. In addition, he married in 1889 Sophia of Prussia, a younger sister of William II, German Emperor. The United Kingdom had hoped that this familial connection might persuade Constantine to join the cause of the Allies of World War I; Constantine signaled his intention to join the Triple Entente (UK, France and Russia) and actually gave a tentative promise to that effect, but took no concrete steps towards doing so. As a result, he was forced into exile.

Though Constantine remained decidedly neutral, the influence of the Prime Minister of Greece, Venizelos is evident. In May 1917, after the exile of Constantine, Venizelos returned to Athens and allied with the Entente. Greek military forces (though divided between supporters of the monarchy and supporters of Venizelos) began to take part in military operations against the Bulgarian Army on the border. If Greece had followed King Constantine's wishes in 1916, Greece would have lost all of Macedonia to Serbia. All those Greeks of Macedonia, who were killed by the Bulgarians during the Balkan Wars, would have sacrificed their lives for nothing. The Bulgarians and Serbs contested this area, populated by Greeks, for obvious reasons, because it gave them access to the Aegean Sea. As shown in history, since the Byzantine times they came time after time and slaughtered the local population, with the hope that through ethic cleansing, their population would be the dominant one. Serbia would have been out of a Balkan union without Venizelos' shrewd political move to negotiate with their Prime Minister, giving Serbia free zone access to the port of Thessaloniki. That is how Greece managed to reclaim Eastern Macedonia and Thrace. All this would not have happened if the King were still in power.[122]

Venizelos went to the Paris peace talks armed with the assurances he had received from the Allies during the war and focused on recovering territories of Greece. He showed all of his considerable diplomatic skills at the peace talks. He wooed the United States president, Woodrow Wilson, and Britain's Prime Minister David Lloyd George. Venizelos quickly offered the services of the Greek military as policing agents and as peacekeepers in the occupied territories. Foreign leaders were indebted to the wily Venizelos for this assistance, but the offer fostered domestic discontent. The Greek armed forces had been mobilized almost continuously since 1912, and the nation was becoming war weary. In addition, Venizelos neglected urgent domestic issues as he put all of his energies into winning the peace talks. He would eventually pay for this neglect.

The Greeks were in Eastern Thrace and western coast of Asia Minor, including Smyrna (Izmir), having signed the treaty of Sevres with Turkey. After two years of intense negotiations, Greece stood on the verge of realizing what was started in 1912. Venizelos started the war with Turkey with one primary reason: the liberation a sizeable Greek-speaking Orthodox Christian population inhabiting Anatolia.

---

122 A. Boinodiris, Book 1, p.272-274.

Greeks have lived In Asia Minor since antiquity. Before the outbreak of the First World War, over 2.5 million Greeks lived in Turkey. In 1915, the Young Turk government enacted genocidal policies against the minorities in the Ottoman Empire, slaughtering hundreds of thousands of people. While the Armenian Genocide is the best known of these events, there were also severe atrocities towards Greeks in Pontus and western Anatolia.

Venizelos stated to a British newspaper that: "Greece is not making war against Islam, but against the anachronistic Ottoman Government, and its corrupt, ignominious, and bloody administration, with a view to the expelling it from those territories where the majority of the population consists of Greeks." Opponents of the Greek argument have pointed out that the Young Turk government was not in power at that time as its leaders had fled the country at the end of World War I and the Ottoman government in Istanbul was already under British control.

The total population of the Ottoman Empire in 1914 (sum of all millets) was 20,975,345 and the Greek population before the Balkan wars were 2,833,370 (1909 census) was dropped to 1,792,206 (due to the loss of lands to Greece).[123]

Although Venizelos downplayed the concept of "Great Idea," other nationalists and demagogues used it as a prime motivation for initiating the war. The "Great Idea" was a core concept of Greek nationalism, based on the restoration of a new Byzantine Empire on both sides of the Aegean that would incorporate territories with Greek populations outside the borders of a Modern Greek state (in Ionia, Thrace and Constantinople, Pontus etc.). From the time of Greek independence from the Ottoman Empire in 1830, the Great Idea had played a major role in Greek politics, motivated by the will to liberate Greeks under the Ottoman rule. Venizelos understood this idea, but also realized that without the proper economic and political backing from the allies, it could lead to a careless adventure with disastrous results.

The Great Idea was not merely the product of the 19th century nationalism. It was, in one of its aspects, deeply rooted in many Greeks' religious consciousness. This aspect was the recovery of Constantinople for Christendom, the reestablishment of the universal Christian Byzantine

---

123 This is based on a publication Stamford Shaw, of 1914.

Empire, which had fallen in 1453. Ever since this time the recovery of St. Sophia and the city had been handed down from generation to generation as the destiny and aspiration of the Greek Orthodox.

The military aspect of the war began with the Armistice of Mudros. The operations of the Greco-Turkish war can be roughly divided into three main phases: The first phase, spanning the period from May 1919 to October 1920, encompasses the Greek Landings in Asia Minor and their consolidation along the Aegean Coast.

On May 15, 1919, twenty thousand Greek soldiers landed in Izmir or Smyrna and took control of the city and its surroundings under cover of the Greek, French, and British navies. Legal justifications for the landings were found in the article 7 of the Armistice of Moudros, which allowed the Allies "to occupy any strategic points in the event of any situation arising which threatens the security of Allies." The Greeks had already brought their forces into Eastern Thrace (apart from Constantinople and its region).

The Greeks of Smyrna and other Christians, (mainly Greeks and Armenians, who formed a minority according to Turkish sources, a majority according to Greek sources, greeted the Greek troops as liberators. By contrast, the Turkish population saw this as an invading force, as they resented the Greeks. The Greek landings were met by sporadic resistance, mainly by small groups of irregular Turkish troops in the suburbs. However, the majority of the Turkish forces in the region either surrendered peacefully to the Greek Army, or fled to the countryside.

While the Turkish army was ordered not to open fire, a Turkish nationalist (Hasan Tahsin) among the crowd fired a shot and killed the Greek standard-bearer. Greek soldiers then opened fire on the Turkish barracks as well as the government building. Between 300, to 400 Turks and 100 Greeks were killed on the first day. The occupation proved a humiliation for many of the Turkish and Muslim inhabitants. Long lines of killed and wounded were seen along the front.

During the summer of 1920, the Greek army launched a series of successful offensives in the directions of Meander (Menderes) Valley, Peramos and Philadelphia. The overall strategic objective of these operations, which were met by increasingly stiff Turkish resistance, was to provide strategic depth to the defense of Smyrna. To that end, the Greek zone of occupation was extended over all of Western and most of North-Western Asia Minor.

Then, in August 1920, the Treaty of Sevres was signed. In return for the contribution of the Greek army on the side of the Allies, the Allies supported the assignment of eastern Thrace and the millet of Smyrna to Greece. This treaty ended the First World War in Asia Minor and, at the same time, sealed the fate of the Ottoman Empire. Henceforth, the Ottoman Empire would no longer be a European power. More importantly, Turkey renounced to Greece all rights over Imbros and Tenedos, retaining the small territories of Constantinople, the islands of Marmara, and "a tiny strip of European territory." The Straits of Bosporus were placed under an International Commission, as they were now open to all.

Turkey was furthermore forced to transfer to Greece "the exercise of her rights of sovereignty" over Smyrna in addition to "a considerable land, merely retaining a 'flag over an outer fort.'" The treaty was never ratified by the Ottoman Empire, or Greece.

Figure 13 Venizelos (1864-1936)

CRIMEAN EXPEDITION (NOVEMBER, 1920)

In October 1917, the October Revolution in Russia overthrew the provisional government and five months later, the Russian Socialist Republic signed the Treaty of Brest-Litovsk with the Germans, which formally ended the war on the Eastern Front. This allowed the Germans to begin redeploying troops on the Western Front. There, the American Expeditionary Force had not bolstered the depleted British and French armies. Also, worrisome to the Allies was the fact that in April 1918, a division of German troops had landed in Finland, creating fears that they might try to capture the Russian ports to the Arctic Sea. Faced with these series of events, the leaders of the British and French governments decided that the Allies needed to begin a military intervention in North Russia.

Severely short of troops to spare, the British and French decided to request that President Wilson provide U.S. troops for the North Russia Campaign and the Siberian Campaign. In July 1918, against the advice of his War Department, President Wilson finally agreed to a limited participation in the Campaign by 5,000 U.S. troops who were hastily organized as the American North Russia Expeditionary Force (also known as the Polar Bear Expedition) and sent to Archangel as well as 8,000 U.S. troops who were similarly organized as the American Expeditionary Force Siberia and shipped to Vladivostok from the Philippines and Camp Fremont in California. That same month the Canadian government agreed to a British request to command and furnish the majority of troops for a combined British Empire force.

Japan, which sent by far the biggest force, had its own reasons for participating in the intervention. The Empire by then had annexed Korea, Inner Manchuria, parts of China, and had a very strong interest in expanding its influence and territories in the Far East. The Japanese government's intense hostility to communism as a potential threat to its monarchy, a determination to recoup historical losses to Russia following the Treaty of Portsmouth, and the perceived opportunity to settle the "northern problem" in Japan's security by either creating a buffer state, or through outright territorial acquisition, were also factors. American economic and diplomatic pressure and internal political issues along with the military success of the Red Army forced Japan's withdrawal.

A month after the Armistice, namely on December 18, 1918, the French occupied the city of Odessa. That initiated an Allied involvement in the Ukraine and Southern Russia. The intervention was intended to aid and supply the White forces of General Denikin (the Volunteer Army) operating in the area. The campaign involved French, Polish (12,000 men), and Greek troops (24,000 men). The Greek force was led by colonel Nicolas Plastiras.

Plastiras was a soldier, born in Karditsa, Thessaly. He joined the 5th Infantry Regiment as a volunteer in 1904. He entered the Evelpidon Academy[124] in 1910 and, after being assigned to the rank 2nd Lieutenant in 1912, he fought with distinction in the Balkan Wars, where he earned his nickname "The Black Horseman". He first rose to wider prominence when, as a Major he supported the Movement of National Defense of Venizelos during the First World War. He fought with distinction with the Evzones Regiment at the battle of Skra-di-Legen and was promoted to Lieutenant Colonel. In 1919, Colonel Plastiras commanded the Evzones Regiment in the Ukraine.

My father, who was then in Thessaloniki, working for the French decided to go back to Russia with this expedition. With him were also his sister and his brother-in-law. As the expedition passed through Constantinople, he sent us a letter with five gold liras, so that I (then about 13) could go to him in Odessa in the spring of 1919. To my good luck, the destroyed Turkish postal service delayed the delivery of that letter. I received it almost a year later, at the end of 1919. Fate though had it that we encountered a heavy winter in 1919-1920 and Mustafa Kemal had closed all roads to the west, so I was barred from joining my father and was trapped in Cappadocia under Kemal's control. Several classmates of mine, those that had parents in Russia left for Odessa. Years later, when I was reunited with my father, I found out that from all of them only one survived. The rest of my friends and classmates, Michael Tsolakoglou, Stefanos Tsolakoglou and George Vermisoglou died in 1921 from hunger and typhus. The only one that survived was Prodromos Karasavas, who left Odessa and went to Constanza, Romania.[125]

---

124 Evelpidon Military Academy was established in 1828.
125 A. Boinodiris, Book 1, p. 313.

It was fortunate for me that I did not join my father, because the Greek, French and English expedition to support the Czar was ill planned and was doomed to fail. The expedition to Russia ended up in failure, especially after the defeat of the White Russian forces' attempt to march against Moscow. General Wrangel managed to reorganize his army in the Crimea, but in the end he and his men were forced to flee abroad, with their evacuation aboard Allied ships ending on November 14, 1920.

The troops were returned to Greece, but not the civilians that came with them on their own accord. Plastiras and his force were transferred to Smyrna in Asia Minor via Romania. As a result of this hurried flight, my father, his sister and brother-in-law were trapped. There, they had to deal with the terror of civil war and the innumerable deaths from hunger and disease.[126]

THE MONKEY BITE THAT CHANGED GREEK DREAMS (WINTER, 1920)

In October 1920, the Greek army advanced further east into Anatolia, with the encouragement of Lloyd George, who intended to increase pressure on the Turkish and Ottoman governments to sign the Treaty of Sevres. The advance began under the direction of the Liberal government of Venizelos.

When Venizelos announced in triumph that Greece now occupied two continents and touched on five seas, the impossible dream seemed to be coming true. The dream soon turned into a nightmare however. In August, 1920, as he prepared to return to Greece from his talks in France, monarchist assassins shot Venizelos. Venizelos survived the assassination attempt. This was the second one; the first was in 1918, in Lyon, France, as he disembarked from a train. After being wounded, he fell, pretending to be dead. The attackers, members of the Popular Party, mistaken about their success, left the scene.[127]

He survived, but by focusing on foreign affairs, he became out of touch with events in Greece, and his extended convalescence isolated him even more from the domestic scene. On top of that, two months after the attack on Venizelos, in October of 1920 King Alexander

126 A. Boinodiris, Book 1, p. 312.
127 A. Boinodiris Book 1, p. 55.

was bitten by his favorite monkey and died. This incident has been characterized as the "monkey bite that changed the course of Greek history." With the King's death, Venizelos' preference was to declare a Greek republic, and thus end the monarchy. However, he was well aware that this would not be acceptable to the European powers. After King Alexander died leaving no heirs, general elections were held on November 1, 1920 and suddenly became the focus of a new conflict between the supporters of Venizelos and those of King Constantine, who now entered the scene.

The war-weary Greek people opted for change. To the surprise of many, Venizelos won only 118 out of the total 369 seats. The crushing defeat obliged Venizelos and a number of his closest supporters to leave the country. Venizelos was replaced by a royalist demagogue, Dimitrios Gounaris, who appointed inexperienced monarchist officers to senior commands. Instead of peace, the Greeks were tricked into voting for more war. All logic went out the window and was replaced by blind nationalism in view of the recent successes in Asia Minor. The Greeks fell into the same trap that plagued the Turks for centuries: winning against a hated enemy became more important than the logic of winning for humanity as a whole. Sometimes it is more important to patiently bid your time and even lose a battle, to help everyone around you survive and contribute.

Gounaris' campaign slogan revolved around the Great Idea, a concept that King Constantine repeatedly used to rally the masses for his support. Queen Sophia wrote about her husband's preoccupation with the Great Idea: "Constantine is completely possessed by the specter of Byzantium." According to Queen Sophia, Constantine's dream of "marching into the great city and walk to St. Sophia at the head of the Greek army" was still "in his heart" and it appeared as if the King was ready to enter the war against the Ottoman Empire. This turn of events was the mistake Kemal was hoping for. It caused a disaster beyond proportion for the Greeks of Asia Minor.

The new government prepared for a plebiscite on the return of King Constantine. Remembering his pro-German posture during the war, the allies warned the Greek government that if he should be returned to the throne they would cut off all aid to Greece. A month later a plebiscite called for the return of King Constantine. The Greek

Army which had secured Smyrna and the Asia Minor coast was purged of Venizelos supporters while it was marching on Ankara.

POLITICAL CLOUDS (SPRING 1921)

In December 1920, the Greeks had advanced to Eskisehir, about half way between Constantinople and Ankara. By then, their supplies were dwindling. The French, Russians and Italians bitterly opposed the policies of the new government. The French and the Italians concluded private agreements with the Turkish revolutionaries in recognition of their mounting strength. Turkish revolutionaries received arms from Italy and France, who threw in their lot with them against Greece, which was seen as a British client.

The French left Cilicia and left their weapons of war to the Turks. When the French left, a French General of Greek origin was stationed in Cilicia. His name was Theophilou. Soon after Gounaris took over, Paris issued an order to General Theophilou to evacuate Cilicia and move into Syria and Lebanon. France hated the pro-German King that Gounaris brought back, especially after having gone through several grueling years of World War I with Germany. General Theophilou's orders also told him to deliver all heavy armament to the army of Kemal. He was also to leave enough advisors with Kemal to train his troops. Theophilou followed his orders, but true to his conscience he immediately contacted Greek and Armenian leadership to get out of Asia Minor, since they were about to become targets of reprisals by the Turks. Fresh and trained Cilician Turkish troops were the key to Kemal's success in crushing the weak and tired Greek forces that were advancing in Asia Minor. If Venizelos were in power, the French would never make this move.

Even Russia helped the Turks with weapons and money. The new communist regime in Russia hated the pro-German King even more than the French did. Although they hated the Turks, they sent to Kemal 70 (or maybe 700) sacks of Russian gold coins. These coins were commonplace then. I heard this news as a child and could not verify which number was correct. Kemal used the money, since armies cannot move without money.

The Italians used their base in Antalya to assist, especially from the point of view of intelligence, to the Turkish revolutionaries against the Greeks. There was also a positive relationship between the Soviet Union and the Turkish Revolutionaries, which was solidified under Treaty of Moscow (1921).

In early 1921 the Greeks earnestly resumed their advance, but again met stiff resistance from the entrenched Turkish Nationalists, who were increasingly better prepared and equipped like a regular army. The Greek advance was halted for the first time at the First Battle of Inonu on January 11, 1921. This development led to Allied proposals to amend the Treaty of Sevres at a conference in London where both the Turkish Revolutionary and Ottoman governments were represented. Although some agreements were reached with Italy, France and Britain, the decisions were not agreed to by the Greek government, who believed that they still retained the strategic advantage and could negotiate from a stronger point.

The Greeks initiated another attack on March 27th, the Second Battle of Inonu, which was resisted fiercely and finally defeated by the Turkish troops on March 30th. The British favored a Greek territorial expansion but refused to offer any military assistance in order to avoid provoking the French.

At that time, my uncle Charalambos Pavlides was a volunteer, fighting in Asia Minor with the Greek Army. With the Plastiras regiment, he fought at Smyrna, Ala Sehir, Magnesia, and Ak Sehir[128] and reached Kotz Hissar near Lake Tata. He was planning to come to Karvali in 1921, when the Greek Army was defeated. His unit disappointed and frustrated by the lack of supplies and ammunition took the road back in an orderly retreat.

EARLY PARTNERSHIPS (KALIVARION, SPRING 1921)

I was sixteen now and tried to make a living with my newly purchased animal. My work progressed relatively well. My capital was adequate to collaborate with my Aunt Anna, who baked bread in two ovens, which I sold in addition to the items in my inventory. On Mondays, during the bazaar the bread production could not keep up with the demand. We earned about 70% profit on all sales.

---

128 Ak Sehir is the birthplace of the famous Nasreddin Hotza, the story-telling Turk mullah. A. Boinodiris, Book 1, p.24.

Our business expanded into making ouzo. We bought black raisins with seeds, strong in sugar content, and placed them in a barrel or large clay storage jugs for a month with some water. After it fermented, we passed the mixture through our still, adding mint into it and making some of the best mint-flavored ouzo in the area. The Turks and Turkomans of the region used to drink our ouzo in large quantities, using a water glass. We also went through a three level distillation, a lot stronger than today's Metaxa cognac.[129] After Kemal Ataturk made liquor illegal in his region, and closed down major producers of liquor, our homemade products were in high demand.[130]

Early in 1921, my Aunt Anna married her daughter Maria to Minas, who became her son-in-law and I lost my partner, because she now collaborated with him for obvious reasons. Maria died in the quarantined island of St. George, out of Piraeus, later on in 1924.[131] Minas came to Greece and became a clerk in Nea Karvali. He was still a clerk in 1974, when I last saw him.[132]

When I separated from Aunt Anna's business, whose house was near the market, I was forced to open my own store near the market, by renting the store of Charalambos Koulouzoglou. I was now 16-years old. I was lucky, since the previous owner went to the army and he offered it to me at a good price. We were closely associated, since my father had baptized his daughter Anastasia.

I bought my own animal. My grandfather sold the mule that caused all sorts of damage, including the disability of my grandmother.

In my dealings, I met Armenian merchants, like Karabet, Alexander and Haji Lofit. I also met a Turk named Ali, who was part of the salt monopoly in the closed market of Akserai. Although I was still a child, these people helped me out. They became fond of me, because I was so honest. In the back of my mind, I was thinking what I would do when I reached 21, in 1926, when the Turkish army came after me.

---

129 A. Boinodiris, Book 1, p. 310-311.
130 A. Boinodiris, Book 1, p. 316. The Greeks of Cappadocia were involved in bootlegging, especially since the Turkish government was not able to effectively enforce Kemal's ruling in that region.
131 A. Boinodiris, Book 1, p. 310-311.
132 A. Boinodiris, Book 1, p. 314-315.

I was doing relatively well economically and then one of the village elders, named Averkios asked me to take his sickly son Stelios as partner. I did take Stelios as a partner as a favor to that elder.[133]

One day, my partner Stelios wanted to come to Akserai with me. We hardly had any load going to Akserai, and we went riding. We had some ouzo and food with us and we had a pleasant trip.

The next day, on our return, the animals were loaded, so we had to walk. Stelios was so weak, that I had to take some load off one animal, to load it onto the other, so that he could ride. We did that until we reached the lime factory, near Kireslik. There the road was going uphill, where most animals had difficulty negotiating the road. I was forced to ask Stelios to dismount and walk. He barely made it to 100 meters and fell down from exhaustion and tears in his eyes, bless his soul.

"I wish that I was healthy, like you. I would give my entire father's wealth and then some to be healthy," he said crying.

I had to put him on the horse again. He rode to Karvali crying and he never came with me again on a trip. I felt sorry for Stelios. I then realized that health equates to freedom, the most valuable asset anyone can have. Without health, you lose freedom to do what you want to do in life.

THE ROAD TO POLATLI (KALIVARION, JULY, 1921)

In the winter of 1921, in spite of Venizelos' warnings, the Greek government decided on a military confrontation with the Turkish nationalist movement led by Mustafa Kemal that was growing in strength and threatening the Smyrna Protectorate. In March, Athens launched a major offensive. The Greek army pushed eastward into Asia Minor along a broad front. At one point, the Greek line extended across much of Anatolia.

In the middle of 1921, we received governmental orders in Karvali to feed the new troops of Kemal. Each family was to prepare 24 okas[134] of clean bulgur[135] in order for someone to take all this food to

---

133 A. Boinodiris, Book 1, p. 315-316.
134 "Oka" was a weight measure, equivalent to 1.2829 kilograms divided into 400 "drams". One dram is equivalent to 3.2 grams.
135 Bulgur is dried, cracked wheat.

specific military authorities at Polatli. Being under the Turkish guns, the community complied. Karvali, consisting of about 1000 families contributed 24,000 okas (about 30 tons) of bulgur. In addition, we were told to take all our animals, loaded with the bulgur for Polatli, a train station near Ankara to be delivered to the military authority there. The Turkish police officers that received the orders did not know where Polatli was. Being illiterate, they could not read maps. Fortunately, we had a few old Greeks from Karvali that worked as potters in Ankara and Kir Sehir. The police ordered me, a young lad of 16 to be part of the animal drive and take our mule to that station. They made no provisions for our food or night accommodations for either humans or animals.

We started the drive at the end of June 1921 passing near Lake Tata, a salt lake to the Northwest. We passed the mountains, many of them having salt mines, with the scattered and abandoned villages of Haji Pektes. The residents had left their houses to avoid being caught in the rage of war between the advancing Greek Army and the defending Turkish Army. After a few days on the road, we exhausted our own food supplies and started to become hungry. For twelve days, we were traveling six to seven hours per day in the hot sun. The heat was exhausting. It did not take us long to persuade the police officers to share part of the load that we were carrying with us. We started taking little bulgur from each sack, boiled it and ate it.

We managed to find some bread in the abandoned villages too. The residents had abandoned their fields without harvesting them. By rifling through the homes, we found leftover yogurt and ariani (diluted non-fat yogurt, made into a refreshing drink) and abandoned chickens, which we slaughtered and cooked. We and our animals suffered the most from thirst. Every time we found a well, we had to resolve disputes on who would drink first. As we approached the plain of Ankara, a cavalry detachment appeared.

"Halt. " We stopped. "Where are you heading? What are you carrying?

"We are taking these animals, loaded with bulgur for the Army, destined for the railroad station of Polatli."

"Your orders have changed. Polatli is too close to the front. You are ordered to take this load to the warehouse of ... "

He gave a location (that I forgot) that was further to the east of Ankara.

It took us another three days to go to the new location. There, we unloaded the animals and returned back to our previous road. We met again the cavalry detachment.

"Did you deliver your load?"

"We did effendi."

It took us 15 days to return to Karvali. These days were like hell for us. On the return trip, all the farms and fields were put on fire by the Turkish cavalry, refusing to let the Greek cavalry have any food for themselves and their animals.[136] We had no means of foraging on farms to feed our hunger. We felt that we were on an anvil, between the hammering burning sun of that July and the charred earth and countryside.[137][138]

THE UGLY FACE OF HATE (JANUARY, 1922)

Selefkia was a prosperous town, on the coast route from Syria to Constantinople. The house that John Aslanoglou had purchased was small, but fully equipped. It had a large yard with a brick walled fence, where children could grow, unattended if need be. The yard soon became a flower garden, under the hands of Makrina. A new addition to the family was added in a year, a girl, named Marianthi (1914). Basil (1918) followed her. John was also told that his wife was pregnant with yet another baby.[139] John's hopes and aspirations for a better future were high. He made enough money, adequate to support servants, to help Makrina with the house chores and the raising of her five children.

One of them made an impression to the kids, for he was an Arab, wearing nothing but his white robe. What impressed the kids was that he could go to the bathroom in a split second. He just squatted on his path, anywhere and did his business. Then he would get up, made sure he did not step on his mess and walk to his chores without even

---

136 This excerpt of Anthony confirms that the Turks practiced the "scorched earth policy", just as much it was practiced by the Greeks in this war.
137 A. Boinodiris, Book 1, p. 274.
138 A. Boinodiris, Book 4, loose attachment B1 (3, 4).
139 This baby was to be a girl, Fevronia, to be born at the end of the summer of 1922.

blinking. Since he had no underwear, this became a routine, which the children had not seen before and found remarkable.

World War I ended, leaving John Aslanoglou very rich. He was a jovial fellow, mostly bald, with a reddish band of hair, surrounding his baldhead. He was generous to Greeks and Turks alike. His warehouse was expanded, housing everything in quantity, from soap to olive oil and from matches to clothing materials. Meanwhile, Greek politics in the West started a set of events that were to have serious consequences for the family.

The Nameless police officer that helped John bring his family to Selefkia from Karvali was a good friend. He had the rank of regional Major in the Police Force. Before Venizelos lost the elections in Greece, the "nameless police officer" visited John's home and had liberal discussions on everything. He was politically a liberal, wanting to abolish discrimination of minorities. When Venizelos lost the elections, he came and symbolically asked for a bitter cup of coffee. When asked, "What is the matter?" he responded prophetically:

"Since Venizelos lost the elections, things will turn to be worse for you and the rest of the Christians. The English and French liked Venizelos. The only ones that like his opposition of Gounaris are the losing side of Germany. Hard liners in Greece will make Turks even more fanatical, causing the destruction of the Greek Army, which will be starved for supplies. With the defeat of Greece, your position and mine here will become untenable. That is why I drink bitter coffee."

John thought: *"what do you expect from a Turk, but to look after Turkish interests."* He would regret this thought later on.[140]

John Aslanoglou had at least 50 employees to run his business, most of them Turks. One of them was a new face. He came hating Christians, especially Greeks.

The environment was ripe for hate. Gounaris, in spite of advice from Venizelos, the Great Powers and the King, instead of discharging the army, declared war against Turkey, to repay them for their guerilla warfare in Smyrna, breaking the treaty of Sevres. King Constantine assumed personal command of the army at Smyrna (Izmir). The strategic objective of these operations was to defeat the Turkish Nationalists and force Kemal into peace negotiations. The advancing Greeks, with their

---

140 A. Boinodiris, Book 1, p 134.

superiority in modern equipment, had hoped for an early battle in which they were confident of breaking up ill-equipped Turkish forces. Yet they met with little resistance, as the Turks managed to retreat in an orderly fashion and avoid encirclement. Churchill said: "The Greek columns trailed along the country roads passing safely through many ugly defiles, and at their approach the Turks, under strong and sagacious leadership, vanished into the recesses of Anatolia."

The Greek army was on the move again, fighting all the way to the suburbs of Ankara, short of supplies and ammunition because soon the powers started supporting Turkey against Greece. The southern front went to Ak Sehir, the town of the famous comic character Nasreddin Hotza. It was now the turn of the Turkish Army under Kemal to reverse the attack.[141][142]

In spite of this, John was considered an asset to the Turkish government, because his enterprise was supporting the Turkish economy and the Turkish Army. Yet, the protection offered by the authorities eventually failed to protect him against the ugly face of hate. One morning in November of 1921 he was awaken by the "Nameless police officer," informing him of a fire in his warehouse. He found that in a matter of hours, his fortune was turned into ashes. All his hopes and aspirations for a better future for raising his family disappeared that morning.

It would take John months to clear his debts. Makrina encouraged him to start and rebuild his business from scratch, but her words fell on deaf ears. His spirit was beaten. He felt that no matter what he did, things were hopeless within the Turkish justice system. For him, there will always be Turks that hate him and ready to destroy him and he would always be considered a second-class citizen. He started gathering whatever resources he could muster and made plans to leave the country of his forefathers forever. He had to, for the sake of his family.

CHRYSOSTOMOS (VATHY, SAMOS, APRIL, 1922)

"Our major mistake was that we believed that we could change the Turks and make them become a Western society within a few generations. We

141 A. Boinodiris, Book 1, p. 274.
142 A. Boinodiris, Book 4, loose attachment B1 (3, 4).

were wrong, because we underestimated the staying power of Muslim Religion. We should have known better. It took us almost 1000 years for Christianity to eliminate the ancient Greco-Roman idolatry. What made us think that we could do better with Islam in four hundred years? Anyone who thinks that they can unify deeply religious populations, so that they can live in a secular society and not be governed by an iron-fisted dictator is a fool. Even iron-fisted Sultans have tried it and failed. Many have lost their lives trying to bring rule onto the Ottoman Empire. In the almost four centuries, from 1453 to now; it is doubtful that we have managed to persuade one out of five Turks to embrace and defend a secular society."

Bishop Chrysostomos stared at the group. Among them was Paul Magioglou, and other refugees, who were about to move to Drama. They were all gathered in the Church of Metamorphosis of Vathy, Samos, listening to the ex-bishop of Drama. Chrysostomos was transferred to Smyrna from Drama a few years earlier. He came to Samos to meet Asia Minor refugees and give them courage and help.

"Now, Mustafa Kemal, one of those few, secular-minded people, has taken over Turkey. He was born and educated in Thessaloniki. I expect that even he is smart enough to know that he cannot have a secular society under democratic rule. Last August, he won the battle of Sangarios River and he is advancing West. With this war, a great number of Greek refugees will come this way, requiring to be moved to Greece. After dealing with us, Ataturk will probably turn to the internal problems posed by the conservatives and other radical religious forces. He will have the power to do so because we, Greeks have given that power to him by attacking Turkey. Because of that, he will probably turn us Greeks into villains. We represent a problem in the internal stability of Turkey. He has to appease the Moslem fanatic elements and the nationalists. We have seen the Armenian genocide[143] in 1915 and 1919. That mob that perpetrated these atrocities is still at large, and Kemal cannot control them. I expect that we will be uprooted from

---

143 The Turkish government does not recognize either genocide. The issue of Armenian genocide has been reemerging in France. The French parliament adopted a bill making it a crime to deny that Armenians suffered "genocide" at the hands of the Turks, infuriating Turkey and causing a boycott of French goods in Turkey (BBC News http://news.bbc.co.uk/2/hi/europe/6043730.stm, 12 October, 2006).

Asia Minor, because by uprooting us from Asia Minor, Kemal might prevent our genocide. And, by having absolute power over the army, he may cause the changes on Turkey to a Western society that we all worked and died for. We may have failed to bring these changes on the Ottomans for the last four centuries into a western nation, but Kemal may be in a position to carry them out. We left an impression within the Turkish population that they cannot shed, even if they decided to shed us from their midst through an exchange of populations. They will always be different than the rest of the Middle Eastern Nations. For us, it was as if a man grabbed the tail of a tiger and tried to stay safe. Now, after we became free from the tiger, both we and the tiger may want to live in peace, regardless of the pain that we inflicted on each other."

"This brings us to how we, the Philhellenes can recover from this ordeal. I say Philhellenes, because that is who we are. We are people from all sorts of races, who believe in a specific way of life, linked to ancient Hellas. Some of us are descendants of people from Greece that came so long ago here that none knows exactly what happened to them from then to now. If we only look at the last four centuries, the ordeal of our ancestors took a great toll on us. About half the people of Byzantium left for the west. From the remaining, about half was integrated with the Moslem Turks by conversion. What remained was only about one fourth of us. About 1 million of Greeks have established a free country in 1821. By 1913, another 4.5 million have been freed. I expect that soon more than 1.5 million of us will be ready to be absorbed by the 5.5 million Greeks of poor, but free Greece. What we all need is patience, and hard work to convert a small, poor, war-torn country into one that can support us all."

"Among the most promising parts of Greece are the newly liberated areas, those that are evacuated by the Turks. I have served as a bishop in Drama, of Macedonia and the surrounding areas of Macedonia and Thrace. They are very promising, because I can see them after you and your children go there and work on them. Most of these places have been neglected into swampy, infested lands, but they can be converted into rich, productive lands, because they have ample water and fertile soil. I highly recommend that you consider moving there. Please let me know if you are interested, so that I can provide you with some of my contacts, who can make your first difficult years there less painful."

Paul Magioglou nodded, as the Bishop[144] concluded his speech. He was determined to work in his organization and help him move as many immigrants as he could to Macedonia.

KEMAL'S COUNTER-ATTACK (ASIA MINOR, SEPTEMBER, 1922)

The new Turkish government at Ankara appointed Mustafa Kemal as the commander in chief and he did a great job rallying the Turkish population. Owners of private rifles, guns and ammunition had to surrender them to the army and every household was required to provide a pair of underclothing, and sandals. It was envisaged that the Turkish Revolutionaries, who had consistently avoided encirclement would be drawn into battle in defense of their capital.

The advancing Greek Army faced fierce resistance which culminated in the 21-day Battle of Sakarya (August 23 – September 13, 1921). The Turkish defense positions were centered on series of heights, and the Greeks had to storm and occupy them. The Turks held certain hilltops and lost others, while some were lost and recaptured several times over. Yet the Turks had to conserve men, for the Greeks held the numerical advantage. During the war with Turkey, the Turks called Plastiras Kara Biber ("The Black Pepper"), while the Evzones became known as the Satan's Army. His advance was finally halted at Kale-Grotso, just across the Sakarya River. The crucial moment came when the Greek army tried to take Haymana, 40 kilometers south of Ankara but the Turks held out. Greeks also had their problems; their advance into Anatolia lengthened their lines of supply and communication and they were running out of ammunition. The ferocity of the battle exhausted both

---

144 The Metropolitan (Bishop) Chrysostomos Kalafatis of Smyrna was lynched and brutally murdered by a Turkish mob incited by Nureddin Pasha in Smyrna, a few months later, on 9 September 1922, soon after the Turkish army regained control of Smyrna. After the defeat of the Greek Army, the Catholic priests asked him to escape with them, before the Turkish Army comes. He declined, by saying:
"I cannot leave my flock, to be massacred by the Turkish mob."
The Turks killed him, together with many Christians of his flock.

sides to such an extent that they were both contemplating a withdrawal, but the Greeks were the first to withdraw to their previous lines. The thunder of cannon was plainly heard in Ankara throughout the battle.

That was the furthest in Anatolia the Greeks would advance, and within a few weeks they withdrew in an orderly manner back to the lines that they had held in June. Some claim that a major factor contributing to the defeat of the Greeks was the lack of whole-hearted Allied support. One reason for the alleged lack of support was that King Constantine was reviled by the British for his pro-German policies during World War I (in contrast to former Prime Minister Venizelos). Meanwhile, the Turks enjoyed Soviet support.

On August 4th, Turkey's representative in Moscow, Riza Nur, sent a telegram saying that soon 60 Krupp artillery pieces, 30,000 shells, 700,000 grenades, 10,000 mines, 60,000 Romanian swords, 1.5 million captured Ottoman rifles from WWI, 1 million Russian rifles, 1 million Mannlicher rifles, as well as some older British Martini-Henry rifles and 25,000 bayonets would be delivered to the Kemalist forces. Soviets also provided monetary aid to the Turkish national movement, not to the extent that they promised but almost in sufficient amount to make up the large deficiencies in the promised supply of arms. The Turks also received significant military assistance from Italy and France, who threw in their lot with the Kemalists against Greece which was seen as a British client. The Italians used their base in Antalya to arm and train Turkish troops to assist the Kemalists against the Greeks. Italy did not like Greek expansion into Asia Minor because that would bring into focus the liberation of the Greek-populated Dodecanese Islands of the Aegean, which were now under Italian rule.

In his public speeches, Mustafa Kemal built up the idea of Anatolia as a "kind of fortress against all the aggressions directed to the East". The struggle was not about Turkey alone but "it is the cause of the East." Turkish national movement attracted sympathizers especially from the Muslims of the far east countries, who were living under colonial regimes and who saw nationalist Turkey as the only independent Moslem nation. The Khilafet Committee in Bombay started a fund to help the Turkish National struggle and sent constant letters of encouragement:

"Mustafa Kemal Pasha has done wonders and you have no idea how people in India adore his name... We are all waiting to know the terms on which Angora offers peace to the Greeks. The Great Allah will grant victory to the Armies of Gazi Mustafa Kemal and save Turkey from her enemies..."

However, the main reason for the Greek defeat was the poor strategic and operational planning of this ill-conceived advance in depth. Although the Greek Army was not lacking in men, courage or enthusiasm, it was lacking in nearly everything else due to the poor Greek economy, which could not sustain long-term mobilization and had been stretched beyond its limits. Very soon, the Greek Army exceeded the limits of its logistical structure and had no way of retaining such a large territory under constant attack by regular and irregular Turkish troops fighting in their homeland. On the other hand, Turkish troops had an exceptionally good strategic and tactical command. At the climax of the Greek offensive, Mustafa Kemal commanded his troops.

"There is no such thing as a line of defense. Only a land surface is to be defended. That surface consists of the entire Fatherland. Not one inch of our country can be abandoned unless drenched with the blood of its people." The main defense doctrine of the First World War was holding on a line, so this command was unorthodox for its time. However it proved successful. Turkish troops also had high morale since they were defending their homeland.

Having failed to reach a military solution, Greece appealed to the Allies for help, but early in 1922 Britain, France and Italy decided that the Treaty of Sevres could not be enforced. They decided to revise it. In accordance with this decision, under successive treaties, the Italian and French troops evacuated their positions, leaving the Greeks exposed. In March 1922 the Allies proposed an armistice, but Mustafa Kemal feeling that now he had the strategic advantage, declined any settlement while the Greeks remained in Anatolia and intensified his efforts to re-organize the Turkish military for the final offensive against the Greeks. At the same time, the Greeks strengthened their defensive positions, but were increasingly demoralized by the inactivity of remaining on the defensive and the prolongation of the war.

The Turks finally launched a counter-attack on August 26th, 1922 that has come to be known to the Turks as the Great Offensive. The major Greek defense positions were overrun on August 26, and Izmit also fell the same day. On August 30, the Greek army was defeated decisively with half of its soldiers captured, or slain and its equipment entirely lost. This date is celebrated as Victory Day, a national holiday in Turkey. During the Battle, the Turkish forces captured Greek General Trikoupis and General Dionis. General Trikoupis, only after his capture could have learned that he had recently been appointed Commander-in-Chief in General Hajianestis' place. On September 1, Mustafa Kemal issued his famous order to the Turkish army: "Armies, your first goal is the Mediterranean, Forward!"

After the Turkish breakthrough in August 1922, Colonel Plastiras' unit was among the few retaining any coherence, withdrawing orderly to the coast, fighting off superior Turkish forces, rallying around him men from other units and saving several thousands of Anatolian Greeks along the way. For these feats he earned immense popularity, especially among the Ionian Greeks (Greeks of the West Coast of Asia Minor) that he helped save. The remnants of the Greek Army made their way to the islands of the Eastern Aegean, where the Army's resentment of the political leadership in Athens resulted in the outbreak of the 1922 Revolution on September 11, led by Plastiras, Colonel Stylianos Gonatas and Commander Phokas.

On September 2 Eskisehir was captured, and the Greek government asked Britain to arrange a truce that would preserve its rule in Smyrna at least. Balikesir was taken on September 6, and Aydin and Manisa the next day. The government in Athens resigned. Two days later Turkish cavalry entered into Smyrna.

THE RELIGIOUS SPY (SELEFKIA, SEPTEMBER, 1922)

While the Greek-Turkish war was raging, whole bands of drunken Turkish soldiers started robbing, looting and extorting Greek businesses in Mersina and Selefkia. These soldiers started forming mobs, partitioning areas and even fighting among themselves for territorial dominance. It was at this time that the "Nameless police officer" showed his colors in Selefkia. He put his whole command under alert and spent days and nights running through the streets on horseback, trying to protect Greeks from the bands of the Turkish mob. He soon was overwhelmed by the mob. To consolidate his force, he gathered the Greeks of Selefkia in a secure neighborhood. The neighborhood was stormed by the mob. He then decided to move the Greek families to two warehouses at the port of Selefkia.

Some Greeks fled from there with their own boats for Cyprus. It was then that the "Nameless police officer" found an Albanian schooner, which was hired to take 300 Greeks to Cyprus. Among the 300 were John Aslanoglou and his family. At the departure, the "Nameless policeman" took John Aslanoglou on the side and said:

"Forget what you know about me. I am Greek. The irony is that most of these fanatic Turks don't know what they are doing. They persecute Greeks, not realizing that in actuality they persecute their own relatives. Many of them have Greek grandparents. The difference between them and me is that I happened to know my family's background. I took this role so that I can survive. Yet, I can help my Christian relatives, through a crisis such as this. You should go to Greece. There, see if you can settle in Lesbos or Serres. I intend to stay a little longer and resign, so that I can do the same. I hope to see you there. I've had enough with these ignorant oafs. This country is going to hell, and I feel burned out. If I stay, my identity will soon be found out, and I will be assassinated."

John finally realized who his friend was. The Nameless police officer was another closet Christian. He pretended to be a Moslem, to get his post and help Christians. He knew Greek very well and always carried the scriptures with him all the time. As he admitted, it was becoming very hard to be a "religious spy," serving interests of people of a minority faith. Just like the few first Christians in the sea of Roman prosecution, it was much harder to be a "religious spy," than being a spy, serving interests of an enemy nation. He was never heard of again.[145]

News of the Greek catastrophe was coming to us from Turkish news. We learned that the recent Greek government, under Gounaris, replaced all the veteran officers and Anastasios Papoulis took the leadership of the army. The world now faced the ugly truth of organized atrocities leveled by the Turkish propaganda against the Greeks. The Turks also talked about their victory against the Kara Biber army. We later found out that Kara Biber was a nickname they gave to Nikos Plastiras, the colonel in the Greek army who led the Evzones Regiment in the Ukraine, as part of an Allied force aiding the White Army.

---

145 A. Boinodiris, Book 1, p. 133-134.

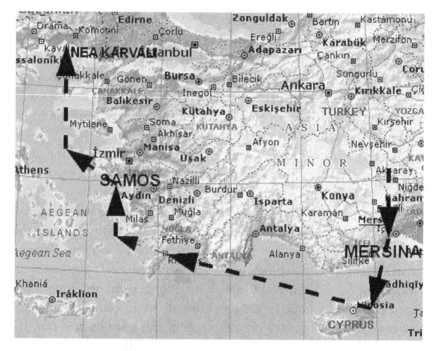

Figure 14 Aslanoglou/Aslanides Return to Greece

SMYRNA: A GREEK, AND YET ANOTHER ARMENIAN MASSACRE (OCTOBER 1922)

While soldiers, sailors, and journalists from around the world watched from ships anchored in the bay, the Turkish forces burned and sacked the great city of Smyrna, slaughtering about 30,000 Greek civilians.

Despite the fact that there were numerous ships from various Allied powers in the harbor of Smyrna, the vast majority of ships, citing "neutrality," did not pick up Greek and Armenian civilians who were forced to flee the fire and Turkish troops. Military bands played loud music to drown out the screams of those who were drowning in the harbor. There were approximately 400,000 Greek and Armenian refugees from Smyrna and the surrounding area who received Red Cross aid immediately after the destruction of the city. Chrysostomos was a fearless bishop, who after serving in Drama, moved to Smyrna. In Smyrna, after the Greek army was defeated, he was asked by the Catholic Church to leave with them before the reconnaissance of the Turkish army arrived. He refused to leave the people of Smyrna, trapped in the city, because the allied forces refused to evacuate them. He wanted to make a statement to the world, for their political inhumanity, when it came to saving women and children. For his statement, Chrysostomos was captured and handed over to a fanatical Muslim mob by the Kemalist General Nureddin Pasha. He was humiliated by having his beard cut off; then he was tortured by having his eyes, ears, nose, and hands cut off, before the Turks hanged him.[146] Some Greeks managed to seek refuge on Greek ships at the harbor of Smyrna and other coastal towns because the Allied (primarily British) ships (with the exception of some Japanese and Italian ships) refused the Greek refugees, even to the point of keeping those who swam out to their ships away, as they had orders not to get involved in the event.

A French journalist, who had covered the war in Smyrna, shortly after the flames had died down, wrote in disbelief:

"The first defeat of the Turkish nationalists had been this enormous fire. Within forty-eight hours, it had destroyed the only hope of immediate economic recovery. For this reason, when I heard that people accused the winners themselves of having provoked it, to get rid of the Greeks and Armenians who still lived in the city, I could only shrug off the absurdity of such talk. One had to know the Turkish leaders very little indeed to attribute to them this unnecessary suicide."

Other scholars give a different account of the events; they argue that the Turks first forbade foreign ships in the harbor to pick up the survivors, but then, under pressure especially from Britain, France, and the United States, they allowed the rescuing of all the Christians except males 17 to 45 years old, whom they aimed to deport into the interior, which "was regarded as a short life sentence to slavery under brutal masters. Most of them ended up being killed by mysterious death." After experiencing the disaster, a Japanese freighter that happened to be there, dumped all of its cargo and filled itself to the brink with refugees, taking them to the Greek port of Piraeus and safety.

A prominent account accusing the Turkish side is the one given by George Horton, the U.S. Consul in the city during the three years of the Greco-Turkish War. His account covers the destruction of the city

---

146 A. Boinodiris, Book 1, p. 346-347.

and its inhabitants in great detail. Quoted from his book "The Blight of Asia":

" ... The last act in the fearful drama of the extermination of Christianity since the Byzantine Empire was the burning of Smyrna by the troops of Mustapha Kemal."

Sir Valentine Chirol, Harris Foundation lecturer at the University of Chicago in 1924, made this statement ("The Occident and the Orient", page 58): "After the Turks had smashed the Greek armies they turned the essentially Greek city (Smyrna) into an ash heap as proof of their victory.

The main facts in regard to the Smyrna fire are:

- Turkish soldier sentinels guarded the streets leading into the Armenian quarter and no one was permitted to enter while the massacre was going on.

- Armed Turks, including many soldiers, entered the quarter thus guarded and went through it looting, massacring and destroying. They made a systematic and horrible "clean up," after which they set fire to it in various places by carrying tins of petroleum or other combustibles into the houses or by saturating bundles of rags in petroleum and throwing these bundles in through the windows.

- They planted small bombs under the paving stones in various places in the European part of the city to explode and act as a supplementary agent in the work of destruction caused by the burning petroleum which Turkish soldiers sprinkled about the streets. The petroleum spread the fire and led it through the European quarter and the bombs shook down the tottering walls. One such bomb was planted near the American Girls' School and another near the American Consulate.

- They set fire to the Armenian quarter on the thirteenth of September 1922. The last Greek soldiers had passed through Smyrna on the evening of the eighth, that is to say, the Turks had been in full, complete and undisputed possession of the city for five days before the fire broke out and for much of this time they had kept the Armenian quarter cut off by military control while conducting a systematic and thorough massacre. If any Armenians were still living in the localities at the time the fires were lighted they hid in cellars, too terrified to move, for Turkish soldiers had overran the whole town, especially the places where the fires had started. In general, all the Christians of the city were keeping to their houses in a state of extreme and justifiable terror for themselves and their families, for the Turks had been in possession of the city for five days, during which time they had been looting, raping and killing. It was the burning of the houses of the Christians, which drove them into the streets and caused the fearful scenes of suffering which will be described later. Of this state of affairs, I was an eyewitness.

- The fire was lit at the edge of the Armenian quarter at a time when a strong wind was blowing toward the Christian section and away from the Turkish. The Turkish quarter was not in any way involved in the catastrophe and during all the abominable scenes that followed and all the indescribable sufferings of the Christians, the Mohammedan quarter was lit up and gay with dancing, singing and joyous celebration.

- Turkish soldiers led the fire down into the well-built, Modern Greek and European section of Smyrna by soaking the narrow streets with petroleum or other highly inflammable matter. They poured petroleum in front of the American Consulate with no other possible purpose than to communicate the fire to that building at a time when C. Clafun Davis, Chairman of the Disaster Relief Committee of the Red Cross, Constantinople Chapter, and others, were standing in the door. Mr. Davis went out and put his hands in the mud thus created and it smelled like petroleum and gasoline mixed. The soldiers seen by Mr. Davis and the others had started from the quay and were proceeding toward the fire.

- Dr. Alexander Mac Lachlan, President of the American College, and a sergeant of American Marines were stripped, the one of his clothes and the other of a portion of his uniform, and beaten with clubs by Turkish soldiers. A squad of American Marines was fired on."

Rudolph J. Rummel blames the Turkish side for the "systematic firing" in the Armenian and Greek quarters of the city. Rummel also argues that after the Turks recaptured the city, Turkish soldiers and Moslem mobs shot and hacked to death Armenians, Greeks, and other Christians in the streets of the city; he estimates the victims of these massacres, by giving reference to the claims of Marjorie Housepian Dobkin, at about 100,000 Christians.

The New York Times in an article published on the 18th of September 1922 titled "Smyrna's ravagers fired on Americans" document the relentless destruction of the Christian quarters of the city and the massacre of its Christian population by the Turkish army. The article gives special emphasis to the attacks against American soldiers and volunteers when they tried to help Armenians and Greeks while they were being attacked.

Rear Adm. Mark Lambert Bristol was the U.S. High Commissioner to Ottoman Empire, serving from 1919 to1927. His initial published statements were as follows:

"Many of us personally saw-- and are ready to affirm the statement-- Turkish soldiers often directed by officers throwing petroleum in the street and houses. Vice-Consul Barnes watched a Turkish officer leisurely fire the Custom House and the Passport Bureau while at least fifty Turkish soldiers stood by. Major Davis saw Turkish soldiers throwing oil in many houses. The Navy patrol reported seeing a complete horseshoe of fires started by the Turks around the American school."

Some Turkish sources accepted Turkish responsibility. Falih Rifki Atay, a Turkish author of national renown is quoted as having lamented that the Turkish army had burnt Smyrna to the ground in the following terms:

"Gavur[147] Izmir burned and came to an end with its flames in the darkness and its smoke in daylight. Were those responsible for the fire really the Armenian arsonists as we were told in those days? ... As I have decided to write the truth as far as I know I want to quote a page from the notes I took in those days. 'The plunderers helped spread the fire ... Why were we burning down Izmir? Were we afraid that if waterfront mansions, hotels and taverns stayed in place, we would never be able to get rid of the minorities? When the Armenians were being deported in the First World War, we had burned down all the habitable districts and neighborhoods in Anatolian towns and cities with this very same fear. This does not solely derive from an urge for destruction. There is also some feeling of inferiority in it. It was as if anywhere that resembled Europe was destined to remain Christian and foreign and to be denied to us. If this was another war and we were defeated, would it be sufficient guarantee of preserving the Turkish nature of the city if we had left Izmir as a devastated expanse of vacant lots? Was it not for Nureddin Pasha, whom I know to be a dyed-in-the-

147 Gavur means infidel.

wool fanatic and rabble rouser, I do not think this tragedy would have gone to the bitter end. He has doubtless been gaining added strength from the unforgiving vengeful feelings of the soldiers and officers who have seen the debris and the weeping and agonized population of the Turkish towns which the Greeks have burned to ashes all the way from Afyon."

Falih Rifkin Atay implied Nureddin Pasha to be the person who is responsible for the fire in his account: "At the time it was said that Armenian arsonists were responsible. But was this so? There were many who assigned a part in it to Nureddin Pasha, commander of the First Army, a man whom Kemal had long disliked..."[148]

As Smyrna was burning, Kemal's forces headed north for Bosporus, the Sea of Marmara, and the Dardanelles where the Allied garrisons were reinforced by British, French and Italian troops from Constantinople. The British cabinet decided to resist the Turks if necessary at the Dardanelles and to ask for French and Italian help to enable the Greeks to remain in eastern Thrace. However Italian and French forces abandoned their positions at the straits and left the British alone to face the Turks. On September 24, Kemal's troops moved into the straits zones and refused British requests to leave. The British cabinet was divided on the matter but eventually any possible armed conflict was prevented. British General Harrington, allied commander in Constantinople, kept his men from firing on Turks and warned the British cabinet against any rash adventure. The Greek fleet left Constantinople upon his request. The British finally decided to force the Greeks to withdraw behind Maritsa in Thrace. This convinced Kemal to accept the opening of Armistice talks.

According to a number of sources, the retreating Greek army carried out a scorched earth policy while fleeing from Anatolia during the final phase of the war after each battle they lost. For instance Middle East historian Sydney Nettleton Fisher wrote that: "The Greek army

---

148 Recently, many Turks have begun to question that nationalist narrative that is taught within their own country. Biray Kolluoglu Kırlı, a Professor of Sociology, published a paper in 2005 in which he pursues an argument based on the claim that the city was burned by the Turks in an attempt to cleanse the predominantly Christian city in order to make way for a new Muslim and Turkish city, and focuses on an examination of the extensions of this viewpoint on the Turkish nationalist narrative since.

in retreat pursued a burned-earth policy and committed every known outrage against defenseless Turkish villagers in its path."

According to many sources and eyewitnesses however, the Turkish government, to cover up their atrocities, fabricated the story of the Greek Scorched Earth policy. The Allies supported the cover-up to maintain a positive relationship with Turkey in the post World War I period to secure access to Turkey's abundant energy reserves. From microfilm, the lead New York Times story from September 15, 1922 clearly states that: "1,000 massacred, as Turks fire city. Kemal threatens to march on capital." Nino Russo of Freeport, Long Island (Ship Engineer on Italian Battleship Vittore Immanuel: "There were so many bodies in the water you couldn't count. Everybody, all the big-shots, the Captain, all those people going back and forth to shore, they knew and they reported that the Turks were burning Smyrna. All the crew, we all knew it was the Turks."

With the possibility of social disorder once the Turkish Army occupied Smyrna, Mustafa Kemal issued a proclamation, sentencing any Turkish soldier to death who harmed non-combatants. A few days before the Turkish capture of the city, Kemal's messengers distributed leaflets with this order written in Greek. Kemal said that Ankara government couldn't be held responsible in the case of an occurrence of a massacre. These orders were largely ignored by the Turkish army, and Nasruddin Pasha, the commander of Turkish forces in the Smyrna district gave orders contradicting Kemal's. Nasruddin Pasha's orders had as their main objective the extermination of the Christian population of the city and were largely followed.

Many of the buildings from which the fire originated were supply depots and warehouses, which would have been to the advantage of the Turks to preserve. On the other hand, Greeks and Armenians owned most of these supply depots and warehouses. Meanwhile, for obvious reasons, the Muslim quarter of the city was largely untouched by the fire. Thus some claimed that the Turks had a motive to burn these buildings to extinguish any Christian presence from the city.

The British historian and journalist, Arnold J. Toynbee, stated that when he toured the region he saw Greek villages that had been burned to the ground. Furthermore, Toynbee stated that the Turkish troops had clearly, individually and deliberately burned down each house.

After the fire, Mustafa Kemal, upon hearing condemnations from foreign embassies, sent a telegram to Hamid Bey:

"FROM COMMANDER IN CHIEF GAZI MUSTAFA KEMAL PASHA TO THE MINISTER OF FOREIGN AFFAIRS YUSUF KEMAL BEY

Tel. 17.9.38 (1922) (Arrived 4.10.38)

To be transmitted with care - Important and urgent.

Find hereunder the instruction I sent to Hamid Bey with Admiral Dumesmil, who left for Istanbul today.

Commander-In-Chief Mustafa KEMAL

Copy to Hamid Bey,

It is necessary to comment on the fire in Izmir for future reference.

Our army took all the necessary measures to protect Izmir from accidents, before entering the city. However, the Greeks and the Armenians, with their pre-arranged plans have decided to destroy Izmir. The Muslims have heard several speeches by Chrysostomos at the churches, and the burning of Izmir was defined to them as a religious duty. The destruction was accomplished by this organization. To confirm this, there are many documents and eyewitness accounts. Our soldiers worked with everything that they had to put out the fires. Those who attribute this to our soldiers may come to Izmir personally and see the situation. However, for a job like this, an official investigation is out of the question. The newspaper correspondents of various nationalities presently in Izmir are already executing this duty. The Christian population is treated with good care and the refugees are being returned to their places."

Despite the telegram, the fact that Kemal explicitly stated that there should be no official investigation leads many Greeks and Armenians to speculate that he wanted to cover up the actions of the Turkish military in Smyrna.

As part of the resolution to this conflict, the map of Turkey with its western borders as specified by the Treaty of Lausanne was defined. The Armistice of Mudanya was concluded on October 11, 1922. The Allies (Britain, France, and Italy) retained control of eastern Thrace and the Bosporus. The Greeks were to evacuate these areas. The agreement came into force starting October 15, one day after the Greek side agreed to sign it. The Treaty of Lausanne, a significant provision of which was an exchange of populations, followed the Armistice of Mudanya. Over one million Greek Orthodox Christians were to be displaced. Among these was my family.

SAMOS (CHRISTMAS, 1922)

The Aslanoglou family, including my mother, now nine years old left Selefkia in September of 1922 through the port of Mersina towards Cyprus. They reached Amohostos (Famagusta), Cyprus, where they asked for asylum from the British. The British, who governed the island, required 30 pounds sterling per person.[149] The Aslanoglou family was broke, consisting of eight souls with only their clothes on. Therefore, the British would not allow them to disembark, keeping them in limbo for weeks. The Albanian captain of the sailing ship that they were on was stuck with 300 passengers of Greek refugees. He proposed to them to go to a Greek island. Rhodes and the Dodecanese belonged to the Italians, who also refused to take them. More delays there, keeping the families aboard. The next closest Greek Island was Samos. On the way, the sailing ship met with a storm, making everyone sick. Many elderly died and were tossed overboard. Finally, they reached Vathy, Samos the day of St. Nicholas, on December 6, 1922 sick and exhausted. During that holiday, right after the defeat of the Greek forces in Asia Minor, the battleship Averof was stationed in Vathy, to support the transfer of thousands of Greeks from Asia Minor to Greece. In support of all these new refugees, the battleship greeted the battered schooner with sirens, while the whole port was ringing from bell tolls. The island of Samos welcomed them.[150]

The people of Samos gave them shelter and fed them for six months at no charge. The islanders, overloaded with refugees from Smyrna, were stretching their resources to their limits. The refugees could not pay anyway, since their property was on whatever rags they had on their backs. Meanwhile, Paul Magioglou fired up after the brutal killing of Metropolitan Chrysostomos was working diligently in an organization to relocate many of the immigrants in Macedonia. Property rights, now abandoned by Turks in the plain of Drama were available for future immigrants that wanted to relocate there. Paul met the Aslanoglou family

149 A. Boinodiris, Book 1, p.133.
150 A. Boinodiris, Book 1, p. 133.

and told them about a specific property, of a farmhouse called Osman Tsiflik, near Drama. John Aslanoglou listened and signed up for it.

Meanwhile, during their stay in Samos, John and his sixteen-year-old son Michael started using their skills. John found out that the Greeks of Samos did not know about making halvah, yet they had a sweet tooth. In their residence, they gathered pots and pans and started making halvah. Initially, they made small quantities, which they sold very fast. Most of the halvah was brought in the island from Piraeus. The people of Samos were very curious about their local product and waited in line to get the fresh batch, produced by one of their local refugees. Soon, it became a sideshow. They were gathering more to see how halvah was made, than to consume it, even though they did that too, since this halvah tasted better. John made the halvah in front of their eyes, with pure ingredients. They used sesame, syrup, cinnamon and other pure ingredients that no factory could afford to use and come up with a profit.

Figure 15 Church of Metamorphosis, Vathy, Samos[151]

---

151 The Church of Metamorphosis is situated on the hill to the west of the harbor. It was constructed in 1833. During the War of Independence, in 1824, the leader of the Greeks in Samos, Lykourgos Logothetis, defeated the Turks on the day of the Metamorphosis (6 August). That is why the chapel of the fortification there was enlarged, made into a church and dedicated to the Metamorphosis.

MAKING ROOM FOR NEW REFUGEES (OCTOBER, 1923)

Having the support of the Army and much of the people, the Plastiras' Revolution quickly assumed control of Greece. Plastiras forced King Constantine to resign, called upon the exiled Venizelos to lead the negotiations with Turkey which culminated in the Treaty of Lausanne, and set about to reorganize the Army to protect the Evros line against any Turkish advance into Western Thrace. One of the most controversial acts of the revolutionary government was the trial and execution of five royalist politicians, including former Prime Minister Dimitrios Gounaris and the former Commander-in-Chief, General Georgios Hatzianestis, on November 28, 1922 as those were mainly responsible for the Asia Minor Disaster, in the infamous "Trial of the Six".

Plastiras faced multiple challenges in governing Greece. The 1.3 million refugees from the population exchange had to be catered for in a country with a ruined economy, internationally isolated and internally divided. The Corfu incident and a botched Royalist coup in October 1923 were evidence of the internal division. After the failed royalist coup, King George II was forced to leave the country. Nonetheless, Plastiras managed to restore some order to the state and to lay the groundwork for the Second Hellenic Republic. After the elections of December 1923 for the new National Assembly, he resigned from the Army on January 2, 1924, retiring to private life. In recognition of his services to the country, the National Assembly conferred to him the rank of Lieutenant General in retirement. Plastiras was even admired by his greatest enemy, Mustafa Kemal. At the end of the war, during the negotiations that took place regarding the exchange of populations between Greece and the newly formed Republic of Turkey, Kemal is quoted telling Plastiras, "I gave gold and you gave me copper."

Meanwhile, John Aslanoglou was doing fine in Samos, making plans to expand his operation, when the Greek government requested that they leave after their six months of stay expired. The rationale was that Samos was becoming overpopulated from refugees and the infrastructure facilities in sewage, water supply and schools were inadequate to support them. Those that had stayed more than six months had to be relocated, to make room for new refugees.

So, after six months, the Aslanoglou family, now named Aslanides, was uprooted one more time to become refugees in Macedonia.[152]

The Plastiras government turned to Venizelos to negotiate an acceptable peace with Turkey. In the Treaty of Lausanne signed in 1923, Greece relinquished all territory in Asia Minor, Eastern Thrace, and two small islands off Turkey's northwest coast. At Lausanne Greece and Turkey agreed to the largest single compulsory exchange of populations known to that time. All Muslims living in Greece, except for the Slavic Pomaks in Thrace and the Dodecanese, and Turkish Muslims in Thrace, were to be relocated to Turkey; they numbered nearly 400,000. In return, approximately 1,300,000 Greeks were expelled to Greece. The determining factor for this shift was religion, not language or culture. Also included in the treaty was protection of Orthodox Greeks and Muslims as religious minorities in Turkey and Greece, respectively.

The Treaty of Lausanne essentially established the boundaries of today's Greece, turning the country into an ethnically homogeneous state by removing almost the entire major minority group. It also ended the possibility of including more Greeks in the nation. Moreover, by instantly increasing Greece's population by about 20 percent, Lausanne posed the huge problem of dealing with over 1 million destitute refugees.

The Asiatic Turks called the Turks remaining in Western Thrace NESRENI. It means that they are turncoats from Christian to survive the Turkish occupation, because they had very fertile farms. To keep these farms they became Muslims. They know very well their origin and for that reason they are discriminated by the Asiatic Turks.[153] The Asiatic Turks also discriminated against the immigrating Turks that came from Greece. Based on reports from Cappadocia by well-founded authorities, their discrimination practices lasted well into the 1970s.

A similar picture can be painted on the Greek side. Christians from Asia Minor and Eastern Thrace were severely discriminated against by the Greeks of southern Greece. They were often called "Turks" in a derogatory way and in one occasion, a murder was attributed to this discrimination. One specific incident even made it into a song. A mother was said to have poisoned her immigrant daughter-in-law, because she did not like her, using poisoned fish with beets with garlic. This led to a well

---

152 A. Boinodiris, Book 1, p. 136.
153 A. Boinodiris, Book 1, p. 26.

known popular song of the thirties. In response to all this discrimination, the Greek refugees remained strongly antiroyalist and they ceaselessly disliked the king, who had to leave Greece under pressure in 1923.

In 1923, the Italians, finding Greece at war with the Turks, did something nasty. In 1914, they had taken Northern Epirus and annexed it to Albania. They found now an excuse that one of the Greeks killed an Albanian mullah and decided to send their fleet to bomb the ports of Corfu and Argostolion, both full of refugees from Asia Minor.[154] This was the first provocation of the fascist regime in Italy, which was starting to gain power. The British responded immediately to the Italian attack. They chased the Italian boats, ordering them to stay out of the region.

Back in Cappadocia, I worked together with my partner Stelios until the end of 1923, having my grandparents beside me for advice and support. In 1923, my grandmother, now incapacitated for five years, died in the arms of my grandfather. He was devastated. From that time on, he aged very fast.

ATROCITIES (1922-1923)

The Greeks were accused on several accounts, since the Greek occupation of Smyrna on the 15th May 1919. Toynbee stated that he and his wife were witnesses to the atrocities perpetrated by Greeks in the Yalova, Gemlik, and Ismit areas and they not only obtained abundant material evidence in the shape of "burnt and plundered houses, recent corpses, and terror stricken survivors." but also witnessed robbery by Greek civilians and arsons by Greek soldiers in uniform in the act of perpetration. Toynbee wrote:

"No sooner had they landed than they began a ruthless warfare against the Turkish population, not omitting the commission the worst of atrocities in the Near Eastern manner. They laid waste to the fertile Meander Valley, and forced thousands of homeless Turks to take refuge beyond the occupied area."

Historian Taner Akcam noted that a British officer claimed:

"The National forces were established solely for the purpose of fighting the Greeks...The Turks are willing to remain under the control of any other state...There was not even an organized resistance at the time of the Greek occupation. Yet the Greeks are persisting in their

---

154 A. Boinodiris, Book 1, p. 33.

oppression, and they have continued to burn villages, kill Turks and rape and kill women and young girls and throttle children to death."

Inter-Allied commission in the Yalova-Gemlik peninsula, in their report of the 23rd May 1921, during the Greek occupation of western Anatolia, wrote that: "A distinct and regular method appears to have been followed in the destruction of villages, group by group, for the last two months. Thus destruction has even reached the neighborhood of the Greek headquarters. The members of the Commission consider that, in Yalova and Gemlike occupied by the Greek army, there is a systematic plan of destruction of Turkish villages and extinction of the Moslem population. This plan is being carried out by Greek and Armenian bands, which appear to operate under Greek instructions and sometimes, even with the assistance of detachments of regular troops."

Arnold J. Toynbee wrote that they obtained convincing evidence that similar atrocities had been started in wide areas all over the remainder of the Greek occupied territories since June 1921. Toynbee argued that: "the situation of the Turks in Smyrna City had become what could be called without exaggeration a 'reign of terror', it was to be inferred that their treatment in the country districts had grown worse in proportion."

According to a number of sources, the retreating Greek army carried out a "scorched earth policy" while fleeing from Anatolia during the final phase of the war after each battle they lost.

Similarly, many Western newspapers reporting gross abuses committed by Turkish forces against Christian, mainly Greek and Armenian civilians. The British historian Toynbee stated that Turkish troops deliberately burned numerous Greek homes, pouring petrol on them and taking care to ensure that they were totally destroyed. There were massacres throughout 1920-1923, the period of the Turkish War of Independence, especially of Armenians in the East and the South, and against the Greeks in the Black Sea Region. There was also significant continuity between the organizers of the massacres between 1915-1917 and 1919-1921 in Eastern Anatolia.

According to the London based Times: "The Turkish authorities frankly state it is their deliberate intention to let all the Greeks die, and their actions support their statement."

An Irish paper, the Belfast News Letter wrote: "The appalling tale of barbarity and cruelty now being practiced by the Angora Turks is part of a systematic policy of extermination of Christian minorities in Asia Minor."

According to the Christian Science Monitor, the Turks felt that they needed to murder their Christian minorities due to Christian superiority in terms of industriousness and the consequent Turkish feelings of jealously and inferiority. The paper wrote: "The result has been to breed feelings of alarm and jealously in the minds of the Turks which in later years have driven them to depression. They believe that they cannot compete with their Christian subjects in the arts of peace and that the Christians and Greeks especially are too industrious and too well educated as rivals. Therefore, from time to time they have striven to try and redress the balance by expulsion and massacre."

A Turkish governor, Ebubekir Hazim Tepeyran in the Sivas Province said in 1919 that the massacres were so horrible that he could not bear to report them. He was referring to the atrocities committed against Greeks in the Black Sea region, and according to the official tally 11,181 Greeks were murdered in 1921 by the Central Army under the command of Nurettin Pasha (who is infamous for the killing of Archbishop Chrysostomos). Some parliamentary deputies demanded Nurettin Pasha to be sentenced to death and it was decided to put him on trial, although the trial was later revoked by the intervention of Mustafa Kemal.

Taner Akcam wrote that according to one newspaper, Nurettin Pasha had suggested killing all the remaining Greek and Armenian populations in Anatolia, a suggestion rejected by Mustafa Kemal. According to the newspaper "the Scotsman," on August 18th of 1920, in the Feival district of Karamusal, South-East of Ismit in Asia Minor, the Turks massacred 5,000 Christians. As well as massacring Greeks, the Turks also massacred Armenians, continuing the policies of the 1915 Armenian Genocide according to many Western newspapers.

The widespread massacres of Greeks in the Pontus region are recognized in Greece and Cyprus as the Pontian Genocide. On February 25, 1922 twenty four Greek villages in the Pontus region were burnt to the ground. An American newspaper, the Atlanta Observer wrote: "The smell of the burning bodies of women and children in Pontus," said the message "comes as a warning of what is awaiting the Christian in Asia Minor after the withdrawal of the Hellenic army."

In the first few months of 1922, advancing Kemalist forces, according to Belfast News Letter, killed 10,000 Greeks. The Turks continued the practice of slavery, seizing women and children for their harems. Many Turkish soldiers would also rape women. American relief works were also treated with extreme disrespect, even when they were aiding Muslim civilians. Christian Science Monitor wrote that Turkish authorities also prevented missionaries and humanitarian aid groups from assisting Greek civilians who had their homes burned, the Turkish authorities leaving these people to die, despite abundant aid. The Christian Science Monitor wrote: "the Turks are trying to exterminate the Greek population with more vigor than they exercised towards the Armenians in 1915."

According to a proclamation made in 2002 by the then-governor of New York (where a sizeable population of Greek Americans resides), George Pataki (of Hungarian origin), Greeks of Asia Minor endured immeasurable cruelty during a Turkish government-sanctioned systematic campaign to displace them; destroying Greek towns and villages and slaughtering additional hundreds of thousands of civilians in areas where Greeks composed a majority, as on the Black Sea coast, Pontus, and areas around Smyrna; those who survived were exiled from Turkey and today they and their descendants live throughout the Greek Diaspora.

In fact, the Greeks who left Anatolia after 1923, were not exiled, but exchanged with Turks in Greece according to the terms of the Treaty of Lausanne signed by both Greek and Turkish governments. A sizable population of Greeks had been forced to leave its ancestral homelands of Ionia, Pontus and Eastern Thrace between 1914 -1922. These refugees, as well as the Greek or Armenian Americans with origins from Anatolia were not allowed to return after 1923 and the signing of the Treaty of Lausanne.

Figure 16 1922 Cartoon of Europe[155]

---

155 "France, England, Austria" written on her skirt) punishes the kid (Greece) for asking too much and not feeling happy with what he got (Crete)

THE UPROOTING
(1924)

EXCHANGE OF POPULATIONS (KARVALI, TURKEY, FALL 1923)

Even before 1923, a torrent of refugees was making its way to Greece. One wave came when the French evacuated Cilicia in 1922 in support of the Kemal regime. The refugees also started arriving in Western Thrace from Eastern Thrace (Adrianople, 40 Churches, Gallipoli, Rhaedestos and Constantinople) with oxen, carts and trains. They were initially about 40,000. They consisted of fishermen, shippers, farmers and vineyard growers, dairy farmers of Silimbria, silk producers of Bursa all of who fed and clothed the citizens of Constantinople. When these initial immigrants came, they were abandoned by the Greek government in Western Thrace like a bunch of uprooted onions in an onion field. They had to fend for their survival on their own.[156]

The winter came, finding the refugees in tents. Volunteers were going from home to home to beg locals, or first-comers to shelter more people. Churches and mosques were full. Meanwhile, we at the center of Asia Minor were reading about the war news from the Turks. The name of Plastiras was prominent, announcing his orderly retreat, to escape capture. He had the nickname of "black pepper- or Kara Bibber," because he was dark and thin. During the negotiations in Paris, between E. Venizelos and Ismet Pasha (later known as Ismet

---

156 A. Boinodiris, Book 1, p. 27.

Inonou), the Turks threatened to invade Greece, contesting land all the way to Thessaly. The Greeks told them that if they did that, they might lose Constantinople. The Turks thought that the Greeks were destroyed irreparably, but they soon realized that they also were too exhausted and had no means of launching an offensive, especially since they had no sea power. I heard the Turks call the Greeks "nine lived-ones," surviving such a massacre.

When the news of the exchange of populations reached us, we started selling what we owned six months prior to our departure. The selling price dropped, to the point of giving everything away. It was then, that Turk refugees from Kozani arrived. They started stealing from us anything they could lay their hands on. The local Turks put a stop to this act, trying to put some order in the town. The local Turks did not like the newcomer Turks from Greece.

With the news of the "exchange of population agreement" between Greece and Turkey, I dissolved my partnership. The store stayed with me until the date that was set that we could not harvest any products from our farms. I started selling all products until only a few items were left on the shelves.

A treaty was signed between Eleftherios Venizelos and Mustafa Kemal to exchange populations of all Greeks living in Turkey and Turks living in Greece. Greeks were defined as Christians, with Greek names, who did not become Moslem before 1916 (7 years earlier). Similarly, Turks were defined as all Muslims in Greece that did not become Christian before 1916. Some exceptions applied in the regions of Constantinople and Western Thrace.

When news of the details reached us, some Turks did not want to part with their Greek assets, especially those that had educational and technical skills. There were several cases, where Greeks were declared Muslims, backed by their Turkish employers, but the police soon discovered their identity and registered them as part of the exchange. Some Turks said to us:

"Where are they going to put you all? Greece is such a small and non-fertile country. In order to relocate you there, they will have to plant you as close as we plant onions. You will be in the Bulgarian borders, fighting with the Bulgarian Mountain raiders, who butcher innocent villagers at night like lambs. " Of course, they were talking from their own experiences with the Bulgarians. "It is a pity that you have to leave all this wealth."

One day, I saw a Turk, refugee from Kozani at my store doorstep.

"How much do you sell this place?" he asked.

We agreed to let him have the whole lot and the key to the store for 20 panganotes (eight gold liras). In August of 1923, we all gathered in the lower neighborhood of Karvali, to leave our homes to Turk refugees from Kozani and double up in other Greek houses. We stayed in those houses until June 1924 (almost 10 months). Then we heard news that each refugee was entitled to carry only 30 kilos of luggage. We immediately started selling our goods at any price we could get. The Turks in the area were getting our furniture, utensils, rugs and other items paying 5% of their value.[157]

In 1923, when the agreement for the exchange of populations was signed we had received instructions in Karvali from my uncle Charalambos, to come to Drama.[158] The elders of Karvali formed the Population Exchange Committee. The top officials of that committee went to Nigde to a meeting with the Greek embassy there. The rest were issuing us passports.

One of the members of that committee was a business competitor, who hated me because I competed with him on the sale of ouzo. I always managed to undersell him and make more profit than he did. He raised an issue of payment to the church of 40 panganotes (10 gold liras) for the burial grounds of my ancestors (one aunt and two grandmothers). As a result, I paid it.

The good news about the exchange was that I was not going to the Turkish army. The bad news was that we were forced to leave our homes, fields and vineyards and venture into the unknown, with only our clothes on our backs.

THE LAST GOOD-BYES (KARVALI, TURKEY, JUNE, 1924)

The four of us were now ready to leave: my 75-year old grandfather Paul, my 36-year old mother Evanthia, my 11-year old sister Irene and me, an 18-year old youngster.[159]

---

157 A. Boinodiris, Book 1, p. 316-318.
158 A. Boinodiris, Book 1, p. 327.
159 A. Boinodiris, Book 4, p.1.

We hired a good coachman, a fifty-year-old Kurd refugee from the Russian frontier, named Mustafa. We loaded his cart with our luggage and mounted the cart. In the cart, we sat silently, the coachman, my grandfather, my mother, Irene and me. We formed a convoy of twenty carts, heading for Akserai. Akserai was in the opposite direction to where we were heading, but it was designated as the meeting point on all the Greeks of the immediate region. As we were passing near our field next to the highway, my grandfather pleaded:

"Please Mustafa. Let us make a stop here." The coachman stopped, stopping the remaining carts of the convoy.

He dismounted and took a last walk on that field, now full of wheat upon which he had spent his whole life. Somewhere near by, under that tree he was born with the help of other relatives. The stalks of wheat swallowed him, while we were waiting. The time passed. The coachman started complaining, about being out of schedule. He had to make stops at a pre-determined time, rest the horses and pray to Mecca, but not now. My mother's eyes were swollen, full of tears.[160]

"Anthony, please go and bring your grandfather back," she said crying.

The coachman joined me. We found him in the north segment of the field, a flat clearing where they separate wheat from straw. There was a small chapel, where we used to find shelter from the rain. We found him there, kneeling, praying and crying all at the same time.

"Mustafa, please kill me and bury me here. I will be happy leaving my last breath on this land of my ancestors. Here I was born, grew up and toiled over in this land. I am old; How can I go to a place I do not know and have no ties to?"

"Pavlo-effendi, I understand your pain, but nobody can do anything about what is written by Allah. I left my land too. My home and ancestors are back in Russian hands. You and I have to follow the will of Allah."

We managed to pull him off his knees and carry him to the cart.[161] We finally reached Akserai. I left the rest of the family at the inn, while Mustafa and I went with his cart to the market.

---

160 A. Boinodiris, Book 1, p. 318-320.
161 A. Boinodiris, Book 1, p. 318-320.

I went straight to my contacts, four wholesalers from whom I bought goods for my business. They trusted me by giving me credit in the past and I had to make sure that I did not let them down, regardless of the circumstances of the times. I had prepared the payoff money ready from Karvali.

"Hello effendi. I have closed business and we are abandoning all our property and heading for Greece. What do I owe you?"

The merchants were left with mouths open. They never expected an infidel child to pay them, on their way out of the country.

"Ten panganotes, Anthony…"

I paid them all, one at a time, about 40 panganotes (ten gold liras). Mustafa looked at me and patted me on the back.

"Well done my child."

When we returned, my grandfather found out what I did from Mustafa.

"God does not abandon people that show honesty in their business transactions," he said, looking approvingly at me.

The merchants were so moved, that that same night they came visiting our family at the inn, bringing food and delicacies for the trip to my grandfather.

The next day, all the gathered families of a group started traveling by cart to Eregli, a city to the south, where the train station was. This was the old Byzantine City of Heraklion. It took us three days to reach it. .[162]

HAJI MILTIADES (EREGLI, TURKEY, JUNE, 1924)

At Eregli, we said good-bye to Mustafa, because our group from Karvali was to board a train to go to Mersina. We stayed three days in that city, under the care of a person named Haji Miltiades. Haji Miltiades was a relatively rich Greek, with lots of property, including hotels, restaurants and houses. He made them all available to all Greeks that passed through Eregli on the way to Greece. He also encouraged young people to get married:

"If you go married to Greece, you are entitled to a house and land."

---

162 A. Boinodiris, Book 1, p. 318-320.

He also had a priest available to do the weddings, while he was offering to pay the expenses of becoming the "best man."

As we were to board the train, Haji Miltiades advised us:

"Brothers, remember. After you board the train, make sure that all doors and windows are closed, in spite of the heat. As you exit the city, some fanatic Turks are waiting to hurt you, by throwing stones at the wagons. We had several deaths by these people."

"How about you, Haji Miltiades…? When are you leaving?" someone asked.

"I am waiting for all of the Greeks from the surrounding areas to board and leave. I will join you, when all of you have left. Good luck."[163]

As we were coming out of Eregli, we realized how fortunate we were to have Haji Miltiades advise us. A mob, of a huge number of Turks was waiting for the train to pass; they were ready to vent their hate on us. The stones were sharpened and thrown as dense as a dense hailstorm, only horizontally. We could not close some small air vents, from which one stone took off the fez of Anestis Kosmidis.[164] The rest of us were down on the floor, to avoid any broken shards from the train windows from hurting us. We speculated that most of these people were displaced Turk refugees, or refugees from Greece, who left their properties and households back and were trying to find a place to stay.

---

163 A. Boinodiris, Book 1, p. 320-321.
164 A. Boinodiris, Book 1, p. 321. The Bulgarians at Kalos Agros, Drama killed Anestis Kosmidis in 1941.

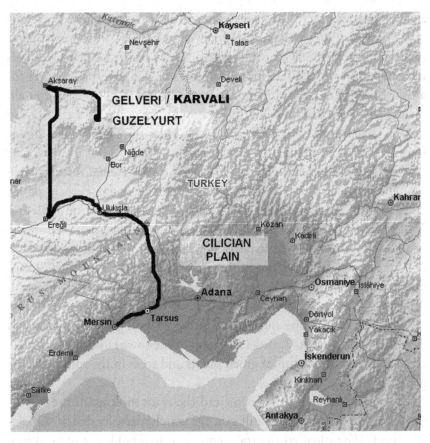

Figure 17 The Boyun-egri-oglu Trip from Karvali to Mersina

FROM EREGLI TO MERSINA (JUNE AND JULY, 1924)

Traveling east, we arrived at Ulukisla, where we saw thousands of refugee tents, spread in the open Cappadocian plain. We stopped at Pozanti and went south to Belemedik and Guluslu. Belemedik means: "can we?" in Turkish. That place was where the railroad line had to be taken through the largest railroad tunnel in Turkey, through the Taurus Mountain, a task which was questioned a lot at that village, where the working crews were based. The major effort took four years to complete and helped connect Baghdad with Constantinople by train.

The tunnel took half hour to traverse, ending at the station of Tas Turmaz (shaking rock). We came to Yenice, entering the plain of Cilicia with its tropical climate. We passed the Kydnos River, the river where it is said that Alexander the Great swam and got sick.[165] At Yenice, we saw how different things were here. Whatever we bought, from watermelon to soda pop was hot. We simply were not used to this hot climate. This was the reason why Cilicia was a winter resort and enterprise center for most of our work force, but in the summer, it was not pleasant at all. That is why my father was working here, before going to Russia. I also suspect that the extreme heat made Alexander the Great take a dip at Kydnos River and made him sick.

Yenice was the place where a few years earlier Kemal Ataturk with his rebels attacked the French garrison, killed some French police officers and several Greek technicians, including two from Karvali. These two were potters, Paul Didimopoulos and his father. We stayed in Yenice one week. If we stayed longer, half of us would be dead in that hot June sun of 1924. The train started going lower into the Cilician plain. We saw beautiful olive groves, cotton and sugar cane fields, carob bean trees, lemon and orange trees. All of these trees were strange to us. Near Yenice, the line split in two lines, one going east to Adana and the other two, west to Tarsus (St. Paul's home town) and Mersina. We came to Tarsus, a city full of green plants and trees in the middle of the plain.

We finally arrived in Mersina and the train took us all the way to the pier. The pier was then full of huge warehouses, loaded with bales of cotton. We unloaded the train and went to Tas Han, the local inn. When we were settled, I ran to the beach to take a dip, because the heat was unbearable for me. It must have been anywhere from 40-45 degrees centigrade. My grandfather knew Mersina well. He and my mother were afraid that, since I did not know how to swim I could drown.[166] They knew that being nineteen and somewhat impetuous, I would try diving into the sea without thinking. To avoid such a behavior, they went in the interior of the city and rented a house for three families from a Catholic woman. We had two other families in our group, rent with us. One of them was the family of Father Kalinikos and the other

---

165 According to the historians, like Plutarch, he arrived in Tarsus just in time to prevent the Persian satrap Arsames from destroying the capital of Cilicia. He stayed at Tarsus and one morning he swam in the frozen waters of ' river. He became seriously ill. The high fever almost killed him and it was Philip the Acarnanian, his personal doctor who saved his life.
166 A. Boinodiris, Book 1, p. 321-324.

was the family of my Aunt Orsia with her daughter Katina and her son-in-law Basil Vermisoglou. The woman rented each flat for 100 grossia per month.

I remember that one night the beating of all sorts of utensils awakened us by the citizens of Mersina. Bells, firearms and all sorts of other noisemakers like bronze pestles and empty tin cans joined the din. The Turkish army was even firing canons in the air. We came out, only to discover that we had a lunar eclipse. The Turks generated such noises to scare the shadow away from the moon. We laughed at their silly superstitions and went back to sleep.

We stayed in that house for about one month.

While we were waiting to board a boat, I held all our passports in my wallet. One day I went to shop for meat. In the crowded market, a pickpocket swiped my wallet. As I was getting ready to pay for the meat, I reached for it in my pocket, only to find it empty.

"It's gone. Oh, no. My wallet is stolen," I yelled.

The butcher was a Turk, but an excellent person.

"Don't worry young man. These things happen here often. There are many pickpockets. Take the meat and pay me another time," he said.

"I had very little money, but our passports were in it." I then wished that I had left them with my mother. Coming from a town where thievery was unknown, I was learning my lessons on big cities the hard way.

"Let me tell you how to go to the Greek embassy, where you can ask for new passports," he said. "You go through these side-streets, because there are many gangs that can kill you by throwing stones at everyone approaching the Greek embassy."

He gave me directions. I took the meat and after thanking him, I left. I paid the butcher the next day. For 15 days, Katherine, the daughter of Father Kalinikos and I were walking half an hour to go to the Greek embassy to get new passports. We avoided most of the gangs, but as we tried to enter the gate, we had to fight our way in, every single of those 15 days. We fought back by throwing stones defensively against the Turks, to suppress their barrage.

When our passports were ready, we formed a boarding committee, representing a group of 105 souls from Karvali. The committee consisted of men who dealt with issues of booking seats on a boat, being transported to the pier and getting aboard, all 105 of us. The president of the committee was Haji Prodromos. He was a venerable old man with an enviable entrepreneurial spirit and originally from Karvali. He owned factories in Tarsus that made linen with a trademark in the form of a harvesting sickle. His company was in a partnership with the Sikalides (originally Tsavdarides) brothers from Beirut, all of them born in Karvali.

TRANSPORT SHIP IOANNIS (MERSINA, TURKEY, JULY 7-14, 1924)

Haji Prodromos knew that he had lost all his business. He was wealthy enough though to board a private ship and go anywhere he wanted. Instead of doing that, he chose to stay behind and guide us to our destination. He took all members of our committee from office to office, until we were all registered in the list of a Greek ship, named IOANNIS.

As we were trying to pass through the market, we became victims of a barbarous trap. Some Turkish hoodlums, full of hate against leading Greeks like Haji Prodromos, tripped him with a curved cane and threw him to the ground. They tore the old man's straw-hat and spat on him. He looked at us with a stern eye:

"Don't talk back at them and do not fight back!" he yelled at us. "I have been doing this for several days now and if I can stand it, you can too."

As we tried to help him up, they started throwing tomatoes and eggplants at our faces. We followed his instructions and did not talk or fight back. As a follow-up to the vegetable barrage, we received a hailstorm of stones. We ran away with minor wounds on many of our group, wondering why this venerable old man took all this punishment for helping us, risking his own life. When we were told that it was time to board, we moved our families and our luggage to the pier we realized that our life in Turkey was at an end. My guts went into a tight knot, as I felt that I would probably never see again the place that I grew up and spent my childhood. I felt that this was the worst day of my life.

We waited, as each family was counted and boarded onto a small boat. We thanked Haji Prodromos when he left us on the pier, as he and his aids walked back to start working on the next group. Our impression of him as a rich man evaporated, replaced by the satisfaction of meeting a selfless, hard-working human being.[167] Before boarding, I bought a sack of bread for the trip. I was mistaken to do so. We threw it away in two days, because it became mildewed. The ship charged us 25 grossia per person. Our family boarded the boat and took us to the ship, anchored at a distance. As we approached the boat, we saw the Greek flag. There was no other time in my life that can exceed the exhilaration that I had at that moment. Twenty-one years later, after being liberated from the occupational forces of World War II, I would experience something equally exhilarating, but all of a sudden that day, the worst day of my life turned out to be also the best day in my life.

As we came along the ship, we noticed that the sea was red from all the tossed fezzes by the refugees. The fez represented Turkey and Turkish oppression. Several Turks on boats were trying to fish them out, to resell them. We tossed our fezzes into the sea and sang the Greek national anthem, together with songs from Paul Melas, all talking about our freedom. A priest was praying unashamedly with tears in his eyes in front of the flag, as if it was his idol. People were crying from joy.[168] Toddlers and babies that could not understand what was going on also started crying when they saw their mothers and fathers sobbing in joyful tears; the scene was a pandemonium, as every one realized that we were now on Greek territory.

The captain and crew of IOANNIS were watching the whole explosion of emotion surprised and not knowing what to do with us. We started singing songs of Nikolaos Plastiras and Eleftherios Venizelos.

"Venizele, Venizele mas patera tis patridos------- Venizele, Venizele father of our country

Venizele, Venizele mas, patera tis filis ----------- Venizele, Venizele father of our nation

Zito, zito lefteria, Zito ke Lefteris tis Cretis----Long live freedom, long live the liberator of Crete

---

167 Unfortunately, the last name of Haji Prodromos is not known. To the author's point of view, this unknown rich Greek with a compassionate golden heart was a rare, unsung hero.
168 A. Boinodiris, Book 1, p. 324-325.

Cretis to pedi, Venizelaros, kato Germanos-----a child of Crete, oust the German-loving King.[169]

Everyone acted in a crazy manner; a manner that cannot be explained. It is very difficult to describe the feeling of "freedom," to someone who takes it for granted, because they have had it all their lives. We, having experienced enslavement, no matter how much we profited by it, felt as if we were reborn. In spite of our situation, leaving all our lives, wealth and history behind and heading to a place with unknown future and difficulties, we celebrated our freedom with indescribable emotion. I vowed myself then not to ever take my freedom for granted. It cannot be exchanged for anything in this life, including life itself.

We spent the night on the boat, anchored in front of Mersina.[170] The next day, IOANNIS raised anchor and sailed away from the coast. The captain placed a request for help from Greek speaking people. I raised my hand, since we were taught Greek at our elementary school. The crew dressed us in khaki clothes, to identify us as a sort of deputies to restore order. We were placed in charge of keeping order; we provided breakfast of toast, sardines and lemons, lunch and diner.

The captain asked me to become a sailor, but I refused. I told him that I was not too fond of the sea, especially since I could not swim. He seemed to like me because I knew relatively good Greek and I was good in my geography. We had quite a few Greeks who could not speak a word of Greek, other than their names. Those men and women from Andavale (Aktas) and Kiolcuk were especially illiterate; they were rough peasants with no education at all. They never traveled anywhere and had a local Turkish dialect that even the rest of us had tough time understanding.

On the boat, I met Kathryn, the niece to John Aslanoglou, who was a widow and had small children. She was married to Artemios, one of the unfortunate Greeks who was murdered in the Arabian Peninsula, drafted by the Turkish Army and used as an unarmed combatant. I took

---

169 This was in reference to King Constantine, who became king in 1915. Since he was the son-in-law of Kaiser, he was pushing Greece to support Germany. Eleftherios Venizelos revolted against King Constantine at Goudi, taking the side of the allies and deposing the King.
170 A. Boinodiris, Book 1, p. 325.

her and her children under my protection, helping them by bringing them their rations of food.[171]

The trip was especially interesting for me, who had never seen the sea before. I was fascinated with the dolphins that followed the ship. When we reached Rhodes, some Greeks from the town brought us a boatload of oranges, lemons and tangerines. They distributed them to us free of charge. We stayed there only for a few hours before departure.

THE TRIP TO GREECE (JULY 14-AUGUST 5, 1924)

In six days from Mersina, IOANNIS was near the port of Piraeus tooting its whistle. It anchored near the island of St. George, which was used as a quarantine, to make sure no contagious diseases are imported into Greece from Asia Minor. The quarantine lasted for three weeks. At St. George, we met the family of Kyriakos Tsekmezoglou.

As we went through the quarantine, they boiled all of our clothes, sheets and mattresses. Unfortunately, they did not tell us that, and the boiling destroyed all our wool. In Karvali, we had no cotton. All of our clothing was made out of wool and was destroyed. This included 40 kilos of wool, which we carried all the way to Greece with the intent of using it to make clothes. After being boiled, we were forced to throw it away. After they checked us out medically, they registered us and gave us identification papers. The bureaucrats of southern Greece had difficulty with our Turkish last names. By the time, they registered us we ended up being transformed from Boyun-egri-oglu to Boinodiris. Our bureaucrat was someone from Naupactus.

"What is your last name?"

"Boyun-egri-oglou," said my grandfather.

"From now on, your name will be 'Boinodiris.' Here are your papers."

As a result, he transposed the Turkish name into Greek as closely to it as he was able.

They asked us where we wanted to go. In 1923, when the agreement for the exchange of populations was signed we had received instructions in Karvali from my Uncle Charalambos, to come to Drama in Macedonia and when asked, we chose Drama. As a result, we were tagged to sail for Thessaloniki. Our Aunt Orsia chose Piraeus. They and

---

171 A. Boinodiris, Book 1, p. 284.

others that chose southern Greek destinations were tagged for Piraeus. Those for Piraeus were placed again on IOANNIS. We, heading for Thessaloniki boarded a ship named CEPHALONIA. Here we split our families, my Aunt Orsia's family and us.

Orsia, her daughter Katherine had to meet her son-in-law Justinos and Justinos' father Constantine at Piraeus, where they were already established. Justinos Ioakimides and his father were working in Mersina, before 1920. The Greco-French general Theophilou advised them to leave for Constantinople in 1920, after Venizelos lost the elections. After the Greek army was destroyed in 1922, they left Constantinople and settled in Piraeus.[172]

If we had not received that letter from Uncle Charalambos, we would be probably with my Aunt Orsia. Uncle Constantine was well to do and we could stay and become partners with him. Nevertheless, our fate was different and we ended up in northern Greece, something that we would regret in the following years.

SS CEPHALONIA (AUGUST 5-10, 1924)

We were about 2,000 souls that boarded the cargo ship CEPHALONIA, heading for Thessaloniki. There was hardly any room to sit. The only space left was the suffocating ship's hold, which was shut by huge doors. When the doors closed, there was a battle on who would occupy the space on top of the doors. I set up a rug for my grandfather, my mother and Irene on it.

"Anthony, see if you can find Katherine and her children, so that we can accommodate them here," my grandfather pleaded. Katherine, the daughter of Father Kalinikos was traveling with two babies, Vlasis and Marina. They were heading for Komotini via Thessaloniki, because her brother had sent a letter from Komotini, asking her to come.

I did not know how to go about finding such space. There was no place to step on, without stepping on the flesh of some person.[173] I decided to climb up and do my search for our relatives. I climbed on the mast of the ship and started looking around. The ship was partitioned in three parts. The front portion, lower than the rest, was accessible via

---

172 A. Boinodiris, Book 1, p. 326-327.

173 A. Boinodiris, Book 1, p. 327-328.

staircases. The center part contained the openings of the hold where we were located. A number of others were placed on top of the large wooden doors placed on the hold openings. The rear was also lower than the middle and accessible via staircases. The whole ship was wall-to-wall lined with people. I started walking on forward masts, seeking Katherine. I was dead-ended. From the masts, I managed to reach the railings of the center section. As I approached the rear, walking on the railing, I saw Katherine and her two babies Vlasis and Marina on the rear section, right in front of the toilets, their feet wallowing in human excrement. They were in bad shape. When I called them, they started crying.

"God must have sent you Anthony. Please save us from this."

I grabbed one child on my back, while she took the other on her back and climbing again on the railing, we inched our way to the place where my grandfather was located. I went back to get her luggage, which I carried over, one at a time. I settled them there, but there was no space for me.

I had to find another place for me to sleep. There were two leaning masts. One of them had a stepping platform. I sat on it, leaned against the mast and tied myself with ropes, so that I do not fall down. I went to sleep, feeling the breeze in my face.

The trip to Thessaloniki lasted five days. All through those days, I slept against the mast on a place high up, tied up with ropes, so that I would not fall on top of the people below.[174]

THESSALONIKI (11TH AUGUST, 1924)

By the time we reached Thessaloniki, my right arm was numb and slightly swollen from the ropes with which I tied myself. As we were disembarking, we saw the Turk refugees leaving Thessaloniki for Asia Minor. They were waiting for a Turkish ship. We were all accounted for on our way out. A committee was processing us, taking us to various destinations. It took us some time to take our luggage out. We were all in a large camp in front of the pier.

My mother sent me to get some charcoal to cook with in an outdoor fire. As I was searching for charcoal in the market, I bumped into a police officer that happened to be my cousin and classmate; his

174 A. Boinodiris, Book 1, p. 328-329.

name was Chris Makisoglou. He left in 1922 from Constantinople and became a police officer in Thessaloniki. He showed me a charcoal shop, from which I purchased some for my mother. My mother set a few rocks on the ground of the waiting compound, lit the fire and placed a pot on it. For the first time since Mersina, we prepared our own food. In the boat and at the quarantine island we were not allowed to cook, being dependent on government-assigned cooks to feed us with mess hall food. We had with us a sack of about twenty kilos of bulgur and a pot of butter from Karvali. After my mother finished boiling the bulgur and placed the butter in it, the whole pier was filled with the familiar aroma of home cooked food. Two, well-dressed men, both wearing fedora hats and milling around the refugees approached us.

"Good morning. Whatever you are cooking smells heavenly. Can you allow us to have a taste of it?"

My mother smiled. "Of course…"

"How much does it cost?"

"I am afraid that it is not for sale. It can only be offered free of charge. Eat as much as you please." She offered them two bowls with spoons. They tasted it.

"It is very tasty. We do not have this wheat in Greece. It seems that this variety grows only in Asia Minor. Where do you come from?"

"Karvali, in Cappadocia…"

They smiled. "We were officers in the Greek army and went all the way to Haymana, about 70 km SW of Ankara." I knew Haymana. It was 18 hours by foot from Karvali.

"What are you doing here?"

"We are part of the committee to help Greeks like you get settled at your destinations. Who are you and where are you heading?"

"We are a family of four," said my mother. "Here is my father-in-law Paul, my son Anthony, my daughter Irene and myself. Here are our papers. We are traveling together with the family of Kyriakos Tsekmezoglou. " She showed them the boarding papers. Kyriakos also came by and gave them his papers.

"Where are you heading to?"

"We are going to meet my brother-in law Charalambos Pavlides in Drama. The Tsekmezoglou family is meeting the Aslanoglou family, also in Drama. Kyriakos' sister Makrina is married to John Aslanoglou and they came to Drama a few years earlier." They took notes.

In two hours a bus appeared. The bus driver started calling our names. Both families were loaded in the bus. It took us to the railroad station of Thessaloniki, in a neighborhood called Harmankoi. The two bowls of bulgur paid off. We were among the first to arrive at the train station.

While we were waiting for the train, I tried to find some medical help for my arm, which was hurting from sleeping on the mast of the ship. Someone told me about an old woman chiropractor at Harmankoi. I went to her home and she helped me recover, by using homemade remedies.[175]

DRAMA AND NEW KARVALI (28 AUGUST 1924-DECEMBER 1925)

We arrived in Drama on August 28, 1924. We came by train that day but had Nea Karvali as the final destination. I did not know it then, but destiny had it for me to make Drama my hometown for the rest of my life. I ended up loving this town and it never passed through my mind to change residence. It has mostly peaceful people, with good climate, with the exception that we have more humidity than I care for, especially during the winter months.

We got the short end of the stick, since other Greek refugees from Thrace and the western coast of Asia Minor got there earlier and received houses left behind by the Turks. By the time we arrived all houses were occupied. The estimated Turks that left Greece were 450,000, while the Greeks that left Asia Minor were close to 2 million. In that sense, we thought that the treaty that Venizelos signed with Kemal Ataturk was unfair.

As soon as we arrived, I started looking for my Uncle Charalambos, now named Pavlides. He took the name of his grandfather and turned it into his last name, to escape being assassinated by Bulgarians and Turks alike. I found him out in a village in Komotini, with the job of field warden. He did not have a home or shelter for us to stay either.

On my return from Komotini, I stopped at Nea Karvali, a new village that the Population Repatriation Committee chose for the residents

---

175 A. Boinodiris, Book 1, p. 328-329.

of Karvali. This committee had such members as Didactopoulos and Haji Mouratis Vafiades. They chose a location on the coast, 10 kilometers east of Kavala, in a location called Ginar Tepe by the Turks. It was a swampy place, without good water, full of mosquitoes and malaria. The place had no housing facilities, most of the refugee tents being under water. In one month, there were 70 refugees dead from malaria.[176] Malaria was rampant in those days, until the swamplands east of Kavala were cleared, and DDT killed the swarms of mosquitoes that lived there. Even though Karvali residents lived among friends and relatives, I was not envious of their position.

There were fields in the area, which was then called Ginar Tepe, or Tsorpagi Tsiflik (Cook's farm) full of burial grounds of convicts that left their bones in the swamps. The village of Nea Karvali now covers these burial grounds. The Turks sent the most hardened criminals here in forced, agricultural labor. By the time a criminal spent a few years at Ginar Tepe (the Turkish name of the region) if he survived his energy for any criminal tendencies was sapped. All he wanted to do is sit and do nothing. No criminal ever returned to this place for a second term.[177]

I immediately decided that Nea Karvali was not suitable for us.

I left Nea Karvali, saying to myself:

"It is a pity that they could not find a better location for our new village. Half of them will die in a year or so from malaria. I am young, ready for life and did not bring my family all this way to die from malaria in that swamp. We need good water, dry climate, similar to what we left behind."[178]

Meanwhile, my family was living in tents at the train station in Drama. We managed to secure a train wagon as temporary residence, among many other refugees. The churches and mosques of Drama were full of people, sleeping on the floor. We registered to the repatriation committee to acquire a residence, but that process took time. The train wagon was getting very hot during that August of 1924. Then, two people appeared to help us out. They were Paul Magioglou and Pandelis Gazopoulos. They felt sorry for us, talked to the mayor, and

---

176 A. Boinodiris, Book 4, p. 2.
177 A. Boinodiris, Book 1, p.2.
178 A. Boinodiris, Book 4, p.2.

they came and picked up our things from the train station.[179] Our next residence was a barn, assigned to us by the mayor.

After a plebiscite favoring a republican form of government, the parliament proclaimed Greece a republic in 1924. The economic World Crisis started at that time. Venizelos started building houses in 1924 and 1925 for the relief of refugees in Drama, which helped in the recovery. He established the Housing Authority Bank. The biggest subdivision was called "PERITHALPSI," or "relief." The houses of that area were one-story, small (less than 30 sq. meters), fast and cheap, but were built with bricks and had roof tiles. They typically housed families of 4-8 people. He had already started on the construction of the Drama High School, near this subdivision

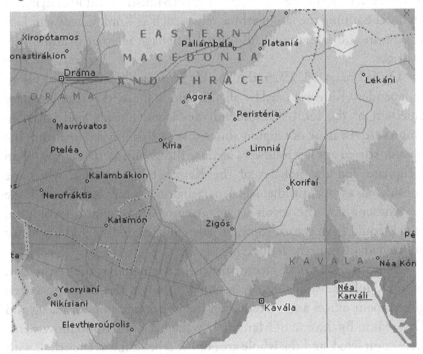

Figure 18 Drama Kavala and Nea Karvali

179 A. Boinodiris, Book 4, p.3.

Kemal's Initial Reforms and Rebellions (Anatolia, March, 1925)

After his victory against the Greeks, Kemal moved to reform the Turkish political system and promote the abolition of the Caliphate. On March 1, 1924, at the Assembly, Mustafa Kemal said:

"The religion of Islam will be elevated if it will cease to be a political instrument, as had been the case in the past."

On March 3, 1924, the Caliphate was officially abolished and its powers within Turkey were transferred to the Turkish Grand National Assembly. During the years of the War of Independence, Kemal recognized the multiethnic character of the Muslim population in Turkey. On December 8, 1925, the Turkish Ministry of Education issued an order banning the use of ethnic terms such as Kurd, Circassian, Laz, Kurdistan and Lazistan.[180] All official language referred to minorities as Turks.

On February 13, 1925, the Sheikh Said rebellion broke out for an independent Kurdistan, led by Sheikh Said of Piran, the rich hereditary chieftain of the local Nakshibendi dervishes. Sheikh Said chose to emphasize the issue of religion above that of Kurdish nationalism. The Sheikh stirred up his followers against the abolition of the Ottoman Caliphate and the policies of the Kemalist government, which he considered as against the Moslem religion. Some members of the government saw the revolt as an attempt at a counter-revolution, which could have spread to other parts of the country, and urged for an immediate military action.

Beneath the Islamic green banner, in the name of the restoration of the Holy Law, his forces roamed through the country, seized government offices and marched on the important cities of Elazıg and Diyarbakır. By the end of March 1925, the necessary troop movements were completed, and the whole area of the rebellion was encircled, with

---

180 Ataturk explained his new policy in the manual of civics which he dedicated to his adopted daughter Afet Inan in 1930:
"Within the political and social unity of today's Turkish nation, there are citizens and co-nationals who have been incited to think of themselves as Kurds, Circassians, Laz or Bosnians. But these erroneous terms have brought nothing but sorrow to individual members of the nation, with the exception of a few brainless reactionaries, who became the enemy's instruments."

Sheikh Said blockaded within his own territory of revolt. The revolt was put down quickly, when Said and thirty-six of his followers were condemned to death for treason and hanged.[181]

The legal reforms included the complete separation of government and religious affairs and the adoption of a strict interpretation of the constitution. This was coupled with the closure of Islamic courts and the replacement of Islamic canon law with a secular civil code, modeled after the Swiss Civil Code; the penal code was modeled after the Italian Penal Code. The seeds planted by Greeks within the Ottoman Empire during the past 400 years brought fruit. Not only were the Greeks denied any credit for this, but because of the recent bloody war, they were considered villains. Kemal said on one occasion that: "We must liberate our concepts of justice, our laws and our legal institutions from the bonds which, even though they are incompatible with the needs of our century, still hold a tight grip on us"

Mustafa Kemal's revolution faced quite an opposition. In 1925, the establishment of another political party was seen as a way to ease the tensions. Mustafa Kemal aided in establishing the Progressive Republican Party as an opposition party in the Assembly, and the first two-party era began. After some time though, the new party was taken over by people Kemal considered as Islamic fundamentalists. In 1925, partly in response to a rebellion, the "Maintenance of Order Law" was passed, giving Kemal the authority to shut down subversive groups. Soon after the Sheikh Said Rebellion, the Progressive Republican Party was disestablished under the new law; an act Mustafa Kemal claimed was necessary for preserving the Turkish state. The closure of the party was seen as an act of dictatorship by some later biographers, such

---

181 Two other revolts occurred one in Agrı and other in Dersim in 1930 and 1937 respectively. Turkish Air Force used aerial bombardments effectively against Kurdish uprisings. Sabiha Gokcen, the first female combat pilot of the world and the adopted daughter of Kemal, took part in the bombing raids against the Dersim Kurds.

On 12 November 1937, Kemal visited southeast Anatolia. During his visit, he issued an order that the cities Diyarbekir and Elaziz should be renamed as Diyarbakır and Elazığ. This was in accordance with the Sun Theory of Languages, which maintained that all words of foreign origin had Turkish roots.

as Harold C. Armstrong, who was captured as a POW by Turks in WWI.

Many Greek immigrants from Turkey believe that if anyone else, other than Kemal, or even Kemal at any other time tried to implement these changes on Turkey, they would not be able to do them. It was the combination of the right person, at the right time, after a bloody war for Turkish survival and after all the preparatory work that the desperate Greeks did on the Ottoman Empire for over 400 years that made Turkey what it is today.

Figure 19 New St. Gregory Church in Nea Karvali

RESETTLING

NEW COUNTRY, NEW PROBLEMS (DRAMA, SUMMER 1926)

After the ethnic exchange, Greece's poor fiscal situation was strained past its limits by the refugees' need for food and shelter. Tent cities sprang up around Athens, Thessaloniki and most other cities. Most refugees had fled with only the few items that they could carry; many had nothing at all. A disproportionate number of them were women, children, and elderly men because the Turks had detained young Greek men in labor camps. Massive foreign aid, organized by the League of Nations was a major contribution toward alleviating the immediate needs of the refugees. Eventually, refugee makeshift neighborhoods developed around Athens and its port city of Piraeus. Many of these enclaves retain a distinctive identity even today.

Most refugees settled in areas of Macedonia and Crete from which Muslims had departed. The hellenization of these regions included the introduction by New Greek settlers of tobacco farming, which became an important factor in Macedonia's agricultural economy. Many of the newcomers who settled in the cities were professionals or entrepreneurs, who helped to invigorate the industrial sector of Greece. The manufacture of cigarettes, cigars, carpets, and textiles grew dramatically, primarily because of the Asia Minor Greeks. Nevertheless, for many years, the general economic condition of the refugee population was grim, and many suffered from discrimination and cultural isolation after leaving Asia Minor.

In 1925 and 1926 Greece was under the dictatorship of Generals Pangalos and Eftaxias. They had expelled the Royal family from Greece because these individuals were blamed for the destruction of Asia Minor. Pangalos was a moral fanatic. He was born on the island of Salamis and like Plastiras had graduated from the Hellenic Army Officer Cadet Academy (Evelpidon) in 1900 and continued his studies in Paris, France. In 1916 he supported Venizelos in his struggle against King Constantine I, and was rewarded with a senior position in the War Ministry. He participated in the Asia Minor Campaign in senior staff positions, but was demoted after Constantine returned to power in 1920.

In 1922, Pangalos supported the coup by Plastiras, which abolished the monarchy and declared the Second Hellenic Republic, and was made War Minister. His first job was to prosecute a number of prominent pro-monarchist government leaders by military court in what became known as the Trial of the Six. This trial resulted in six executions. He then rushed to Thessaloniki, from where he successfully reorganized the Greek army in Macedonia and Thrace, as the war with Turkey was not over, and an attack in the region was imminent. The reorganization was so successful that the Greek High Command prepared for a possible advance into Eastern Thrace in the face of the Turkish demands in the Lausanne peace talks. A sudden reversal of the Turks in April preempted the new war, and the Treaty of Lausanne was signed.

A staunch nationalist, Pangalos objected to the terms of the treaty, and declared that his troops would attack Turkey nonetheless in order to block the deal. He was forced to resign, but his stance made him popular with the many segments of Greek society that objected to the treaty. During the period of political instability that followed, Pangalos jumped into the fray, gaining and losing a number of ministerial positions as governments came and went.

On June 24, 1925, officers loyal to Pangalos, fearing that the political instability was putting the country at risk, overthrew the government in a coup that infuriated the Great Powers. Pangalos immediately abolished the young republic and began to prosecute anyone who could possibly challenge his authority, including his old chief, Plastiras. Freedom of the press was abolished, and a number of repressive laws were enacted (including a law dictating the length of women's skirts - no more than

30cm above the ground). The police was required to carry rulers in their pockets measuring the length of a woman's skirt. Meanwhile, Pangalos awarded himself the Grand Cross of the Order of the Redeemer. The police was ordered to request marriage certificates from dating couples. This act, added to the friction between local Greeks and refugees and the existing poverty added to the public aggravation.

Pangalos was declared dictator on 3 January 1926 and had himself elected president in April 1926. On the economic front Pangalos attempted to devalue the currency by ordering paper notes cut in half. His lack of political and diplomatic ability however became soon apparent. He conceded too many rights to Yugoslav commerce in Thessaloniki, but worst of all, he embroiled Greece in the so-called War of the Stray Dog,[182] harming Greece's already strained international relations.

RESIDING IN A BARN (DRAMA, MACEDONIA, DECEMBER, 1925)

After Macedonia was liberated from Turks and Bulgarians, Drama had a very mixed population. It consisted of local Greeks, Greeks from Epirus, Jews, Turks and Armenians, refugees from Black Sea Thracians, Eastern Thracians, Black Sea Greeks and Asia Minor Greeks. The first

---

182 The "War of the Stray Dog," or the "incident at Petrich," named after the Bulgarian border town Petrich, was a short occupation by Greek forces of Bulgaria, on 22 October 1925. It started when a Greek soldier ran after his dog, which had strayed across the border from Macedonia. The Greek soldier was shot. The Greeks claimed repeated Bulgarian border violations, in an attempt to destabilize the region during the Greek-Turkish War. In response, the Greek dictatorial government under General Pangalos sent soldiers into Bulgaria and occupied Petrich, only to vacate the area a week later under the pressure of the League of Nations. The League did indeed condemn the Greek invasion, and called for both Greek withdrawal and compensation to Bulgaria. Greece ceded to this demand and was imposed a fine of £45,000. Over 50 people were killed before Greece complied. Greece complained about the disparity between its treatment and that of Italy in the Corfu incident in 1923, when the Italian armed forces occupied the Greek island of Corfu in retaliation for the murder of Italian general Enrico Tellini while surveying the Greek border with Albania.

mayor of the city was a tobacco merchant from Cappadocia, named Alexander Dermentzoglou. The immigrants henceforth began to play an integral part of the growth and economic prosperity in Drama.[183]

The second mayor was Michael Fessas and the third was Athanasios Anagnostou. The mayors showed us of a place to stay. This was a barn, which was converted as a shelter for refugees. There were two bulls, one cow, one mule and one donkey there. The barn had hay at the end wall. It was partitioned in two by a reed fence, separating the animals in the inner section, from the human quarters, closer to the entrance. There was also a wagon full of potatoes parked in it. We slept there, 10 souls, all members of both families. Although cramped, it was better than the tents that the rest of the refugees used. Nevertheless, it had rats, no water and no toilet facilities.[184]

The Tsekmezoglou family stayed in that barn with us until the end of the year. Around Christmas, his brother-in-law from Nea Karvali came to visit him and talked him into moving to Nea Karvali. So, we were left alone in the stable, all four of us.[185] We stayed there for 15 months. The owner of the stable was none other than Paul Magioglou. Paul had arrived earlier, in 1922 from Samos and he became a tobacco grower. He was a successful merchant in Smyrna, and even though he escaped with just his clothes, he managed to own some property in Drama. He was a relative of my mother's. The wagon of potatoes belonged to Pandelis Gazopoulos, another merchant. He was also from Karvali.[186]

While we were still living in the barn, I worked on different jobs. I was selling seasonal produce in the local bazaar. The bazaar was located on the south end of the normally dry riverbed of a gulch that ran through the city of Drama. Yet, when it rained at the distant foothills of Mount Falakron, the gulch became unexpectedly a deadly river, whose water burst into the bazaar, flooding it and taking with it shopping stands, carts, animals and all their goods. All these were later fished out from the banks of the gulch at Nea Amissos, the village next to Drama to the South.

Near the church of St. Nicholas, on Venizelos Street was a tiny bridge, which used to be plugged by rocks and trees that the gulch brought down

183 A. Boinodiris, Book 4, p. 192.
184 A. Boinodiris, Book 4, p.2.
185 A. Boinodiris, Book 1, p. 328-329 and Book 4, p.2.
186 A. Boinodiris, Book 4, p.3.

from the mountains. When this happened, the water level went up, the streets, and the central square of the city flooded. When it unplugged, the force was so large that it caused a lot of damage. Once at a later time, the rushing water took automobiles and trucks. In one of these destructive rains, I lost most of my capital that I brought from Asia Minor. The water took my stand with all the produce and even my scale.[187] This terminated my business as a peddler for the time being.

In January of 1925, my mother became sick. My grandfather, Paul went to Komotini to stay with his brother, Charalambos, taking all his stuff plus his money of 15 gold liras.

I started working as a garbage collector for the city of Drama. I was also being used as a laborer, watering the dirt streets of Drama in the summertime to suppress the dust. At that time, I was being paid 140 drachmas per week. I also doubled as a firefighter, until a new Mayor arrived, named Lazarus Danielides, who unjustly decided to fire me to put one of his own people in the job. At that time, the workers had no unions or rights. As an excuse, he used a mishap, when a woman crossed the street right in front of the water truck on its downhill path. The truck driver, a person from Corfu, named Gerasimos, stopped on time, but broke the gears of the truck. It was loaded with two tons of water, but he managed to stop on the downhill slope of Venizelos Street. The event happened on the second alley below the store of Trakasopoulos. I was not even driving, but was using the hose to water the street. He fired us both and put his own people on the job.[188] I had to pay 2000 drachmas damage for the truck gears from my salary, while my weekly salary was only 140 drachmas. Fourteen weeks of no pay was extremely harsh punishment for me at that time. After he fired us, the Mayor placed a man from Epirus in my job and I was forced to become a laborer again, working in construction.[189]

I worked near the springs of Santa Barbara, at the site of a large new tobacco factory, named Austrian-Greek Company. An Austrian of Greek-Jewish background named Herman Spearer was the financial muscle behind the operation. An Austrian, named Wella, was the engineer. The builder was a Greek-Albanian, named Thanasis. There

187 A. Boinodiris, Book 4, p. 5-6.
188 A. Boinodiris, Book 1, p. 330-331.
189 A. Boinodiris, Book 4, p. 5-6.

were about 200 people working around the clock in three shifts. I worked there for nine months. We were mixing cement like ants and poured it by hand buckets, using scaffolding. When I started, we were pumping water from the foundations. When I finished, we placed the roof tiles and delivered the building for interior finishing.[190]

When the job was done, Thanasis gave us references to other builders, like the one at the school of Stenimachos, at a house near Santa Sophia and the railroad station construction. I worked in all these places. Then, I started working in a private house of a Jewish family, named Aaron Haim at Armen and K. Paleologos Streets. There, I found out how bad it is to work for someone else. His contractor, someone named Michael was a crook, who stole hours of work from his workers, even though we were, paid 40 drachmas per day. He was from Bursa, had a hunched back and had a loud voice, which he used to swear against Holy Personages, something that made me furious. I could bear all, except that. I had not experienced such an insult as that in previous jobs. Having to bear daily insults of blaspheming against Christ and God reduced my will to work to nothing. After one week's work, the contractor's behavior became worse. At the end of that week, we had the task to pour concrete in the main entrance.

"Do you want more concrete?" I asked.

"No," He responded.

I went with the others to wash my hands in a water barrel. The contractor got upset, because we were quitting on time. He gets down from the scaffold, approaches me and starts using his foul mouth against my Christ; then he slaps me at my face. "Get back to work," he said, concluding the string of obscenities.

I was surprised. He chose me for being the youngest and thinnest. The rest were older veterans and sported moustaches. I grabbed the contractor, raised him over my head and tossed him in the foundations of the house (about 1.5 meters deep), which I had dug up previously.

"I have not received a slap from my father in my life," I yelled. "How dare you filthy hunchback raise a hand at me?"

I jumped over him into the ditch, jumping up and down on his hunched back.

"Let me straighten up your body, with the hope that it straightens up your filthy ways."

---

190 A. Boinodiris, Book 4, p. 6-7.

At that time, his secretary rushes out to his aid. He came to attack me by kicking me. I grabbed him by his leg and dragged him into the ditch, flattening him on top of his boss.

I got out of the ditch and dirty as I was I walked into the police station. There, I met the commander, a Cretan named Stamatakis. He knew of us and was good friends with my friend Michael Aslanides and my future brother in law. Michael's little sister, Marianthi was babysitting Stamatakis' children.

I told him what happened.

"Did you straighten him up?" he asked me.

"A little…"

"What do you want from us?"

"I worked for a full week. If I go to be paid, we may get into a fight again. How can I get my money?"

"Where did you find this contractor my friend? This person has several lawsuits against him from workers and technicians alike."

"How am I supposed to know? I worked for almost a year for jobs like the Austrian-Greek Company and nothing like that happened to me. I never had to sustain insults like those addressed to Holy Personages in my life and stealing up to 1.5 hours a day from his workers."

"Is it pay time?" asked the commander, getting up.

"Yes," I responded.

"You go up front and I will be behind you."

I went to the café, near the construction site, where the rest of the workers were being paid. I was careful, afraid that the contractor might send a brick towards my head the minute he saw me. He was sitting outside and had a glass of water in his hand when he saw me. I closed the glass door behind me, when I heard his water glass shatter the glass behind me as he hurled it towards me. Fortunately, he missed me. I turned and looked behind me, as commander Stamatakis rushed in and faced the contractor:

"Contractor Michael, are you again causing disturbances? You need to be sent to the mental hospital, instead of being a contractor. I have a lawsuit ready to be sent to the district attorney. However, before we deal with that, you will pay this kid to go to his home. He is a family man."

Suddenly, the café went up in commotion. The rest of the workers took courage and started their own complaints. I was paid and left this crazy contractor for good. I subsequently worked at the new orphanage that was being built in Drama, together with George Krotopoulos and Angelos Seitanides.[191] By the end of 1925, the trials of living in the barn were close to the end. In November of 1925, we were given a house at Perithalpsi.[192] The muddy tobacco fields in the northwest side of the city were converted into small residences. The Treasury of Housing for the Homeless, or Perithalpsi built these residences for all the refugees.

These houses were built on a shoestring budget, without having either sewage or water lines in the streets. All the streets were lined with dirt and every house had a mud-scraper, to avoid bringing mud inside the house during the rainy days. After several families moved into their houses I realized that, these residences could open a hole in the ground for a septic tank, but having no water, forced the residents to carry water from a long distance for home consumption. This lack of facilities created an opportunity for me to go into the water carrying business.[193]

Figure 20 Drama Center in 1935: The Falakron Mountain is seen at the horizon.

191 A. Boinodiris, Book 4, p. 7-11.
192 A. Boinodiris, Book 4, p. 11.
193 A. Boinodiris, Book 4, p.3.

ASLANOGLOU SAGA (DRAMA, EASTER, 1926)

The Aslanoglou family was now registered as Aslanides. They had arrived in Kavala on April 1923. Soon after, they came to Drama. Some groups, related to the Aslanoglou family remained in a mosquito infested area, near Kavala, which was named Nea Karvali. These were the Tsekmezoglou family consisting of Makrina's brothers, sisters, and other relatives, like the Zopoglou family. They were part of the core of refugees that established the village of Nea Karvali.

When the Aslanides family arrived, they reported to the immigration authorities; they were given a number, and a ruffle was held on the location of the lot, where they could reside. The lot was in Drama, in a newly developed neighborhood for refugees, called "PERITHALPSI" (meaning "relief"). There they met Paul Magioglou, the merchant from Smyrna. He was looking after anyone that came from Samos, to see if he recognized anyone among them. He took them to a farmhouse called Osman Tsiflik. This farmhouse was later to become a prosperous village, called Kalos Agros (Good Farm). In that farm, the government let them have a parcel of land, where they could build a home. They built their own home, while the government provided lumber, lime and roof tiles. The immigrants provided all the labor. They laid the foundations out of stones, which they dug and carried from the fields. They made the straw mud-bricks, which made the walls and laid the roof.

The land was fertile and they started cultivating it. One more child had been born, Fevronia (1922). The family now consisted of John (1875), Makrina (1880), Kyriaki (1904), Michael (1906), Elisabeth (1910), Marianthi (1914), Basil (1918) and Fevronia (1922). Even though water was plentiful, drinking water was a problem. Many died from fever by drinking the polluted waters of the river, flowing next to their farms. These people did not know about country living, since most of them were from cities, like Smyrna, where water is filtered and bacteria are killed. Soon, the wet fields became breeding grounds for mosquitoes and malaria fever started killing old people. Since they had no facilities to combat such epidemic, they had to flee back to Drama in 1924.

Not having a place to stay, the Aslanides family went to the yard of a surviving mosque of Drama, called Kursumnu, in which site is now the church of Holy Trinity. It was half torn down then, being rebuilt, but it managed to house five families in its yard, in tents. They stayed there for 18 months, until the "PERITHALPSI" building caught up to allow them to be housed (around the end of 1925).

During that period, John was cultivating a piece of land near Drama, growing and selling vegetables. John Aslanoglou was a very honest, hard working person, who considered himself unlucky. He found a small plot of land to cultivate, near the dry bed of Drama's drainage canal. There he was planting vegetables, to feed the family of eight souls. In his field, he had a frequent young man, who was visiting him often, especially when his daughter Elisabeth was bringing him lunch. He was another refugee, who was trying to make a living by carrying spring water with his two donkeys from Santa Barbara springs to all the neighborhoods. The young man's name was yours truly (Anthony Boinodiris). To feed my donkeys, I visited the drainage canal, where grass was plentiful to be picked. John and I became friends, exchanging stories. He was depressed, because he depended on his young children to survive. At times, tears came to his eyes reminiscing where he was only seven years ago, with his fifty employees and lots of money.

ELISABETH (DRAMA, 1926)

Drama had no water distribution system in those years. Because of that, I was using two donkeys to haul and sell drinking water from the springs of St. Barbara to immigrant camps. To feed these donkeys, I was passing by John Aslanides's farm to pick leftover weeds and vegetable leftovers. He was talking to me about his life.

"My son Anthony, never count your chickens before they hatch. Few years ago, I would have never imagined my life now. I was a rich merchant with a bright future. I had no worries about raising 60 children. Look at me now. Now, I do not know how to raise six. I ask my children to help me bring some income. I had to let my ten-year-old Marianthi to go and live at Papadakis' house and take care of his two children. "

"Who is Papadakis?"

"He is the police commander of Drama. He comes from Crete. His wife requested Marianthi, to help her with her housework, providing her room and board."

John continued talking about the fire in Selefkia, the rebuilding of the store, the war and his escape from the draft with the help of his "nameless policeman" friend. He described his struggle to rebuild his business, only to abandon everything and leave. He was getting old (51) and weak, both bodily and in spirit to start all over again. Occasionally I saw him crying.[194]

It was then that I became good friends with John's son, Michael. I also met the whole family and immediately fell in love with Michael's sister, Elisabeth. Ever since then, I looked forward to doing my runs to John's farm, to feed my donkeys.

Few months after moving to his new home, by Easter time of 1926, John became ill from an unknown cause. In four days, he was dead, leaving his children orphan.

Elisabeth Aslanoglou, now Aslanides grew in a well-to-do household until the age of eleven, when her father had to move his whole family to Greece. She was the third child of six in that family. Although the family was going through a traumatic trial, the trauma of their plight brought them very close together. Ever since she was fourteen, Elisabeth was forced to help her mother Makrina raise the eleven-year-old Marianthi. Soon Marianthi went on loan to a family as a babysitter. She also looked after the seven year old Basil and the rather sickly three year old Fevronia. Fevronia was still sick from the polluted waters of Kalos Agros, having a rather enlarged spleen. Regardless of their suffering and health problems, it seems that the work ethic embedded in the Aslanides family, from father and mother to all the siblings was so strong, that they excelled in every task they undertook.[195] When those children lost their father, the family's bond grew even more by the sheer necessity of survival. From that time on, the family members would form a close support group, continuously supporting each other and their families. That work ethic remained with them through the rest of their lives. There was no task too menial, or too overwhelming that they would not try to tackle, if it meant that the task served their families.

Like the rest of the siblings, Elisabeth felt helpless as she and the rest of the family saw their fairly rich father, wither to his death in

---

194 A. Boinodiris, Book 1, p. 138.
195 A. Boinodiris, Book 1, p. 137.

poverty, because of the circumstances of the Greco-Turkish war. They clang around their mother Makrina, who instilled upon them their family anthem: "the family will survive and succeed, regardless of what has happened in the past." Makrina's words hit a chord on every member of the Aslanides clan. She was a woman of action and strong work ethic. She wiped her tears, pulled her sleeves and set to raise the whole family on her own.[196] Initially, the twenty-one year old Kyriaki and the nineteen-year-old Michael went to work in tobacco factories. Elisabeth also volunteered to work at fourteen in 1925. When the tobacco factory manager saw her, he told her:

"Little girl, I want you to go home and play with your dolls until you are old enough."

In those days, women were the primary workers that did the rather unhealthy and labor-intensive tobacco factory tasks. They processed leaf tobacco, sorted it before it is blended in silos and then brought it to the cutting machines where the tobacco is cut to a carefully specified width which ensures perfect filling of the cigarettes later in the manufacturing process. These processes were done in other factories in Kavala. There, the factory added flavor in the form of various aromas as the last step, before the tobacco was ready for cigarette production. These, later to become quite controversial aromas are sprayed onto the tobacco in rotating cylinders. The aroma sprays have been known to contain dozens of chemicals, most of them quite harmful, including some amount of tar and arsenic. The factories were huge warehouses, with very poor ventilation systems. The air was so full of tobacco leaf dust that most people with weak respiratory systems got sick. Around 1926, Kyriaki got sick from asthma and allergies in the unhealthy environment of these factories, so she stopped working there. To supplement their income, Kyriaki started working in farms, part-timing during the fall and winter, harvesting and processing tobacco for drying.

The tobacco leaves were harvested from plants in the early hours of the day in the fall. The leaves were piled in a dry area, from where workers picked the leaves and using a long, thin, flat needle, they passed a string through the main vein of each leaf. The strung tobacco leaves then were hung in a "drying room," where throughout the winter, it was dried up. In the spring, the leaves were taken out of the strings,

---

196 A. Boinodiris, Book 4, p.18-19.

inspected, sorted, and finally placed on carrier containers, which were weighed and sold. To string these leaves, it requires people that were fast with their fingers and capable of sustaining for months the boring chore of doing this repetitive work. Yet, for that time, tobacco processing offered the Aslanides family the income potential they needed.

For the family to maintain a year-round steady income, Elisabeth went to work in tobacco factories in 1926, at the age of 15. After that, the Aslanides family had two full-time working members: Michael and Elisabeth.

In 1927, Marianthi kept on working as a babysitter. At that time, the family received a small amount of reparation money for all the property that the Turks destroyed and confiscated in Asia Minor. When Makrina received the reparation money, she used it to get a knitting machine that Marianthi could make socks. These machines were mechanical monsters in terms of maintenance. They were about the size of a small table and were driven manually by foot and weights. If you were good, you could produce a pair of socks every half-hour.[197]

Early in 1927, Elisabeth and I were engaged. As I dated Elisabeth and made plans for our future, I tried to pitch in and support —as much as I could- the proud Makrina Aslanides raise her family.

Figure 21 St. Barbara Springs in Drama, with Tobacco Factories, Built and Ran by Asia Minor Refugees

---

197 This machine was passed from Marianthi on to Fevronia, when she came of age. The author remembers that machine, sitting in the family room of Fevronia's family when he visited her house, thirty years later.

Water Carrier (Drama, Spring 1926)

The lack of a water distribution system at the new settlement of Perithalpsi in Drama was a temporary boon for me. I changed from construction work and went in the water business (which I practiced for two years) until the city installed piping and neighborhood faucets on the sidewalks of the streets of PERITHALPSI and a pump house in the springs of St. Barbara. I was supplying water to the tents and newly built houses of the region using first my back and then donkeys when I could afford them.[198]

Perithalpsi was becoming large, to the size of about 400 families, representing 1550 people. The refugees had many children, some of them up to eight children per family. I constructed a shed behind our house, to hold two donkeys and bought two animals with my construction work earnings. I was loading four large tin cans on each animal, full of water and distributing it to the neighborhoods. I was charging one drachma per tin. By making 20 runs each day was netting me 160 drachmas of earnings per day, a lot more than the 40-45 drachmas of daily wages I was getting for construction work. On Saturdays, I had a lot more demand for water, because the wives did their laundry that day. I managed to do 25 runs, netting me 200 drachmas per day. This was good money at that time. Soon, others saw my success and went into the water business competing with me.[199]

I had to go back and forth 25 times a day to the springs of St. Barbara and fill my cans with fresh water. I carried water and filled containers in tents and houses for a small fee. This is how homemakers could cook the daily beans and soups for their husbands and children. Water was precious, because it had to be carried 0.5-2 kilometers by hand.

In 1926, my grandfather Paul (1855-1926) wanted us to come and visit him and my uncle Charalambos at Komotini, but I was too busy, trying to make a living. Early in 1926, we made plans for mother and me to go and see him, but when we got ready to go, we got news of his death at the age of 77. He was buried in Komotini. My mother managed to be there in his 40-day memorial. I was extremely sad and cried for days.

198 A. Boinodiris, Book 1, p.153 and Book 4, p. 3.
199 A. Boinodiris, Book 4, p. 4.

In absence of a father, my grandfather was the person who raised me, taking the role of a father. He was the person who pulled us through during the difficult days of both wars. He was an honest man, truthful in his words, hard working and a great artist in pottery. Although hard working, he was not workaholic like Haji John, balancing his life to eight hours hard work, eight hours spiritual and social activities and a full eight hours of sleep. His health had deteriorated by the hardships of the war, the loss of his wife and his mental fixation that he actually belonged back at his fields in Karvali, rather than in Greece. He died of a broken heart, deeply depressed in his old age. He was one of the countless victims of this cruel relocation.

NEWS FROM ABROAD (DRAMA, NOVEMBER, 1926)

In November of 1926, we received almost simultaneously two letters. One was from America, from my Uncle Pandel Mayo and the other was from Russia, from my father. We were extremely happy. We were not sure if they were dead or alive after all these years of continuous wars.[200]

Pandel Mayo (changed from Pandelis Magioglou) found us through a search of the Red Cross. They located the remains of the Magioglou family and us. We started corresponding, exchanging information.

My father sent us 2000 drachmas from Saint Petersburg and asked us to get him a visa for his return. I asked Justin Ioakimides in Athens for help with the visa.

At almost the same time, I received a letter from someone named Nikos Kanakis, from the island of Chios. He was working in the same factory with my father in St. Petersburg (Leningrad).

"Dear Anthony," he was writing, "we work together with your father and with your Uncle Dimitris in Leningrad. You are trying to get your father's visa to come near you, but if he comes, your family's peace will be destroyed. You will regret it bitterly. He is very obnoxious and has many problems. He is obliged to help economically in settling his daughter Irene. Don't help him come home, for you will regret it."

I read the letter stunned.

---

200 A. Boinodiris, Book 1, p.182.

"Who is this islander, named Kanakis," I wondered. *"What does he have against my father? Why does he hate him so?"*

It took some time to realize that Nikos Kanakis was trying to save us some grief.[201] What we did not know at that time was that my father found another woman in Russia, married her and had another family there. The conditions were such that nobody could check on him to accuse him of bigamy. During the confusion of war, such infractions as infidelity were set aside.

THE MOBILE STAND (DRAMA, SUMMER 1927)

I worked as a water carrier until 1927, living in tents with my mother and sister Irene. Irene was going to the elementary school at Ekpedeftiria.

By 1927, we were five water carriers. It was then that the city of Drama managed to place a pumping station and a few water faucets in the neighborhoods. The business was declining at a fast rate. The only use for water carriers was for taking water to the tobacco fields and that was not paying much. Like all things in life, my job had to change.[202] At the start of 1927, my water business job ended. Having had bad experiences working for others as a laborer, I decided to open my own business. I realized later that my bad experience was incidental. If I worked for an honest employer, I work with zest and I can be productive. If your employer mistreats you and abuses you by degrading all you hold dear, you cannot work at all. I was not expecting much, but we were very thrifty and did not need much to survive. I kept some of my water business by carrying 15 tins of water to the bread bakery of Tsaganos and 10 to a pie-and-sweets shop near-by, thus collecting 25 drachmas per day. When the city got organized, the neighborhoods received running water and so did bakeries and other shops.[203] Bread consumption was in high demand. I was planning to open a store in Perithalpsi, which with a population of 1500 souls in a very small area would do well. They needed a neighborhood store, since they were all forced to walk downtown to shop.

---

201 A. Boinodiris, Book 4, p. 16-17.
202 A. Boinodiris, Book 4, p. 4.
203 Water to individual houses was not installed and had to wait until the 1950s and 1960s for it to be realized.

In that spring of 1927, I became a milkman, dealing with farmers in Nea Amissos; this was a community, established a short distance from Drama by Greeks from the shores of the Black Sea. With the horse I bought for 4500 Drachmas, I started making and distributing yogurt. I worked with Simeon Merakoglou in a partnership. Simeon had all the tools and I had the transportation. I distributed milk and yogurt for about six months. We made the yogurt in a place of Sinai Street. By bad luck, that summer was a cool, rainy one; as a result, yogurt consumption dropped. Yogurt was consumed as a thirst quencher in the old times and was a favorite treat in hot summers, like ice cream is today. If yogurt is not consumed, it is turned into a strained, thick paste of yogurt, similar to sour cream. With low consumption, we ran into some tough spots with cash flow, but I managed to pull through and pay every one of the milk suppliers from Nea Amissos.[204] That same year, Elisabeth's older brother, Michael Aslanoglou was engaged to Urania Rafailides from Pontus.

The whole family pitched in to help me; this included Makrina Aslanides, the widow of John Aslanides, my mother in law to be. I was carrying and selling milk twice a day. Simeon and his elderly father were pasteurizing the milk. Makrina was helping to clean all utensils during the yogurt making process. She also cleaned all used clay containers, since these containers were re-cycled. Families had to place a deposit for each clay container of yogurt. The containers were of 0.5, 1 and 2 Oka size.[205][206]

As I was looking for a store, I found a ready portable one. It was a strong, tobacco stand at the railroad station.[207] I sold the two animals used for the water carrying business and with money that I saved from that business I opened up a store in my mobile stand. I was supposed to go to the service in 1926, but the paperwork made an error and registered me two years younger. So, I was destined to go to the service in 1928. Since I was the only male supporter in my family, the Greek Government allowed a special dispensation, upon which I had to be trained, serve for four months and go home. So, all I had to do is leave

---

204 A. Boinodiris, Book 1, p.155.
205 A. Boinodiris, Book 1, p.155.
206 A unit of mass used in 19th century, 2.834 pounds avoirdupois was used in Greece until the 1950s.
207 A. Boinodiris, Book 4, p. 12-13.

my mother and my sister for a few months and come back to resume my business. Having planned such a transition, I purchased this 3.5x4 meter mobile stand with ceramic roof and glass. The owner was a retired old man. When he died, his wife sold it to one of our compatriots. This compatriot was then a street peddler, named Joachim. He purchased it, but then changed his mind and sold it to me at no profit.

I had to move this huge stand from the railroad station to an opening at PERITHALPSI without destroying it. To move it to the new location, I got help from Jordan Zoumboulides from Kavala. After dismantling the stand, we loaded it on a large railroad cart with small wheels and attached it to a horse-drawn cart, which I hired. The cart driver was an Armenian, who used this cart to carry heavy and bulky loads for railroad work. The wheels were small, so that these loads can be loaded with minimum lift. He charged me 250 drachmas (200 for the store and 50 for the tiles). We moved it with great difficulty and slowly up the somewhat steep Venizelos and Chrysostomou Streets, using the railroad cart.

On the way to the new location, another stand owner, a refugee from Russia, named Tzoras who had a grocery stand near by, and fearing competition attempted to stop me. He starts yelling and screaming for me to stop; he brings over a friend that worked as a night watchman for PERITHALPSI.

"How dare you set up business here? Don't you see that we are trying to make a living? Go somewhere else."

The builder of PERITHALPSI, named Constantopoulos hired night watchmen to look after half-finished housing, so that none steals any building materials. One of them was Costas Mavrides, a fellow from Pontus, who favored his own friends, like Tzoras. Mavrides and Tzoras came close to the cart and would not allow the horse to proceed.

I became upset, considering that I had just as much right to set my business in that location as anyone else.

"Where is your license?" He asked angrily.

"Under what authority are you asking me for a license? " I responded. "You are just a guard here, making sure that none steals materials."

"I will not let you move this stuff in here," Costas responded.

"You are not the only refugees in this place. What do you think we are? We also want to survive as much as you do. The sun rises for all humanity, not only you."

"If you don't leave, we will break every bone in your body."

I leaped on top of them from the cart and flattened Tzoras to the ground. As Costas rushed towards me, I grabbed Costas from his collar and tossed him to the ground, almost five yards away, primarily from his own speed.

"You do that again and you will really get hurt," I shouted.

The Armenian coachman and Jordan intervened and held Costas.

"Don't start anything that you may regret," the coachman said.

"Get him out of here," Tzoras yelled.

The cart driver took my side.

"I will not. This is public land, Tzora. Just as you placed your stand on it, this man has the right to do the same."

"I hope you rot in hell," yelled Tzoras. The two men got up and left. I looked at them as they left. I realized that I had to fight to survive. A person has to be just, but never give in to the threats of others that are unjustly attacking him for their own survival or pleasure. Victory belongs to the daring, as the ancient Greeks were saying and daring becomes fortified when you are on moral high ground. We all wanted to survive, but some of us became unscrupulous in the way they went about it.

We slowly unloaded the stand. To me, it was the most beautiful stand I ever saw. It had wooden floors, thick planks and a roof made out of ceramic tiles. I started with a number of customers, who worked at the tobacco factories during the warm months. In the cold months, they worked in drying the tobacco at individual farms. I gave them weekly credit until their payday. My sister Irene was an elementary school student. She and my mother were coming to help me out, by keeping the store while I did the shopping to stock it.

My saga with Tzoras was just beginning. He would be my nemesis for the years to come. He wanted to have monopoly on this site and was using criminal, mafia-style tactics by hiring Costas as his muscle. In the future, he would use other tactics, like harassment. He accused us to the police that we were dirty, or that we were selling goods with deficient weight. The police checked us out, finding that his complaints were unfounded and started getting irritated with him.

My grocery store business did well because I was well known by the people that I served through my water business. Since many of those people were speaking only Turkish, I was a preferred source for their groceries. Most of my clients were Greeks that could not speak a word of Greek.[208] Storeowners like Tzoras spoke no Turkish and he had difficulties communicating with many of his customers. This gave me an edge, which I could have used, except that I had to go to the army.[209]

At that same time, someone called Costas from Kerasus of Pontus opened up a café, using a barn like mine. He painted it to beautify it and made it the center in which youth from Pontus were gathering. I occasionally visited the café at night. One night, four youngsters from Pontus set an ambush and suddenly attacked me, without provocation. After recovering from the surprise, I counter-attacked and tossed them to the ground, one after the other.

"Why don't you come up and fight like men," I yelled, "instead of trying to sneak up on me?"

Glasses were broken, which I had to pay, since the attackers disappeared.

In those years, I was afraid of none, except God.[210]

George Boyun-egri-oglou, my long lost father returned from Russia in March of 1927, running away from the bloodbath of the Russian revolution and leaving his family in Russia to join with his family in Greece. He had little money with which he bought cloth for his wife and daughter.

George, as he entered the country, had different immigration officials and was registered in a different way than us. He was registered as Boidaris. Mistakes like that went undetected for many years in the Greek bureaucracy and the people had more important priorities than to go through the courts to fix such mistakes. My father's coming brought me the first disadvantage; it changed my military status from a supporting male, to a regular service. Supporting males served only for four months, while a regular service was for eighteen months. Military service in Greece was compulsory.

208 A. Boinodiris, Book 1, p.154 and Book 4, p.13-16.
209 A. Boinodiris, Book 4, p.157-158.
210 A. Boinodiris, Book 4, p.17-18.

I made the mistake of entrusting the grocery store to my father, after my father arrived from Russia. Even during that period I supported my father in that stand for three months. To supplement our income, I bought a horse and started selling produce at the farmer's markets.

THE MILK HORSE (DRAMA, SPRING 1928)

In the spring of 1928 I purchased a young horse (4 year old) for 8000 Drachmas to be used with a cart. My previous horse could only carry things on a saddle. The new horse, light red in color[211] was from Caucasus and liked music. Every time it heard music, it lifted its front legs and danced. I bought this new horse from a horse dealer called Costas from Smyrna. He found it somewhere in Sidirokastron. I gave Costas a down payment, shoed the horse and promised to pay the rest of the money at home. I purchased a bale of hay and started with Costas towards my home. The new horse was bare backed, led only by its reigns, walking next to Costa's horse.[212]

We watered the two horses in the lake of St. Barbara and started up the hill towards Chrysostomou Street. There, I tried riding bareback the horse, carrying the bail of hay on its back. Then we set my horse next to the horse of the merchant and urging them to race. This was a mistake. It revealed that my horse was a thoroughbred racer, for it took off at high speed. When we reached a tobacco kiosk of Antavalis, I see a street cleaner, cleaning the road from animal dung. I was afraid that the horse would kill him. Instead, the horse jumped over him, without touching him at all. There I turned left, tossing the bail of hay, which I was clutching until then. I grabbed onto the horse's mane for life. The horse was heading straight towards a tobacco factory. A number of children were playing there. To avoid them and turn towards the Chrysostomou Street to the right, I took a wide turn, keeping the horse to the left of the street. The animal must have thought that I was planning a left turn, until I swung its head to the right. It was too late. The horse took the turn so fast, that the centrifugal force tossed me on the turn against the house of Lazarus Eleminoglou. The house had a rough, tossed plaster on it. I had no saddle to control my body and I flew up in the air. Fortunately, I kept my hands in front of my face and

211 A. Boinodiris, Book 1, p.171.
212 A. Boinodiris, Book 1, p.156.

did not get hurt seriously. Yet, I was pulling sand and plaster out of my hand wounds for one week.

The horse went for a few yards and turned back, lowering its head to mine and neighing. I could hear the animal talk to me: *"what happened to you, stupid? I am sorry for throwing you off like that, but you should have let me know which way you wanted to go. "*

The horse dealer approached with a deathly white face.

"It is all my fault, son. I did not know I had this kind of an animal. I bought it yesterday and did not have a chance to test it." Then, after checking me out, he continued. "When I saw you fly off, I shut my eyes. When I opened them again and saw you come up and the horse next to you like it was its fault I breathed easy. If it were me in your place, I would be dead."

I looked at him wincing from the pain of my raw hands; he was in his fifties; I was in my twenties and full of energy. We reached my father's home on foot and paid him the rest of the money. The horse dealer turned to my father, before departing:

"You have a strong son here George. He just purchased an equally strong horse to match. I hope they have fun together. "[213]

And, so it was. I bought a buggy and started chasing after bazaars, where I sold everything in season. The horse was used to pull the buggy with produce to markets. I loved that horse so much I fed it raisins, costing me 4 Drachmas per Oka.

On Mondays, I was selling produce in Drama and on Tuesday, I was at Kyrgia. On Wednesday, I was at Chrysoupolis and on Thursday, I was at Eleftheroupolis, both in the district of Kavala. On Friday, I hauled grain from Prosotsani and on Saturday, I hauled clothing for the Arvanitis brothers of the Alexander the Great Street. These brothers kept a store for knit, cotton and wool clothing. I also hauled shoes for shoe stores. The horse stayed with me until I left for the army in October of 1928. It was so well trained that it kept on the right side of the road.

A fellow named Zacharias Katranzis was a refugee from Asia Minor; he was buying and selling grain in bazaars. We were bringing excellent quality grain from Thrace at that time. The wheat was very hard and was used for seed. One Thursday we were exchanging it with softer

---

213 A. Boinodiris, Book 1, p.157.

grain of Kalos Agros, 2 kilos of soft grain for each kilo of hard grain. Both of us loaded two carts, each with 400 Okas of hard grain and exchanged it for 800 of soft grain in each cart. We started coming to Drama from Kalos Agros around 4 PM that August day, my light red horse and his fish-speckled white horse.

When we reached the estate of the agriculturist Kisagislis, it started raining. Roads at that time were made out of dirt and gravel and that section had a steep uphill stretch. Zacharias' horse could not pull the weight and stopped. To help him out, I took half his load on my cart. His horse was exhausted. A little further, we added some more. By the time we reached the uphill stretch of the electricity-producing factory of Hatzopoulos, we had loaded almost all sacks onto my cart. Then, the horse started backwards, pushing cart and Zacharias towards the river bank, nearly 8 meters above the riverbed. I immediately jumped to his aid, placing a large stone to stop his wheels from rolling, grabbing his wheels and preventing him, his horse and his cart from falling into the river.

We finally reached his home, unloaded his grain, each sack about 80 Okas (100 kilos). I reached home around midnight with a tummy ache and sore hands from grabbing the cart's wheels.[214]

Next day (Friday) I woke up to go to Prosotsani. After delivering the grain and returned to the market, a fierce tummy ache began, forcing me to enter the café of John, from Adrianople. He used to be an experienced cart owner and knew the trade, but because of his age and his rheumatism, he became a café owner. He served me 50 drams of cognac and while I was trying to recover, I told him what happened to me the night before.

"Didn't you have a revolver to shoot that blasted horse?" he replied. "It is a very handsome horse, good for shows, but it certainly lacks stamina. I feel sorry for Zacharias." Then he turned to me.

"Come on over. Let me check you out."

He took me in a private room and checked my belly button area. Indeed, my belly button looked different. It was out of its place. He laid me flat, with my knees bent. Then he put a heat-activated suction glass on my belly button. I stayed in his bed for two hours, while John was rubbing my belly with alcohol. He sent someone to take my horse

---

214 A. Boinodiris, Book 1, p.171-172.

and cart to the nearby inn. The horse was unhitched, but it had its bridles on.

I started feeling somewhat better. I got up, and after thanking John, hitched my horse to the cart, and went home. It was about 9 PM.[215] As I got off the horse, ready to unhitch it, two kids run to me. "Mr. Anthony, the men in the square are looking for you."

"What men?"

"Please come."

They took me to the square of PERITHALPSI, where a number of young men of my age were gathered near the police station. Among them were two brothers and fish peddlers, Theophilos and Chris. A lively young police officer from Volos, named Michael was there with police officers George Monastirides and Nick Kanakis. They had a friendly wrestling match. The young police officer wrestled the older police officers to the ground and then he also wrestled the two fish peddlers. The young man was challenging the rest into a wrestling match, chasing them around the square. Theophilos then told the kids to look for me, knowing very well that I used to wrestle in Asia Minor. He knew that I was supposed to come home any time from Prosotsani. He told the young man to stop chasing them and save his energy for me.

I approached and told them about my condition, pleading them to give me a rain check. They would not hear of it. Then Michael comes and taunts me,

"This guy is a halvah," meaning "an easy prey," in front of my father and my brother in law Michael.[216]

"Anthony, give this brat a lesson, will you?" said the rest.

I decided to take him on. With one wrestling maneuver, I pinned him on his back. To avoid hurting him, I got up immediately and started walking home. The young police officer got up and jumped on me from behind. Frustrated, I toss him over me and pin him down with a hand lock until he started pleading with me to let him go.

"Say please..." I responded.

"Please..." I finally went home, unhitched my horse and went in to lie down. "What a day!" I exclaimed.

---

215 A. Boinodiris, Book 1, p.173.
216 A. Boinodiris, Book 1, p.173.

At that time, bridges were scarce, most roads having to cross uphill, sandy stream banks. One such stream bank was that of the river near Doxato, on the main highway from Drama to Kavala. There was a bridge once at that location, but it was destroyed during the war. Looking back at those times, I wonder how poor a nation we were, not having a small bridge between two good-size cities. We suffered, the animals suffered and the whole mess was resolved when the government rebuilt the bridge later on, only to be destroyed again during World War II.

Most carts could not manage to cross these banks, loaded with 1000 Oka load. My horse did. Many times, after crossing I helped others cross it, by unhitching my horse and hitching it to their cart. The buggy users of that time had a code of mutual help, similar to today's truckers. We helped each other and traveled together from place to place in convoys.[217]

I worked, using my horse and cart until I was called in to serve in the military. I was supposed to be called in the spring of 1928. So, early that spring I was forced to sell my beautiful horse, since it would have been too expensive to maintain. The person that bought it used it for another 25 years, making a living with it until well after the war.[218] Shortly after I sold the horse, I found out that the military delayed my calling until the fall of 1928, because of an epidemic disease, called "Dengue."[219]

I (now 23) was drafted to go to the Greek military service in October of 1928, leaving my savings with my mother (banks were not known then). Before leaving, on the same month we engaged Elisabeth's sister, Kyriaki Aslanides to Jordan Zoumboulides from Nea Karvali, the same person that helped me carry my stand. This was Kyriaki's second engagement. The first one, to another fellow from Nea Karvali did not work out, since that fellow was found to be chronically ill. Their wedding followed in November, when I was a rookie in the army.

---

217 A. Boinodiris, Book 1, p.158.

218 A. Boinodiris, Book 1, p.158.

219 A. Boinodiris, Book 4, p. 20. Dengue and dengue hemorrhagic fever (DHF) result from infection by any of four serotypes of dengue viruses. Transmission occurs through the bite of infected Aedes mosquitoes, principally Aedes aegypti, which is also the principal urban vector of yellow fever. Hundreds of thousands of cases of dengue and DHF are reported each year in tropical regions of the Americas, Africa, Asia and Oceania.

My father's coming from Russia was a mixed blessing. I was really happy to see him. Yet, if he did not appear at that time, I would not have served as long as I did, since I would have been the sole supporter of the family. I would have served for three months, trained until I knew how to use a weapon and then the army would let me go home. One of my friends, Theophilos served a short time while his mother and his brother Chris kept the store. He was let go soon after.[220] Now, I had to serve eighteen months and as my luck had in store for me, would get destroyed economically because of my father. I left a grocery to a father that I did not know at all. My father had left me when I was only five years old and came back when I was 22. When I left for the army, the store (consisting of the 3.5x4 meter mobile stand) was full of supplies.[221] When I came back, it was all gone.

VENIZELOS (DRAMA, 1928)

The dictatorship of Pangalos ended when a General, called George Kondylis, nicknamed "lightning" for his fast maneuvering in war, captured Pangalos and Eftaxias with just a pistol in his hand and placed them both in the a jail of Crete, named Tsetin.[222] It seems that Pangalos had burned a few villages there.

Many of his officers, who had helped him come to power, became convinced that he had to be removed.[223] In the elections held a few months later, the republican majority was so small that a coalition government including the royalist Populist Party had to be formed. The coalition

220 A. Boinodiris, Book 1, p.179.
221 A. Boinodiris, Book 1, p.158.
222 "Kondylis was an ambitious man, who did not finish the military academy, yet from an ex-teacher and corporal rises to Prime Minister, with a very short time title of Viceroy. Some compared him with Hitler. He was initially a democrat, later to switch sides and become royalist." A. Boinodiris, Book 1, P.60.
223 In 1930, Pangalos was sent to prison for a building scandal. He remained in prison for two years and was released during a period when Venizelos gave a number of amnesties. He never regained the popular support he had before the coup, and never again played a role in Greek politics. He was accused of collaboration with the Germans in Italians in World War II, but these claims were never substantiated. He unsuccessfully ran for parliament in 1950 and died in Athens two years later. His grandson today is a member of the Parliament.

government finished drafting and, in 1927, promulgated a republican constitution, work on which had been begun in 1925. The royal family was in exile in England. As the government passed through successive crises and was beginning to lose control, in 1928, Venizelos surprised them all by returning to Greek politics. After being appointed prime minister by the temporary president, Admiral Koundouriotis, Venizelos and his Liberal Party won a 90% landslide against Panagiotis Tsaldaris, who was a good and honest politician, but did not have the power of Venizelos. Koundouriotis then became the Prime Minister.[224]

Venizelos, instead of rejoicing at the landslide (in which he had 270 representatives to 30 of the opposition) he called the new government a farce. He could not govern, according to him, without a strong opposition, a necessary condition for having a democratic government. He ordered some of his closest twenty friends to join the opposition party, in spite of their protests. "[225]

Venizelos visited Drama in 1928, in his tour for determining the needs of the nation. He was quite impressive, with his beard and two-cornered hat, as he spoke. He wanted to separate agriculture from tobacco, by helping farmers plant other crops. To do this, the malaria-infested swamps of Macedonia, Thessaly and other parts of Greece had to be cleaned. Drama, especially the southern part of its plain, near Philippi was immersed in water, full of mosquitoes. He impressed upon the people a vision: that they could turn these places into a rich land, capable of feeding Greece, instead of Greece being dependent on foreign grain imports from the United States and Canada.

Several opposition representatives wanted military works, in the form of defensive forts against Bulgaria and Serbia. He defeated such moves, by being one of the few that foresaw that defensive forts, like the Maginot line were useless and economic strength was mightier than any fixed fortification. He contracted an engineering firm from England (Manx Yulen) led by a lead engineer called Hamilton, who established his office at the village of Fotolivos. Hamilton was paid 70,000 drachmas per month, which at that the time was worth 210-pound sterling per month. His second in command was a Greek from Constantinople, called Pandelis Sargos.

---

224 A. Boinodiris, Book 1, p. 60.
225 A. Boinodiris, Book 1, p. 53.

He was being paid half, what Hamilton was getting. I worked six months under Sargos, as a messenger, supplier and mail carrier. When they were measuring the hilly land and riverbanks of Touloumbari and Livaderon I supplied the workers with food, mail messages and diagrams.[226]

The operation proceeded, by using large excavators, bulldozers and paving machines. They formed dykes draining the waters of the Kefalari spring (near Philippi), Santa Barbara spring (inside Drama), and the banks of river Angitis, which was draining into the Strymon River. The areas of Drama, Kavala and Serres were drained with dykes of running water, reducing vastly the breeding grounds of mosquitoes. Similar works were executed in Chrysoupolis of Kavala, near the delta of Nestos River, the plain of Thessaloniki and Gianitsa, the plain of Arta and other works.

DENGUE HEMORRHAGIC FEVER (DRAMA, 1929)

Meanwhile in Drama, a new, plusher subdivision began construction. This was the "Central Subdivision," which started early in 1929. It had bigger lots parceled for sale to refugees that could afford it.

In that period, a strain of malaria, called Dengue Hemorrhagic Fever hit the population with devastating effects. Until the drainage works were completed, mosquitoes ruled over the land. The Army was especially hit hard. Quinine pills were dispersed to everyone. In Drama, a lead physician and pharmacist, called Galopoulos, prepared the quinines locally. He was also from Cyclades and a black marketer. He was stealing the drug from the army and selling it to the farmers, who worked a lot in the mosquito-infested fields and needed plenty of this stuff. The drug was supposed to be dispensed freely to the army, who were getting instead colored placebos.

One day, one psychotic soldier decided to terminate his life. Quinine pills were lethal, if someone gets more than five in one day. Therefore, he eats five and nothing happens. He goes and gets 50, with the same result. He gets so upset for not being able to kill himself that he goes to the local newspaper and spills the beans. Galopoulos decides to escape abroad, but since the Venizelos government had placed him in this position, the heat fell on his administration for the crooked physician.

---

226 A. Boinodiris, Book 1, p. 54.

**Figure 22 Drama, Greece; Wintry Scenery of the Santa Barbara Springs and
Church**

MILITARY SERVICE (DRAMA, JUNE 1929)

I was drafted in the army and had to serve from October 1928 to March 1930.

I was lucky, for I did escape malaria during my whole stay in the Greek Army. Few of us can claim that. I was put in the machine gun corps on the 9th month of the first infantry group of the 26th Brigade in Drama. I was checked out medically and placed in that unit.[227] This was a mobile artillery corps, using mules to carry light artillery pieces in the mountains. These corps would be vital later on in defeating the Italians in World War II. I was trained as a machine gunner on St Etienne, Hotchkiss and Maxim guns. I also was trained on using my personal weapon, a short carbine.

To avoid being an officer and remain in the army longer, I declared second grade of Elementary School education. This was not true, because I completed my fifth grade. In those years, they needed educated people so badly, that they immediately made them officers and kept them in the army for much longer service. This was a lot of hard work in comparison to infantry. You have your own gun, a machine gun, and a mule, all of which you are responsible for. We had to clean the weapons and wash, water and feed our naked mules, three times per day, from the springs of St. Barbara, two miles away from the barracks. We had guard duty for barracks, stables and ammunition. I became used to this hard work, since I worked hard all my life.

It was not the cleaning or the watering, but the riding of bareback mules that was the worst. Riding bareback caused us to have blisters and heat rash on our rear. For this reason, I was praying to God to transfer me elsewhere. Often, I was loaded with that heavy (26-kilo) St. Etienne machine gun on my back and was told to take it up to Korilovo, a hill of over 700 meters high. To exercise, my Sergeant Anthony Georgakopoulos used to take us to marble quarries. His favorite one was the quarry of Giorgantopoulos, where we did aerobic exercises.

He also put us in pairs to wrestle with each other. This was not with the agreement of the lieutenant, but he did not care. In fact, he put one of us on guard, in case some "male goat" showed up unexpectedly. That is what we called "the brass."

---

227 A. Boinodiris, Book 1, p.159.

Soon it was my turn to wrestle. I was good in wrestling, because I had wrestled in Karvali since I was in grammar school. I ended up winning one after the other. In the final match, I had to face a soldier called Moustakas, refugee from Sokia near Smyrna. This was a strong young man, who gave me a lot of trouble before I managed to throw him. Unfortunately, he fell on a hard place and when I turned him to pin his back down, he yelled angrily to me to stop. I had broken his right arm. I got up somewhat embarrassed and helped take him to the Military Hospital.

The lieutenant was now in trouble. I was under Lieutenant Alexander Hatzioannou. To save his platoon commander they blamed the whole event on me. None of the platoon wanted to hurt the officers, so they claimed that it was a friendly fight, in which accidentally I broke Moustakas' arm. As a private, I was not given an opportunity to defend myself. I became extremely upset when I heard Moustakas' mother curse me for hurting her son. It was then that I vowed not to wrestle again in my life, except in self-defense.[228] Lt. Major John Hatzakis did not want to dig further. He consulted with Lt. Colonel George Lavdas and Major Basil Kekas and he simply advised us to be careful and covered it up.

I was relatively good with my carbine. This was a small weapon, much lighter than that of the infantry and used primarily by the cavalry. For four months, we target practiced from 30 to 200 meters continuously. I was always hitting bull's eye and as a reward, I was first in the food line. My officers asked if my father or I were ever a hunter. When I told them that I had never used a weapon before, they were surprised. My commanding officer was Colonel Michael Nicolareas.

The eye doctor, named Pistolas, checked me out. He affirmed that I had excellent eyesight and good reflexes. They decided to send me to Athens, for a national competition. I was also good with the machine gun. As targets, we had a moving, large flag-like cloth, with horizontal stripes of three different colors, green on top, black in the middle and white on the bottom. The objective was to hit black only. After a competition, where all my rounds ended on black, General Kimisis came and gave me personally congratulations. Although I was recognized as a sharpshooter and wrestler in my unit, when the time came for becoming a specialist I asked to be transferred as a harness technician to the military supply depot of Drama.

---

228 A. Boinodiris, Book 1, p.160.

I was learning to cut and sew reigns and saddles for the mounted infantry. At that time, this was the equivalent of mechanized infantry today. I spent another four months there and learned a lot. There were 24 men in the saddle making shop. Five of them knew the trade from their parents, who were in the saddle making business. In the whole company of 120 men, there was only one person that had even attended high school. His name was Palas and he was a gun machinist. The rest had very little schooling, if any at all. Some could not even sign their names.

I felt sorry for many that could not read and write and helped them with letters home. Soon the officer found out about my lie and put me in an office, to be an accountant of the supply depot.

Palas and I were put on daily report duty to the brass, alternating each week. Reports included such things as who was put on report, which soldier was put on commendation, etc. In addition, I had to do all the paperwork of my lead saddle making technician, a commissioned lieutenant. This lieutenant was a family man with three children and needed help. At the end of the day, he left his office and went home, leaving all the work on my shoulders. This work included orders for saddles, reigns and other parts, raw material orders and tools. A sergeant, George Koros, was a good technician but he was a pain in the butt. He was the one who decided that I had enough time to cover the lieutenant's office work as well.

One day, after my three months of training ended, a messenger arrived from the 26th Regiment (that of Drama) with a request to the Commander of Military Provisions. The request was from a Colonel, asking the Commander to send Anthony Boinodiris to be present on the National Rifle and Machine Gun Marksmanship Competition in Athens, since he was recognized as a top sharpshooter of the Regiment. I left my office and ran to the Commander, who was a Lt. Colonel. After a proper salute, I show him the message. After seeing the note he said:[229]

"Congratulations my son; it is a great honor to have the best sharpshooter in the Regiment in the Unit of Military Provisions. You need to bring this to the attention of your lieutenant. Then, go and report this message to the technical core. After that, clean your weapons put clean clothes on and report to the regiment. They will give you orders to travel by train to Athens."

---

229 A. Boinodiris, Book 1, p.162.

I came to the technical core. When I reported the news, sergeant Koros was upset. He went straight to the lieutenant. "Anthony is trying to destroy your livelihood," he said.

The lieutenant hit the roof. Then read the letter carefully.

"The Regiment is not ordering us. They are making a request. We get our orders from Division Headquarters."

Then he turns to me.

"I am sorry Anthony, but we have need of you here at the office. If I guess correctly, you will not make it to Athens."

And so it was. The Commander called me to his office:

"I am sorry son that you will not see Athens. I would have really liked to see us get a medal in our unit. But your lieutenant objected, because of the great amount of work he has for you."

I started crying from grief. From that day on, I vowed to leave that unit, which made me lose a chance for a medal. The second best in our brigade, someone called George Veranis from Doxato, got the silver medal. From what I heard about Veranis, the Bulgarians killed him during the brutal massacre of 1941.[230] Being upset with my officer, I asked for a transfer.[231] Now I was a specialist in making all fittings for animals, required to carry field artillery, from burden saddles, to leather straps. We had many animals to outfit. They were enough, to require a fully equipped workshop, with many technicians.

While I was in the army, I met my father's first cousin, George, youngest son of Father Kalinikos. He was a great Marathon runner and about the same age as I. He came first in covering the Marathon from Eleftheroupolis to Kavala in 1928. He later became a shoemaker in Athens and had four children.

After four months, I asked for a transfer. In spite of protests from the lieutenant, I was transferred to Komotini, as harness technician of the 12th Division. The commander there was the Lt. General Kotoulas. The captain was a man from Smyrna, called Tsiparis. I stayed 15 days on a company of new transferees, finding out all the ropes, including local saddle makers, Greeks and Greeks of Turkish origin. Then, I was asked to be part of a new saddle shop, since none was available in Komotini. The Lt. Major in charge of the workshop was Constantine

---

230 See "Andros Odyssey- The Return, 1940-1997," by Stavros Boinodiris.
231 A. Boinodiris, Book 1, p.161, 163.

Exarchopoulos. He was partially deaf, having lost his hearing from an explosion in World War I. His chief technician was Emmanuel Emmanuilides, who ran the gun shop.

In June of 1929, when I came home on leave, I found my store closed and my mother alone in a newly purchased, two-room home. I asked her to give me more details.

Figure 23 Anthony Boinodiris while in his Military Service.[232]

---

232 A Note behind it says: "Komotini, 13 Nov 1929. Dear parents, Merry Christmas. I am sending you this photo (object without a soul) as a memory of my military life."

A Destructive Father (Drama, June 1929)

"What happened to my store?"

My mother told me that my father became bankrupt. He was now working harvesting wheat for wages. He gave credit to all who wanted to buy, but were unwilling to pay. By then, the family had very little to eat, since the store was empty and his wages very small.

I knew that I had to restrict my father's actions otherwise my family would starve.

"Mother, in nine months I will be out of the army. He wasted the store, but with the money I gave you, I will buy another horse and cart and we will recover. We will restart my business."

When my mother started crying, I became alarmed.

"Why are you crying mom?"

She would not talk. "What happened mom?"

Then, after pressuring her she told me.[233]

My father forced my mother to give him all of my savings (15000 Drachmas) for a horse (9000 Drachmas) and cart (6000 Drachmas), which he spent. My existing cart he sold with a 500 Drachmas down payment to Nikos Skabanis from Adriani, a known crook who never paid for it. This was all my money, saved working in the water carrying business. I discovered that my father had no head for business and my mother was too gullible and trusted him too much. He loaned my money to people that never paid him back. He gave credit to an untrustworthy person, called Anestis Katemides who also never paid him back. He managed to buy also a small house in PERITHALPSI in his name, with my own money, and left me without a drachma. This forced me to move in with him after my service.

While on leave, I became furious and had violent arguments with my father. How could I have known what kind of a person my father was, when he left me when I was seven years old?[234] How could I have imagined that I had left a wolf to guard sheep?

The following Sunday, after I found out about my father's doings, a teacher named Mirodes approaches me at church. Mirodes was working on a summer job, weighing and making inventory of the wheat harvesting. "I saw your father work in the wheat harvester. I admired

233 A. Boinodiris, Book 1, p.167-168.
234 A. Boinodiris, Book 1, p.152, 167.

his strength and stamina," he confided to me. Then he continued. "He worked very hard. The only problem he had was with the swearing of the Greeks from Southern Greece. Those people blaspheme, using Holy Personages. He hates swearing, but mostly one directed against Saints. He got so upset, that he attacked a whole bunch of them at once, flattening many on the ground. It seems that the heat of the sun hit him on the head some. When the rest saw four of them with broken noses on the ground, they backed off."

When I came home, after my encounter with Mirodes, the family was asleep. I found out on Monday morning that he did not tell his family about the event.

I saw Mirodes that morning and he told me that my father did not collect his pay that week. It seems that among the people that he attacked, the paymaster was one of them. I grabbed my father. "Let's go to get your pay."

When the paymaster saw me in my uniform with my father, he did not say anything. He just handed him the envelope with his money.[235]

MY ARMY CONNECTION (DRAMA, SPRING 1930)

The Komotini Division had other shops, like gun shop, cart shop, smith shop, etc., but not a saddle shop. The unit was forced to use civilian shops in Komotini, as a temporary measure.

The Lt. Major showed me an empty room, which was to be used as the shop and told me to get it going. There were no tools and no materials. I ordered all the tools and material from the Army Depot, which came in ten days. I brought them over by cart and started putting out new saddles, with numbers, with shoes, based on the animal type and size. I ordered wood from private shops and tailor-fitted saddles and bridles carefully for each animal. I had hundreds of orders all of them fulfilled satisfactorily. I was then assigned two soldiers of Turkish origin. Their parents were indeed saddlers. To summarize my time in Komotini, I had a great time there.

One day I was told to report to Lt. General Kotoulas. After cleaning up and getting dressed, I went to Kotoulas' office at Division Headquarters. After knocking and told to come in, I stepped inside. To

235 A. Boinodiris, Book 1, p. 168.

my surprise, my uncle Charalambos was sitting near Kotoulas, sipping coffee together. After saluting, Kotoulas asked me about myself.

"Where are you from, son?"

"From Drama, sir..."

"Any family there...?"

"Yes, sir"

"Who...?"

"My parents, sister, a baby brother and my fiancé, sir..."

"Do you want to visit your fiancée?"

I was stunned, and then smiled somewhat embarrassed. "Yes sir."

He looked at Charalambos. "Yes, he is my nephew," Charalambos said. "He is the oldest son of my brother George."

"Yes, but why is his name different than yours?"

"That's a long story. My name is now Pavlides; but before that, it was Boyun-egri-oglou. I changed it to escape the Bulgarian and Turkish reprisals during troubling times. Pavlides was used because my father's name was Paul. You know how the bureaucrats like to alter names of people from Asia Minor. They turned it into ..." he looked at me, "what is your last name Anthony?"

"Boinodiris, uncle..."

Kotoulas laughed heartily, as he was getting up. "Is he as crazy as you?"

Charalambos started laughing too. "What do you expect? He is my blood." He went to the next office, still laughing and asked his secretary to give me a 15-day leave. Soon, I had my orders in my hands. I thanked them both and exited.

I found out later that the two served in the front of Asia Minor against the Turks. Kotoulas seems to have been a man of action, achieving the rank of Lt. Colonel by his war deeds. Of course, Charalambos was a common farmer now, but Kotoulas respected Charalambos more than he respected his superiors. The two fought side-by-side in the Plastiras Regiment. In 1922, their Regiment, left without supplies had to retreat from the center of Asia Minor all the way to Smyrna, fighting its way through hostile territory. Then they were transferred to Chios, given supplies, regrouped and taken to Evros River, where they held their ground.[236]

---

236 A. Boinodiris, Book 1, p.166.

I was in Drama on 6 January 1930, on the eve of Epiphany for 15 days.

After my leave, I returned to my unit. From that time on, Kotoulas was my friend.

The army fed me, clothed me and housed me. I even had enough time in my hands to go and work out in the city, in civilian saddle shops and earn my pocket money. I spent little, mostly in cinemas or in bakeries, to take care of my sweet tooth cravings. As a result, I had left all my money in my mother's care untouched, or so I thought.

I was soon told that I was eligible to be commissioned as a professional soldier, since I was a specialist. Emmanuilides pleaded with me:

"Anthony, please sign up. We badly need technicians like you."

"I am engaged Emmanuel."

"So much the better; I will become your best man."

"I have a whole family in Drama. They depend on me."

I made a mistake for not staying there. If I knew how bad the years ahead would be, I would have signed up. If I knew that the upcoming crisis would be so severe, I would not have hesitated to stay in the army. How could I predict that it would be so bad that it would not allow anybody with debts to repay us and we would be completely broke. I also felt sorry for my father and his young children. As a result, I returned to Drama to help him out.[237] I am sure that after I disclosed that I had fifth grade elementary education in Asia Minor, the army would give me a rank (a corporal or sergeant) and even may have helped me go to school.

When it was time to be discharged from the army, I found my replacement, George Vamvakas, another immigrant from Asia Minor. George was a saddle maker, living in Komotini. After I certified him, I got my discharge papers. I started regretting my decision the instant I was handed my papers and told that I was a civilian now.

STARTING A FAMILY (DRAMA, CHRISTMAS 1930)

When I was discharged from the army at the end of March of 1930, the store was dissolved and there was no stock on the shelves. At that

---

237 A. Boinodiris, Book 1, p.164.

time, my father would make his living by being a common laborer. He wasted all my savings of 10,000 drachmas, and another 8000 drachmas from the sale of the cart. After forcing my mother to give him my money, he loaned the money to a crooked fellow and the cart to another one, never to see them again. By the time I came out of the army, I was economically destroyed.[238]

While I was in the army (or shortly after) two new children were born by my mother Evanthia, Paul Boidaris (1928) and Georgia Boidaris (26th December 1930). When my father arrived, the bureaucracy managed to give him a yet different name than mine, namely "George Boidaris." That is why my brother and sister had different last names, a common occurrence in those times.[239]

When I came out of the army, the great depression, which started in America, hit Greece in full force. Depression affected Greece, to a degree, not unlike that of many other countries of the West. Workers that had pay coming were not paid due to bankruptcies. Cash was scarce. Loans were cut on 24 October of 1929 and slowly, until 1931, the economic depression spread from the United States into Europe.[240]

In 1930, I married Elisabeth Aslanoglou, attaining my ultimate achievement. I liked Elisabeth a lot and if you like something or someone, you sacrifice personal freedom and act irrationally fast to get what you like. Achievement is attained with some sacrifices and marriage is quite an achievement. Human freedom is associated with likes, not needs. A human that likes something is willing to sacrifice even freedom to get it. As wedding presents, among other items Elisabeth received two Singer sewing machines. These machines became our salvation in times of need. My new family now embraced the Aslanides clan.

When Fevronia became of age, she inherited Marianthi's sock knitting machine and started making socks.[241] In 1931, Michael Aslanides married Urania Rafailides, daughter of Charalambos and Despina from Kalos Agros, all immigrants from Pontus. As a result, the Aslanides family was left with Makrina and Marianthi working, Basil and Fevronia in school. They now had two members married,

238 A. Boinodiris, Book 4, p.20.
239 A. Boinodiris, Book 1, p.151.
240 A. Boinodiris, Book 4, loose attachment A1.
241 The author remembers that machine, located in the family room when he visited Fevronia's house, thirty years later.

Michael and Elisabeth. Basil was very artistic. He often went to villages around Drama, making toys for children (shadow-theater figurines of Karagiozis, and others) coming back loaded with eggs as a payment.[242]

In my family, Irene was a 17-year-old teenager. When I returned home, the store was dissolved and I had to start from scratch. I found nothing right. Every item in the store was gone and not replaced. What was left was only some school supplies, canned goods and sealed bottles.

My small grocery store went under, because the workers could not pay for their purchases. My clients owed me 70,000 drachmas (210 gold sterling), when the store closed. I owed 2500 drachmas to my suppliers, which had to be paid off. The store was empty. The other storeowner of the area, Tzoras asked to borrow from my father the empty wine and ouzo large containers. He loaned them to him not knowing how much trouble the person caused me when I was setting up my store. Later, he completely denied that the containers were ours.

I was broke because of my father. We started selling nuts and school supplies in the store.[243]

After my discharge, I started doing odd jobs, waiting for summer to go into ice cream business. Naturally, I had no capital to get started. I had to get some money. After Easter I went to the annual fair of Zoodohos Pigi at Monastiraki, a village north of Drama, loaded with two ice-cream barrels of about 60 Okas. It took me a long time to carry that load to the village through the ravines of Damnatza, formed by the gulch of the river that crosses the city of Drama. As I was struggling to carry them uphill, I started crying, feeling sorry for myself.

"Why me God...?" I yelled. "I left a fortune in a store, prior to going to the army. I left it to my father, a father that as a good Christian I was taught to respect and honor. I am trying to form a family. I am engaged to a great girl for three years now. I have not even gone to bed with her, just as a good Christian is supposed to do before their marriage. What did I do wrong and you punish me so?"

I was yelling on the road to Monastiraki, looking at the sky and receiving no answer. I was devastated and angry.[244]

---

242 A. Boinodiris, Book 1, p. 58 and Book 4, p. 34-35.
243 A. Boinodiris, Book 4, p. 34-35 and Book 4, p. 34-35.
244 A. Boinodiris, Book 4, p. 33-34.

Why did I have to have a father like that? Why did he turn out to be so mean and destroyed me economically within 22 months? Why did I ever send him the visa to Russia? I did not blame his customers. They came in and started shopping, initially with cash, later on credit promising to pay as soon as they got the next paycheck. When the next paycheck did not come, they were begging my father to extend their time. When the store was empty, they were gone forever. I advised my father on this, but he never listened. He knew better. I kept on going to fairs like that, trying to survive by selling ice cream, which was carried on my shoulder.

In the summer of 1930, 50% of the tobacco was sold. Half of the workers went to work. This was a good omen. After the 17th of August 1930 I was married and living with my father's family in a two-room house of PERITHALPSI. By Christmas of 1930, my mother gave birth to a little girl, that she named Georgia. Paul was a two-year old then. Irene was a 19-year old girl. My father got a place to stay with my money, but we were forced to live with him, all of us cramped in two rooms, soon with my new, now pregnant bride Elisabeth.

LOOKING FOR A SHACK (DRAMA, JANUARY 1930)

I went to a lumberyard and asked more wood to make a shack for storing charcoal. All heating those days was done in charcoal pots (mangali), which were lit outside and then placed indoors, to heat up the space. These pots were lethal, generating plenty of carbon monoxide if the people did not wait before bringing them indoors. Even then, they generated some amount of carbon dioxide. Yet, most houses were not well sealed and the natural aeration from the cracks prevented massive number of deaths. These pots were used for small space heating, cooking, roasting and heating hot water bottles, which were inserted in beds, under the bed covers. Bedrooms had no heating at all at nights.

The charcoal shack I was planning required a permit, which even if the city issued it to me, it would cost so much money, that we did not have. What was yet worse, the city stopped giving permits because the subdivision was becoming a shantytown. The lumberyard owner, named Kioses gave me the price of the lumber. I did not have the cash with me. I promised to send my father with the cart and the remaining payment, since I had to run on an errant that was paying well. And so I did. I gave my father the rest of the money and told him:

"Take the cart, pay Kiose and load all the lumber and the tin roof I ordered. Remember, do not come from Chrysostomou Street, since that storeowner Tzoras will bring the police on us and stop us from expanding the store. Come from the side road, in front of the Magioglou house. We cannot build the shack next to the store in the square, because that is next to the police station. Our neighbors agreed to help us raise it in our back yard at night."[245]

Naturally, I needed the shack next to my store, not behind the house. Being poor refugees, most people evaded paying for permits when they built added spaces. They also helped each other in any such endeavor to survive looking at the government as a bunch of meddling bureaucrats that wanted to make the poor folks pay, so that they can keep their jobs.

TZORAS (DRAMA, JANUARY 1931)

My father decided to do his thing, in spite of my warnings. He loaded the cart and paraded it in front of Tzoras' store. I see him from a distance driving his cart on Chrysostomou Street. In fact he stopped in the middle of serving a customer, came out and asked my father in Russian:

"What do you have there George? What are you going to do with it?"

"We are going to put a shed behind our house," my father replied.

"I don't believe you."

When my father came home, I became furious. "You really wrote my advice on the soles of your old shoes, didn't you?"

When we started building the shack the next day, Tzoras appeared, pretending to buy some eggs from Peter Katsikopoulos next door. From his wife he asked details about our operation.

"What is Anthony doing back there?"

"I don't know and I don't care. They can do whatever they want in their land."

---

245 A. Boinodiris, Book 1, p. 175.

The next day he appeared again and asked the carpenter, named Panagiotis:

"What are you building?"

"They need a shed. It is a large family and they need the space. Anyway, it is not any of your business and I don't need you as my supervisor."

I heard all this and decided to delay the raising of the shack for a week, so that the whole thing is forgotten. Meanwhile, I noticed that Tzoras was around us day and night, so that when we moved to raise it, he could go to the police and stop us.

Finally one night, around one in the morning, Demosthenes Tselepides, Michael Aslanides, Lazarus Oreopoulos, Charalambos Kirtsekides, Stefanos Ectaroglou, the carpenter Panagiotis, my father and I started raising the shed. I made a T with some studs and raised the electric cables so that we would not hit them. The rest were loaded with the pre-built shack and started on Chrysostomou Street. Unfortunately, Tzoras was on watch that night. He placed a chair across from us and was snoozing with one eye open. When he saw the activity, he ran straight to the police. In the police station were two police officers, one of them a sergeant, named Andreas Pitsikas while the other was someone called Dimitris Kelesakos. Both of them were sleeping when Tzoras pounded on their door and started yelling for their intervention. They thought that somebody was on fire or was being killed, so they were not dressed fully. They had pants on, but no top or hat. Tzoras was running up front, urging them to hurry, while they were trying to catch up and find out what was going on. Meanwhile, most of the shed was already up.

"He is trying to expand his store."

'Who…?" the sergeant asked.

"Anthony; hurry up; you can sleep tomorrow. If you don't stop him, I will report you tomorrow to your commander."

As they approached, I became furious and attacked him, only to be held by the police officers. He was on the ground. "You are a Judas and a hypocrite. You, having a family of two have expanded your shack four times illegally, and we said nothing. We, with eight souls are trying to survive with one shack and you have bellyaches. I was destroyed because I had to serve as a soldier, making sure you are safe. If you try to destroy me, I will burn you. If I don't, my name is not Anthony."

"If you don't take him in, I will file a complaint against you both."

The sergeant talked to the police officer privately and then loudly asked the police officer to take me in. The police officer quietly obeyed. As I was led downtown, around 2 A.M., the police officer turned to me. "Listen to me Anthony. We feel sorry for you. We hate that person. If I take you in, you will get 2000 to 3000 Drachmas fine. I do not know whether you have that money, but if you disappear for ten days, we can make sure that nothing happens. He is very busy and will eventually forget the whole thing. Do you agree?"

"Does the sergeant agree?"

"Yes. He suggested it to me himself."

"I agree; thank you officer."

I went home to sleep. In a few hours, I was on my way to Nea Karvali, staying at the house of my cousin Galaktides for ten days.[246] Since that day, my fury put a bug in me for revenge one day. It never passed from my mind to hurt him physically, but I had to find a way to hurt him monetarily. If I did not do anything, the act of passiveness would eat me up.

I remember the events with that scum that I had to deal with, like yesterday. A great number of these nasty people were destroyed later on, in the Greek civil war. At that time, people went on revenge, killing, or accusing them to others who killed anyone who had done them wrong in the past. I was not the only one who ran into trouble. From that moment on, the jealous and greedy Tzoras was in trouble. The neighborhood, the police and even his own relatives, like his brother-in-law Mirodes would not talk to him.

After the ten days were up, I came back from Karvali and put out the rumor that the police kept me ten days in jail and had to pay a fine. The police had no orders to tear down the shack, which I proceeded to complete. I started selling charcoal that winter, while all other sales activities stopped. The store was kept, but we were not making any money.

I found out later that the police officers Pitsikas and Kelesakos turned and started harassing Tzoras. In a period of six months, the

---

246 A. Boinodiris, Book 1, p. 178.

police placed seven citations against Tzoras. The more the police harassed him, the more he hated me. Some of the citations were very severe and he had to pay large fines. One of them was especially serious. He was so driven to desperation, that one night he entered his store pulling the roll of the store behind him. Then he proceeds to tie a hanging rope on his roof beam. He rubbed soap on the rope, climbed up on a chair, put the noose around his neck and kicked the chair. As soon as he did that, his brother appeared, rolling up the store roll. He hurried up and pushed him up just in time to save him.

"What are you doing? What is wrong with you?"

"I can't live like that any more. The police cannot let me breathe."

The following morning, his two brother-in-laws, Constantinides and Mirodes, together with his brother Christopher went to the police station and filed a complaint to the commander against Pitsikas and Kelesakos. The two police officers were transferred very soon to Kalifitos. I found out later that Andreas Pitsikas was killed on duty, trying to save a man from a drunk that wielded a knife.[247]

Had Tzoras succeeded in committing suicide, I might have had an easier time with his successor. Tzoras was a man who was jealous, and eager to get rich over someone else's misfortune.[248]

We had to find something to make money. We had no money for a horse and cart, so we bought a small-bodied male donkey. We named the donkey "Kitsos." We tried selling charcoal, but we faced competition from the producers, who sold it in retail at the same price we were getting it wholesale. Then we started using Kitsos for peddling small articles to mountain villages. He was small but fast and able to carry twice its weight in loads. The trek to the mountains was done either by me, or by my father. The villages at the plains had no money, since tobacco was not selling. The only people that had food were the shepherds in the mountains. They had animals and their by-products, which we could barter with. My father did well there, since he was treating every kid with candy. The only currency the villagers could use to pay for goods was eggs. My father did not distinguish small, medium or large eggs. An egg was an egg to him.[249]

247 A. Boinodiris, Book 1, p. 208.
248 A. Boinodiris, Book 1, p. 209 and Book 4, p. 47-48.
249 A. Boinodiris, Book 1, p. 178.

My friend, Theophilos, who later became a fish peddler, one day met with Tzoras.

"Listen Tzora, Anthony is my friend and a good neighbor. He has the right to make a living, as much as anyone else. He has a large family that needs food on the table. Besides my groceries, I do not sell fruit, so that Anthony can make a living selling fruit. George, his father is an old man who is forced to plow the mountains to sell in villages of less than 50 families. It is very rough for them. Give them a break and stop selling fruit. There are too many of us here. "

"I will tell you Theophilos. If he comes to Christopher's (his brother) café and treats us as many beers as we can drink, I will stop selling fruit."

"Are you serious?"

"Yes."

Theophilos told me. I decided to take him on. The café was in front of the Drama High School before a cedar forest was planted there. The three of us consumed 200 Drachmas worth of beer. I paid for it in spite of my poverty. We left, with his promise to stop selling fruit. I hoped to be able to make some cash after Easter of 1931. I got me a stand, where I started selling cherries, then moved to apricots and pears. When melon season came around June, I saw Tzoras walk to me, while I was placing them on the stand.

"I changed my mind Anthony. I cannot pass up the opportunity to sell fruit."

"But, you promised…"

"I know what I promised, but I changed my mind. Show me where I signed such promise. "

Then he came closer. "I have though an offer for you. You let me get fruit from you for my family without pay and I will delay selling it; with one stipulation though, do not tell Theophilos on our agreement."

I was dumbfounded. I knew extortion when I saw it. I had no economic strength to withstand such an attack. If he opened up a fruit stand, I would be ruined.

"I agree only to one Oka fruit per day; no more."

I kept my promise and did not tell Theophilos. He was coming and buying fruit from me regularly, paying for it, like everyone else. This extortion went on from June to October. The fruit season finished, but

I still had 50 sturdy watermelons that I was selling to workers toiling in construction work in the area. I also had some second-grade grapes from Larissa and some beaten up apples from Volos. Tzoras walks in; without talking, he grabs a watermelon and is about to leave. My anger took over my better sense.

"You put that watermelon down Tzora. You are welcome to some apples or grapes."

He put the watermelon down. As he departed, I heard: "I will show you."

Next day, Tzoras brought a whole cart full of fruit, including tangerines, oranges, apples and whatever else he could get in the market. When Theophilos saw it, he started doing the same. I was forced to start traveling more frequently to the mountain villages.

At this time, the ex-Turkish stores, which were part of the exchange agreement, went on the auction block. The government also made accommodations for loans, requiring you to pay only 25% as down payment. My father and mother also were given a reparation grant of 7000 Drachmas each. If I added my money to their money, we would get a proper store, like Theophilos did, but unfortunately my delinquent father wasted it all.

THE GREAT DEPRESSION (DRAMA, 1931)

Tobacco sales dropped drastically during the Great Depression. Since our region was exclusively dependent on tobacco, it was hit the hardest. Our farmers were not planting wheat or corn, but only tobacco.[250] By the time our farmers were trained to plant new crops, the crisis was over. Fortunately, Venizelos had started the agricultural infrastructure for the conversion to occur. All the swamps of the Philippi plain were now dry, ready to be planted with wheat, corn and other produce. The conversion was taking time. Meanwhile, tobacco prices fell to five drachmas per Oka. In the past, the lowest quality tobacco sold for 80 drachmas per Oka, while the best quality (from Kyrgia or Xanthi) sold for 150 drachmas per Oka. Rumanian corn was purchased for two drachmas per Oka, since American corn was out of reach at five drachmas per Oka (same price as the tobacco). The bakeries were selling

---

250 The government of Greece went into bankruptcy between the years of 1930 an1935 (A. Boinodiris)

corn bread for one drachma per slice (like we used to buy fancy sweets) so that people do not die from hunger.[251]

We opened the grocery store, but there were no buyers. We were newlyweds with a baby, waiting for someone to come with cash and purchase something, so that we could buy some bread. Meanwhile, I had to support eight souls, not only my family, but also my mother, father, my sister Irene (17) and my two siblings Paul and Georgia. My father was of no use, but I was taught to respect and provide for our elders, even if they were worthless.

It was around that time that I discovered that my father was by no means faithful to my mother while he lived in Russia. I discovered that during his 15 years in Russia he had married there and had another family there, which he proceeded to abandon, as he did us. I could only rationalize his actions, based on what my grandfather Paul -a wise old man- had taught me. I still remember his words:

"The fundamental clause of our Greek culture is to focus on improving humanity unbounded by time and space. As human beings, we are given certain gifts. These gifts could be a strong, reproductive body, a keen mind, and other combined attributes that make each one of us unique. These gifts did not happen by chance. They are the result of eons of struggle by our ancestors, who lived and died struggling to make you what you are. You may criticize them now, but if you lived in their time and had their limitations, physical or mental, you probably would have acted the same way. As a result, you must respect your ancestors, no matter how badly they behaved. You also owe it to your species to try to contribute to their struggle. You cannot sit idly and simply take all these gifts without giving some benefits to newer generations. If you idle, you are a thief, who steals from your own species and heritage. Inactivity and ignorance are not bliss. They speed up the destruction of humanity. A lifetime does not bound human progress, if everyone adds something in improving our lives. Location does not bound human progress either. You can go anywhere and do your best, setting the stage for the next generations, wherever you are. That is our culture; it is your inheritance, and one must try to relay it to the next generations."

---

251 A. Boinodiris, Book 4, p.20-21.

I was ashamed of him, but could do nothing about it. It was not my doing, but my father's. I owed him respect, no matter how bad his behavior seemed to be. In addition, when I found out about my father, I tried to push it aside, claiming that I was too busy in my daily survival. Yet, I now realize that subconsciously it was burning me out.

In 1930 and 1931, the economic crisis was at its peak. Tobacco crops were unsold. The government bought it for very little (about 5 drachmas per Oka – or 2.5 kilos) and proceeded to burn it. Workers were laid off. The farmers had to buy mildewed Rumanian corn, destined for animals, in order to feed their families. In Drama's square, the peddlers sold bread by the slice, one drachma per slice.

A sack of 50 Oka flour cost a gold sterling.[252] In Russia, people starved because the government took all production for export, leaving very small quantities for people to eat. They were selling flour, worth seven drachmas per Oka at our ports for one drachma per Oka. Venizelos realized what was going on. They were selling the flour for less than its transportation costs, to compete with the Americans.

He immediately declined purchases of the flour, asking the Russian Communists to take it back and feed their people. The Communists were furious. The Russian captains were ordered not take it back. Instead, they dumped it in the sea. For several years, we had a bumper crop of fish that benefited from that act. Venizelos was also tough against the new Communists, by passing a law prohibiting their propaganda in Greece.

In 1930, the relationship between Greece and Turkey improved. Kemal Ataturk changed the whole structure of Turkey, by changing the letters from Arabic to Latin, the calendar to that of the West and giving liberty to women. Many from the opposition, like Topal Osman, who was a menace to the Greeks, were hanged. Kemal invited Venizelos and his staff to Ankara. They had a formal dance; each Prime Minister danced with the other's wife. They promised friendship and cooperation. It was then, that St. Sophia stopped being a minaret and became a museum. Each reiterated that they had interests on populations in the other's territory. Constantinople had 120,000 Greeks then. Western Thrace had 80,000 Turks.

---

252 Each Oka cost seven drachmas.

Village Peddlers (Drama, Spring 1932)

By 1931, the good omens of 1930 frizzled as the economy worsened. After John was born on October 5, 1931 Elisabeth had a tough time living in the same two-room house with her mother in law's family. The situation became unbearable. We were seven people in a house of less than 30 square meters. That means that we had about foursquare meters per person. We decided to rent a small place near by.

We looked for a place at the Central Neighborhood, near the northern cistern (now a little park). The owner asked for 250 drachmas per month. I had no means of paying 200. We had to find another place for 150. The owner of this place was John Katemides.

My son John was born on 5 October of 1931, in the midst of hunger. The winter was upon us and I had no money to purchase wood for fuel. Fortunately, a friend from the army from Xiropotamos named John helped us out in our time in need. Every other day, he managed to bring me an animal-load of birch-wood at the store. I cut the wood in front of the store and brought it home on my back. This saved us from freezing that winter. Elisabeth, with the new baby was doing the wash for the baby change. My sister-in-law Marianthi and my mother-in-law Makrina were helping her out once in awhile.

Irene came to me one day crying. "What is going to happen to us, now that you left?"

"What do you mean?"

"Father goes to the villages but does not bring enough money for us. He eats out, but when it comes to bring something for us to eat, he does not. Mother does not have enough to feed us. I must go to work; otherwise mother will not have food for Paul and Georgia on the table."

"Fine; what do you want me to do about it?" I responded. "Go and see if you can find some work."

Irene kept on crying. "Do you know of anyone that could use me?"

"Wait a minute," Elisabeth intervened. "I am out of work, since I have my baby to look after. Why doesn't Irene use my work permit, until I am ready to work?"

We agreed to do exactly that, even though it was illegal. Irene started working at the tobacco factories instead of Elisabeth. After some months of work though, Irene's illegal work permit was discovered and 750 days of benefits were deducted from Elisabeth as a penalty.

Little John got sick. Nikos Kutahialis brought the doctor, because I had no money for him. He checked him out and declared: "The child's mother must have had the malaria and transferred it to the child. The child will possibly be deprived from normal growth, but he is healthy. He will recover with the medicine I am prescribing and may maintain his growth with some good nutrition."

Indeed, we recalled that Elisabeth had gone to Nea Karvali. She stayed for two months there at the house of her uncle Kyriakos Tsekmezoglou, while she was pregnant. It was there that she had contracted the malaria. Now, medicine was available, but good nutrition was not. Where could I find money for good nutrition? I barely had money to buy two loaves of bread. Meat was 40 drachmas per kilo, about one-quarter of my monthly rental. Beans and bread were our main staples. Everyone was starving, including my landowner John Katemides. He and his wife Katina were struggling as tobacco factory workers to feed themselves and their boy. They were begging me to pay my rent on a daily basis (5 drachmas per day) so that they can eat themselves.

No matter how I express myself, none can fathom the hunger of those days in 1931, unless they have lived through hunger themselves. While we had the store, I was purchasing goods from a Jewish merchant named Abraham Cohen. After going bankrupt, I owed him 2500 drachmas that I could not repay. People owed me 70000 drachmas, which was never paid to me because of the economic crisis. I was so ashamed, that every time I saw him I changed direction, so that I would not have to face him.[253]

The men of the family decided to go to the mountainous villages, peddling goods bartered for foodstuff. It was then, that we found our base at Taxiarchis. Taxiarchis is a village to the north of Drama, near the Nestos River. We spent the winter of 1931-1932 traveling the mountain villages of Drama. The customers would be villagers, but primarily those that are called Saracatsanei, a local, ancient Macedonian group of people that still lived nomadic lives. They move around with their animals to seek suitable pastures because the mountainous areas do not have adequate sustenance in one location. These people produced

---

253 A. Boinodiris, Book 4, p. 74-75.

wool, cheese, hides and meat, which can be traded for flour, tools, pharmaceuticals and other products.[254]

On 25 February 1932, we were late coming down from the village of Rezenik, eight hours from Drama. We decided to sleep in a friend's house at Taxiarchis. It belonged to Joachim and his father's George. George had an ugly face and was married to his second wife, a very religious woman. Every time we were peddling small items in that village, she was treating us to lunch. Joachim was also married and had two small boys. They took Kitsos (our little donkey) and us in and they warmed us up. Kitsos ate well in the stable. We were talking at dinnertime, when Joachim proposed in front of his wife:[255]

"Why don't you rent our old store on the main road of the village, near the church? The store could be your base for the distant villages, so that you do not have to transport your products that far."

"How much do you rent it for?"

"300 Drachmas per month..."

"I will agree on 200 Drachmas per month."

"No; it is not worth it to me."

Then, George's wife intervened.

"They are going to help the village by serving us with a store. Why don't you agree for 250 Drachmas per month?"

"Alright; when are you moving in?"

"I am coming in on the first of March."

"Fine; it will be ready for you."

"How much deposit do you want?"

"I don't need a deposit. Your word is good enough."

"Let's shake on it."

Therefore, we did. We tried again to talk them into putting earnest money, but they refused. We found out that they had attempted to run that store themselves, but they failed miserably.[256] We saw the old store, which had space in a back room to sleep, and a kitchen behind it.

That last week of February, we hired Lazarus Oreopoulos who had a cart, peddling goods in villages for 150 Drachmas to carry our material to Taxiarchis. We loaded tools, goods to sell, beds and clothes

254 A. Boinodiris, Book 4, p. 36.
255 A. Boinodiris, Book 1, p. 183.
256 A. Boinodiris, Book 1, p. 192 and Book 4, p. 37.

and took them to the village. We planned to stack up the general store with a variety of goods, from tools, to soap and to medicines. We were limited in the amount, since we did not have adequate capital. It took us two hours to reach the place. We stopped the cart in front of the store and I went to pick up the keys from Joachim. He was not there, but George was.[257]

"Good morning Mr. George. Can we have the key to the store? We brought our stuff from Drama." He looked at me and with an accent from Pontus[258] responded sternly:

"I don't want to rent that store. I changed my mind."

"What are you telling us? We hired a cart and bought all this stuff for this place. You simply cannot go back on our agreement."

"No. I will not rent that store."

I became extremely depressed. Why is every nut out to get me? Is my fate to fail on all fronts? I was walking back to the cart when his wife rushes out and grabs my arm.

"Go and talk to Joachim. He is in our field near the river, across the road. He can help you."

I left Lazarus with the cart and walked to the field. I saw Joachim was resting, after plowing the field with his mule. As I walked to him, he decided to restart plowing but made the mistake not to warn the animal with his human voice. A typical "whoa," would warn the mule that he was approaching. Well, this time he did not. A surprised mule can react violently, instinctively for self-defense. The mule was surprised from the noise behind it and responding instinctively to a predator attack, it let go of a powerful kick. I saw him fall flat on the ground. When I saw what happened, I started running to help him. By the time I reached him, he was lifting his head, but not quite sitting up. The mule caught him on the forehead, which was bleeding. I took off my handkerchief and my cigarettes. I tore off a few cigarettes and poured the tobacco on it, then pressed it onto his forehead. I was taught to use tobacco as an antiseptic, and as a means to stop bleeding from my grandfather. Tobacco is one of the readily available blood

---

257 A. Boinodiris, Book 1, p. 185.

258 The people of Pontus speak Greek using a large portion of words and grammar, derived straight from ancient Greek, from the classical period. The rest of the Greeks have a bit of tough time understanding them.

coagulants, namely substances that help bind the platelets together to form a permanent plug (clot) that seals the leak. His cut was too large for the small amount of tobacco I had. I helped him to his feet. He emptied his whole tobacco pouch on my handkerchief, which I helped wrap around his forehead.

"Let's go to my cart Joachim. I have iodine and gauge there. I am going up there to get things ready. Can you make it up there?"

He nodded. I had prepared the medical supplies by the time he arrived. Fortunately, the bleeding stopped. "What are you doing here?" he asked.

"We are waiting here because your father refused to give us the keys."

"Let me handle this."

He started walking to his house, while I followed him. We came right across from his father, sitting on a chair in front of his house. "Father, why didn't you give the keys to the man?"

George saw his son's head with blood all over the handkerchief. He turned to him and talked in Pontian language: "Ne pe do pathes?"[259] This meant: "What happened to you son?"

"The mule kicked me and this man took care of me with the medical supplies he brought from Drama; he brought them to place them in our store, if and only if you give him the keys to open it up."

"Oh God...! How Great You Are and how Great are Your Deeds," said George, crossing himself and quoting from the Bible. He turned to me, giving me the keys.

"I am sorry Anthony. Thank you God for straightening me out."

Nobody was more stunned than I. I never expected such a sudden change on the behavior of a man. I asked his wife if she knew what happened. She shrugged, showing that she was just as surprised. God works in mysterious ways.[260]

We started well, hoping that this event was a sign of good things to come. We added shelving, but could not sustain large quantities of goods. Due to the failure of the economy, most loans failed to be

---

259 "Ne pe do pathes," is derived directly from Ancient Greek, "Ne pedion tion epathes." The Pontic people, being isolated for many years from Roman, Arab and even Turkish influence have maintained many of their ancient attributes, including their language from Ancient Greek times.

260 A. Boinodiris, Book 4, p. 37-38.

paid. Venizelos declared loan payment extensions. The merchants had terminated any new credit and we dealt with small quantities. This forced us to purchase items almost every day. Most of the time, I sent my father, since he could not keep books at the store. I went into Drama about once a week. Among the items we purchased were one large tin of olive oil, kerosene for lamps, some ouzo, and five Oka of different kinds of pasta. We got started with a 200 Drachmas of goods on the donkey and soon we had 1000 Drachmas in capital and goods on the animal.[261] For payment, we receive eggs from women and children, which we sold in Drama, after sorting them by size. This was a different practice, than that used by Joachim and his father, where they placed equal value on all eggs.

The first week of March of 1932, we decided to save our money by regrouping again in the two rooms in PERITHALPSI, living together with my father's family (seven people in a house of less than 30 square meters). Now we used one fire source, one lamp with strict budgeting on food and expenses.[262]

A few times, I supplemented my income by making saddles in exchange for a few loads of wood.

Since I lived at the village, Elisabeth moved again at her mother in law's two-room house with my mother, Irene, Paul, Georgia and baby John. She did not object sleeping there, as long as the men were away at the village.[263]

In April of 1932, the government sent engineers and laborers to build an elementary school at the village. We started bringing bread and preparing food to feed them, turning our store into a small restaurant. Soon, the whole family joined us at the village, preparing the food to feed the workers. In addition to the workers, other government employees (tax collectors) and local teachers started eating at our place, including passing carts with loads of lumber from the mountains. We now had to carry daily lots of bread and food for at least 20 people, including us.[264] They consumed 30 Okas of bread, a pot of beans,

---

261 A. Boinodiris, Book 1, p. 186 and Book 4, p. 37-38.
262 A. Boinodiris, Book 4, p. 34-36.
263 A. Boinodiris, Book 1, p. 186.
264 A. Boinodiris, Book 1, p. 188.

chicken souvlaki, a large tin of feta and a large basket of grapes. By cooking a bit more, our family had to eat too.

Every night I was making the list of items that we needed, so that my father can purchase them the next morning. He had to be back by noon, so that we can feed our clientele. One morning he came back, having purchased everything except bread. He got only 2.5 Okas of bread. Instead, he brought 10 Okas of hand soap.

When the workers saw him, they rushed to the store to eat. We prepared the plates with the beans and we were waiting for the bread. To hurry things up, I ran down the road to get the bread. "Where is the bread father?"

"Stop acting so hungry. I did not get much bread this time, only 2.5 Okas. I brought you soap, which lasts longer."

"Are you nuts? This bread is not enough to feed us. We have 30 people waiting for you to eat. If I tell them that we have no bread, they would beat us up and then eat us. "

I started throwing the soap all over the place. When he saw me, he got out of the cart and started walking away. I threw a few bars at him, catching him on his back and butt. The women saw me and ran to calm me down. They saved the situation. They picked up the soap and pulled the cart and me in. Elisabeth rushed to a neighbor's house and managed to find five large loaves of freshly baked bread from their oven. By sheer luck, a trucker named Euthimius was passing by, coming from Livaderon. He was distributing bread. I was lucky enough to find two sacks of bread in his truck, which I purchased. The women served the customers carefully, so that the bread suffices. Naturally, we had no bread that day for ourselves.

My luck in Taxiarchis improved, but I still had my nutty father to deal with.[265] We bought a second donkey. The contractor Nick Ioanides took over the work to build the road to those villages. The original roads were narrow and full of potholes. He started work with 40 workers, 10 carts with drivers, a supervisor an engineer and his nephews who drove the paving equipment. After drinking coffee, they approach me.

"Can you undertake the job of feeding us and our animals? If you can, we will give you 15,000 Drachmas as down payment."

---

265 A. Boinodiris, Book 1, p. 189.

I started thinking. I had no means of taking care of his animals. No feeding supply for them either. I have a lousy means of getting even bread.

"What we can supply is cigarettes, dry food, feta and fruits. We will do what we can on the rest."

The contractor paid me the 15000 Drachmas. I gave to each worker a booklet with his name on it and kept count of what they purchased. In addition I had a central book, which I recorded all purchases. In this manner, I planned to keep accurate count of purchases by the end of the week. We asked from the merchants to give us information on the contractor. His credit was excellent.

I started instructing my father on the process. I gave him the money and told him to go, sell the donkeys and buy a horse and a cart and the rest to purchase a list of goods to feed the workers with.

He disappeared for several days in Drama. I had to go there and discover that he went and spent 8000 Drachmas on buying lots of cloth, which he stuff ed in a trunk of his house. I barely managed to get back the 7000 Drachmas, which he had not used. I found a cart man and bought the supplies myself. I had to face the workers, who now started complaining and Ioanides, who called us crooks, a characterization, which we rightly deserved. Ioanides cleared with me in the second payment, saying: "I saw your large family and felt sorry for you. However, I cannot trust your father, but that is something that you have to deal with personally. Whatever we ask, he does not care to listen, bringing things that we are not interested in. I cannot afford to deal with you any longer."[266]

They got very upset and slowly I lost their business. They moved to the 18th kilometer from Drama and on the 20th, Stelios Makris set up a shack where he started a similar business. They paid me what they owed and left to do business with him. Makris did well with them. The son of Stelios Makris became a mayor in Drama many years later.[267] This was my father. Because of him, we lost a very good income opportunity during a very critical period, when most people in Drama were without work. In that environment, we could have made 50000-100000 Drachmas, if I had a father that had an inkling of common

266 A. Boinodiris, Book 1, p. 191 and Book 4, p. 39-40.
267 A. Boinodiris, Book 4, p. 40-41.

sense. During that period, people were starving in Drama. My mother Evanthia was upset, but would hold all her bitterness inside her. A few times, when she thought I was not listening, I heard her talk about him to one of her friends.

"I curse the boat that brought him back from Russia. Why didn't it sink? We had a descent family here."

His acts defied logic. Any time the women made food he did not like what they made.

"What is for lunch?"

"Lentils...."

"Lentils again...? Why don't you make some spaghetti?"

The next day, the women prepared spaghetti.

"Spaghetti again...? Why don't you make some lentils?"[268]

In my life, I learned the hard way that certain people are born and become insensitive to all responsibilities. That is what they are. Unfortunately, even though I was getting all indications of my father's behavior, I was naïve enough to continue to believe that he would eventually get to his senses and become the father that I always hoped for. That was my fault and my downfall. My judgment was based more on a dream than on sound evaluation of my father's character. Every time he proved me wrong, I blamed him and God for making him my father, but never myself, who was responsible for trusting him. I realized my mistakes too late, well after my father's death and after repeatedly allowing him to destroy my loved ones and me. If you are taken in by someone for the first time, shame on him; if you are taken in more than once, shame on you. I am ashamed for this, regardless of the fact that the person I am talking about was my own father, because by blindly following my dreams for a better father, I placed my family in danger. Life consists not in holding good cards, but in playing well those cards that you are dealt.

PONTIC LAMENTATION (TAXIARCHIS, 14 AUGUST 1932)

The 15th of August is a very important holiday in the Greek calendar, at the same level as Easter and Christmas. The day is dedicated to the

---

268 These are direct memories from the narration of Elisabeth Boinodiris to the author.

Repose of Virgin Mary. Greeks throughout the country go to summer fairs, or cool springs and they indulge in family picnics.

On August 14 of 1932, two families of Taxiarchis[269] agreed to share a male goat in such a picnic. The families were that of the tax collector Savas Mizamtzis and ours. Savas had his brother Simon, sister Marika, his brother-in-law Abraham, the son of Marika and his partner Demosthenes. We were eight of us. In addition, Marianthi Aslanides, my sister-in-law was there, because she often visited us at Taxiarchis.

The male goat was a good animal, which cost me only 100 Drachmas. We prepared it and took it to a location, which had two faucets, below the main road, being led there by a side road leading to the gulch. The faucets were placed in a green field and trees. There we prepared the skewer and pit, where we roasted the goat. We had a gramophone, playing records with Pontic songs, about the destruction of Asia Minor Greek communities, and their slaughter by the Turks.

Savas, Simon and Marika started crying, singing and dancing like children. This was their time to heal their psychic wounds from their experience of the war through the catharsis of self-expression in singing, dancing and crying.

Savas had served in the military, in the infantry of Pontus. Simon, Marika and a younger brother named Themistocles were small children then, lost in the massacre and ended up at different locations. Their parents were massacred and years later, brothers and sister would find each other after many ordeals, thanks to the efforts of the International Red Cross. The oldest, a soldier would run from city to city, in orphanages and hospitals to locate the lost children of his family. Finally, they would find each other. The fourth brother (Themistocles) was found in a village near Drama, called Kalithea.

At one time they were laughing and dancing, celebrating their reunion. A minute later, the song would change the mood, making them cry over the deaths in their family and their ordeals in the hands of the Turks.[270]

This catharsis lasted all day long. We all rejoiced on our freedom, thanking God for our deliverance from those awful years.

---

269 Taxiarchis is a village, North of Drama, located at 41°14⊠N 24°13⊠E.
270 A. Boinodiris, Book 1, p. 201.

STRUGGLE FOR SURVIVAL (DRAMA, SPRING 1933)

It was time for the construction workers of the Taxiarchis elementary school to leave. We were left alone, with a teacher, a tax collector and any cart man who happened to pass by. In a few days a group of surveyors from Manx Yulen appeared. They were taking measurements of rivers and mountains, to assess dimensions for making canals, to dry the plain of Drama. The group was led by an engineer, named Hamilton. His second in command was a Greek from Constantinople, called Pandelis Sargos. They made their own meals, stayed in tents, but I supplied coffee and drinks.

I slowly built friendly relations with these people.[271] I asked them for a job, since I could leave the women to run the store and my father do the small purchases that we now needed. Some of these people talked to the engineer Sargos, who assigned me as a messenger, supplier and mail carrier. I was to supply the workers with food, mail messages and diagrams,[272] when they were measuring the hilly land and riverbanks of Touloumbari and Livaderon. For transportation, I did no longer have to use a donkey (we now had two), but a horse. I decided to sell one donkey and buy a hefty 4-year old horse, named Doris. I worked with them for six months, until all measurements had been completed. My wages were 2500 Drachmas per month.

Early in 1933, we completed the annual lease of the store and the owner asked us to vacate. We had built up a clientele and he wanted to run the store himself. The villagers did not like it at all. Some of them told him to extend our stay until our children grew up. They told him to focus on his goats and agriculture, since he does not know how to run a store. They reminded each other of the time when the owner had ran the store, which was a total flop. They told us stories of unhealthy and unclean methods of operation. We were encouraged to stay by the villagers. They even offered us rooms to stay until we built a new store, free lumber for the store from the lumberjacks and the police officers of Livaderon supported us in terms of construction permits. Distances

---

271 A. Boinodiris, Book 1, p. 192 and Book 4, p. 41.
272 A. Boinodiris, Book 1, p. 54, 192.

were great, when you have to traverse them with a donkey or a horse. Livaderon was 5 hours from Drama. Taxiarchis was only two hours.

When Joachim heard all this, he started threatening me with violence.

"If you do not leave now for ever, I will bushwhack you, like I have done several Turks in Pontus in the past. I will get one of you, either you, or your father with my shotgun. I have not decided who would get it first".

"Why Joachim? Is that because I didn't let you bleed to death when your mule hit you on the head?"

"I just decided. I owe you my life, so I decided not to shoot you. But to your father I owe nothing."

I was flabbergasted with his mafia-style talk. "Aren't you afraid of God Joachim for your greediness and your threats to kill an old man? Aren't you ashamed to threaten to take away the father of these young children? Is that what the monk at the monastery is preaching you? I know that you were a guerilla fighter at Pontus against the Turks. There, you had the right to defend yourselves against slaughter. We are not Turks and this is not Turkey. It is about time you stop acting like varmints and join civilization. No wonder the Turks slaughtered your people. I now cannot help wondering, why they slaughtered your people and did not hurt us. I believe that the mule hit you so hard, that you completely lost your senses."

As you may guess, my words did not help the situation. As a result, on March 1, 1933 we decided to vacate and not risk a confrontation with the crazy Joachim. We brought all goods back to the store in PERITHALPSI, but we did not open the store, afraid of the prospects of credit-driven customers. In Taxiarchis, we dealt with credit, but the villagers were very conservative and paid on time with bartered goods.

We were forced to sell the horse, for we could not afford its feed.

Around Easter of 1933, cheese merchants had shortage of large tin containers for feta cheese. We started collecting these containers, cleaning them and selling them to those merchants. We collected containers that were used for olive oil and even kerosene. We cleaned those cans using brine and soda. This job occupied us for two months.

One day I went to Monastiraki, a village north of Drama. There was a grocery man, named Jojos who collected about 40 of these cans outside his store. I bid for them.

"What are you going to do with these cans?"

"What should I do with them? My store got congested with them."

"I will give you four Drachmas per can."

"Four Drachmas…? Wow! It is a deal. Get them."

I selected 40 good ones with the intention of selling them at 7.5 Drachmas, after proper cleaning.

I was without an animal, for my father had the donkey on a business in another village. How do I carry 40 empty cans, each capable of holding 25 liters? I tie up 20 of them together in each bundle and took the two bundles, one on each arm. They must have weighed about 50 Okas only, but the biggest problem was the volume.

"Are you some kind of a nut Anthony? How can you carry 40 cans in one shot?"

To prevent the rope from cutting onto my shoulder, I wrapped two sacks around the ropes and on my shoulders. The cans are all over me, looking like a weird, clanking ball, not allowing me to be seen by anyone. This scary ball, with me in the middle walked all the way to Drama and to PERITHALPSI. Whoever saw me wondered what made that ball of cans move.[273]

NEW STORE (VATHILAKOS, SUMMER 1933)

Vathilakos is a village north of Drama. There lived Panagiotis Papadopoulos, who owned a closed café. Besides having the café, he was also a farmer and a lumberjack. With his two mules, he often brought firewood, which he sold to bread ovens. His wife Penelope took care of a few fields of tobacco, tended several cows, and had chickens, like all farmers. The two of them had three small boys. The oldest one was named Takis and was a somewhat sickly boy; Christopher was the middle aged one; George was the youngest of the three.

"Why don't you come and stay in my place? You can run your business from Vathilakos; "he said one day to me.

---

273 A. Boinodiris, Book 1, p. 194.

"Forget it. I was burned with Taxiarchis and that crazy Joachim from Pontus."

"I am not Joachim. You cannot judge all people in the same manner."

Finally, I signed a 42-month contract to rent his store for 300 Drachmas per month. For an additional 100 Drachmas per month we could have an additional room, so that my family could come in the summer. The summer of 1933 found us at Vathilakos, with Elisabeth, Irene, my mother and all our children. Fevronia also came and stayed there for one month, after Irene left to get married in Komotini. Fevronia was then eleven years old. They all enjoyed village life.

It was in 1933, while we were at Vathilakos that my father arranged for my sister Irene to marry Prodromos Topalides. My mother objected, but my father insisted. Prodromos (now about 40) was a lot older from Irene (now 19). In addition, he was proven to be very stingy.[274]

At that same time, Marianthi Aslanides was married to Lazarus Tsavdaridis and went to live in Ptolemais in Western Macedonia. Lazarus was the son of Ignatius Tsavdaridis. In Turkish, "tsavdar" means fig (in Greek "sika," that is why several of their family members translated their names to Sikalides). Part of the family had migrated to Beirut, where they thrived as merchants.[275] One member of the Sikalides clan was the partner of Haji Prodromos, the old man that helped us in Mersina.

Between the villages of Taxiarchis, Vathilakos and Kranista, on the side of the mountain there is a church, near a cold spring, located near a grassy area with a dozen tall birch trees. The sheepherders used this place to rest their herds during the hot days of the summer. After a long grazing, during the cool morning hours, the sheep were taken in that area to rest and the ewes feed the young with their own milk.

The church is dedicated to Prophet Elias.[276] It so happens that the Prophet Elias churches are typically placed on mountaintops. The

274 A. Boinodiris, Book 1, p. 182 and Book 4, p. 41-42.
275 A. Boinodiris, Book 1, p. 195.
276 Prophet Elias or Elijah -Hebrew meaning "My God is Yah"- was a prophet in Israel in the 9th century BCE. He appears in the Hebrew Bible, Talmud, Mishnah, Christian Bible, and the Qur'an. Elijah is introduced in Kings as Elijah "The Tishbite." He gives a warning to Ahab, king of Israel, that there will be years of drought. This catastrophe will come because Ahab and his

villagers of the surrounding areas celebrate Prophet Elias in a fair, following church liturgy done on the day of July 20.

July 20 of 1933 was one such special day. The mayor of Drama, named Pazionis came there with his family and a number of his friends and his staff. The villagers purchased a big male goat for roasting. After slaughtering it by cutting its throat, the goat was skinned carefully, the entrails taken out and cleaned. A villager dug a long, deep trench on the ground, piled up wood and lit a large pyre. We waited until the trench became white from heat and the smoke subsided completely. In the meanwhile, the carcass was marinated with salt, pepper, lemon juice and oregano. Then, the villagers wrapped it up with its own hide. They sewed it up, so that it stayed wrapped. When the trench was ready, the amber were pushed aside and the carcass was placed in the trench, covered completely by hot amber, having only small openings through the hide seams from which vapors could escape. The goat cooked very well and was extremely tasty.

I had the job of setting up the tables and furnishing drinks (ouzo, retsina, beer and soda). The villages of Vathilakos and Taxiarchis were paying my bill. Kranista provided the orchestra, which included

---

queen -Jezebel- stand at the end of a line of kings of Israel who have "done evil in the sight of the Lord." In particular, Ahab and Jezebel had encouraged the worship of Baal and killed the prophets of the Lord. Jezebel threatens to kill Elijah. Elijah flees to Beersheba in Judah, continues alone into the wilderness, and finally sits down under a juniper tree. He falls asleep under the tree; an angel touches him and tells him to wake and eat. When he wakes he finds a bit of bread and a jar of water. Elijah travels, for forty days and forty nights, to Mount Horeb and seeks shelter in a cave. God again speaks to Elijah: "What doest thou here, Elijah?" Up until this time Elijah has only the word of God to guide him, but now he is told to go outside the cave and "stand before the Lord." A terrible wind passes, but God is not in the wind. A great earthquake shakes the mountain, but God is not in the earthquake. Then a fire passes the mountain, but God is not in the fire. Then a "still small voice" comes to Elijah and asks again, "What doest thou here, Elijah?" God then sends him out again, this time to Damascus to anoint Hazael as king of Syria, Jehu as king of Israel, and Elisha as his replacement.

Because of this connection of the Prophet with Mount Horeb, and the mountainous terrain, Prophet Elias has many churches to his name in Greece. In fact, chances are that if you see a church, or a chapel on a mountaintop, it is dedicated to Prophet Elias.

Chariton and John Tsakalides. Everyone brought their own goodies, like salads, fruits, cheeses, etc. Watermelons were floating in the cold water of the cold spring and served after the meal.

The table seating was segregated in men and women, old and young. My father was with the old men of the villages, having a good time. The young men, including me were toasting to the mayor Pazionis, wishing him good health. In that hot day of July, all of us had a good, memorable time, enjoying the greenery, the fresh air, the music and the goat.[277]

ELENA (LONDON, FALL 1933)

"I had enough of those hoodlums and goat thieves in Greece, that call themselves Greeks," said Elena; "I do not want to step a foot in that God forsaken country." Elena Venizelos was a first generation Greek-English, born as Elena Skilitsi in London, England. Her parents were wealthy Greeks, originally from the island of Chios. She had married Eleftherios Venizelos - who was eleven years her senior - on September 15, 1921.

"I understand," said her English girlfriend; "especially after all that you went through." She paused. "Yet, it is the country of your parents; it is Greece. You cannot call all Greeks hoodlums, just because some assassins attacked you and your husband."

On June 6, 1933, during the second attempt on Venizelos' life, Elena was injured in the hand. This was the second assassination attempt on his life in Athens. He was with his second wife Elena in a car, when bullets started flying. People said that his wife fell on him, taking the bullets in her rather fat body. She took the bullet in one arm. She survived her wounds, but she was still recovering from her ordeal.

"A Greek is not someone that lives in that puny little country, that they call Greece," said the irate Elena. "A Greek is someone that follows certain basic moral and cultural tenets that our Greek ancestors left for us to follow. Greece was never a country, but an idea. Every true Greek since the time of Alexander knows that. Greeks always worked in unison with other nations in various ways to improve human conditions, no matter where they are. Greek conscience and logic does not live in Greece. Centuries of Byzantine Greek immigrants made their way into

---

277 A. Boinodiris, Book 1, p. 200-201.

the West and bled into the Ottoman Empire by a brutal and systematic Janissary Turkish system. If the English or any European wants to see a Greek, they should look in the mirror. There is more Greek spirit and blood in most Europeans, than some of those villains in Greece. Why do you think that most of the English words have Greek roots? It is no accident that many of the Western languages of the West have Greek words, especially in sciences. It is because for many centuries millions of Greeks have left and blended into the Western fabric and became your ancestors and your teachers. Turks, like Kemal are keenly aware of this and very afraid of the Greek conscience abroad and within Turkey itself. Most Turks have Greek grandfathers and grandmothers, whether they know it or not. Greek conscience within the Turkish population had to be squashed by Kemal through laws, edicts and brainwashing, some of them imposing blatant alteration of history, in order to build up a Greek-free Turkish identity. Like the Turks, those hoodlums that attacked me and my husband cannot be called Greeks; they do not know how to use logic. They do not know what is good for them, let alone what is good for humanity; and the sad fact is that they will never know it."

Elena was an ambitious Greek-English woman, who had a great deal of property. She married Eleftherios when he was a widower.[278] After being shot, she declared that she had enough of Greek politics and violence. She cursed the Greeks who shot their benefactor and left most of her property to England, instead of Greece.[279]

Ever since 1928, when Venizelos regained power, he worked to stabilize Greece, both internally and in its foreign relations. In 1928

---

278 Elena Venizelos was the second wife of Greek Prime Minister Eleftherios Venizelos.
She married Eleftherios Venizelos - who was eleven years her senior - on September 15, 1921 and shared his life until the day he died in March of 1936. Elena became active in social matters in Greece. In 1933, she established a much-needed neo-natal hospital in Athens. Later, with her donations, a chapel would be built nearby. Also, she built a stadium at Chania, Crete. On June 6, 1933, during the second attempt on Venizelos' life, Elena was injured in the hand. Elena remained a widow until her death at age 84, on September 10, 1959. Late in life she wrote her memoirs "In the shadow of Venizelos".
279 A. Boinodiris, Book 1. P56.

Greece signed a friendship pact with Italy and, a year later, a pact with Yugoslavia. A treaty with Turkey was signed in 1930.

Domestically, however, Venizelos had met with less success. Although he was a convinced supporter of constitutional monarchy, his patriotism compelled him to support the national republic. Thus, both the royalists and the more radical republicans resented him.

A grave financial crisis was precipitated in 1932 by the falling of demand for Greek exports, caused by the world depression of that time. The desperate financial situation was reflected in the diminished prestige of the Venizelos government and his defeat in the 1932 elections.

THE MAYO SAGA (MT. VERNON, NEW YORK, U.S.A, CHRISTMAS, 1933)

Pandel Mayo was furious. He had just received a letter from his sister in Drama, Greece and he banged his fist on top of his kitchen table, tossing the letter across the room. His two-year old baby boy started crying in his crib, frightened from the noise.

His wife Kathryn picked up her son and tried to quiet him. Kathryn knew the story, so she kept quiet. She knew exactly what irked her husband.

Pandel Mayo (previously Pandelis Magioglou) was a large man. He was several inches taller than six feet and weighed about three hundred pounds. After his discharge from the Navy, Pandel became a cook in Astoria, N.Y. There, he met a young first generation Greek-American woman of the Comnenus family. He married Kathryn Comnenus in 1928. The couple opened a diner. They had a son in 1931. They named him John, after Pandelis' father. The family moved to a farm in Mt. Vernon, NY, where they were involved in farming, meat production and distribution.

Pandel told his wife that in 1912, while in the Navy, Pandelis found out that his sister's husband George had deserted her and escaped to Russia. He never liked this womanizer, who seduced and impregnated his sixteen-year old sister. He knew that his father had to force this bum to marry her, according to the code of that time-period, in order to avoid a scandal. After hearing that he abandoned her, he went berserk. He told everyone that he sent a message to George in Odessa, threatening his life if he ever saw him again.

When his sister arrived in 1924 in Greece, he received news of her arrival. He was elated and communicated with her on a regular basis. Then she started sending letters, that she discovered that her husband in Russia is alive. He sent her a stern message, advising her not to take him back. Then, he received a letter from a friend, telling him that George was back with his sister and Pandel hit the ceiling, especially when he found out that his sister had two more children with him. He stopped all communications with her.

His sister kept on writing letters to him. She was saying absolutely nothing of George, but complaining continuously because he stopped writing to her.

"How can she do that to me?" he yelled to Kathryn. "Who do they think they are dealing with? Every time she writes us a letter full of lies, I feel like killing them both. "

"She is a forty-year old woman Pandel," said Kathryn. "She is not a child any more."

"It is totally my sister's fault for even associating with a 'character' like George. She is responsible for my parent's untimely death." Pandel was quite furious. He would probably be ready for murder if he knew that George was a bigamist as well. A man who abandoned his sister's family, to establish another family in another country, only to abandon that as well, and return to her, and add a few more children to his Zorba-style living.

RAFAEL LEMKIN, A VOICE IN THE DESSERT (MADRID, SPAIN, 1933)

Raphael Lemkin[280] looked at his audience and tried to explain how his interest in genocide began:

---

280 Raphael Lemkin (June 24, 1900 – August 28, 1959) was a lawyer of Polish-Jewish descent. Before World War II, Lemkin was interested in the Armenian Genocide and campaigned in the League of Nations to ban what he called "barbarity" and "vandalism". He is best known for his work against genocide, a word he coined in 1943 from the root words genos (Greek for family, tribe or race) and -cide (Latin for killing). He first used the word in print in Axis Rule in Occupied Europe: Laws of Occupation - Analysis of Government - Proposals for Redress (1944).

"I became interested in genocide because of the Armenians; afterwards, when the Armenians got a very rough deal at the Versailles Conference and when the guilty of genocide were not punished, I became curious. I discovered that the Ottoman Turks had organized a terrorist organization, which took justice into its own hands. The trial of Talaat Pasha in 1921 in Berlin is very instructive. A man, named Soghomon Tehlirian, whose mother was killed in the genocide, killed Talaat Pasha. And he told the court that he did it because his mother came in his sleep and haunted him many times. Here, facing the murder of your mother, you would do something about it! So he committed a crime. So, you see, as a lawyer, I thought that a crime should not involve punishment of the victims, but should be punishing the guilty by a court of law."

Lemkin was born Rafael Lemkin in the village of Bezwodne in Imperial Russia, now the Vilkaviskis district of Lithuania. Not much is known of Lemkin's early life. He grew up in a Polish-Jewish family and was one of three children born to Joseph and Bella (Pomerantz) Lemkin. His father was a farmer and his mother a highly intellectual woman who was a painter, linguist, and philosophy student with a large collection of books on literature and history. With his mother as an influence, Lemkin mastered nine languages by the age of 14, including French, Spanish, Hebrew, Yiddish, and Russian.

After graduating from a local trade school in Bialystok he began the study of linguistics at the John Casimir University in Lwow. It was there that Lemkin became interested in the concept of the crime, which later evolved into the idea of genocide, which was based mostly on the experience of Assyrians massacred in Iraq during the 1933 Simele massacre and the Armenian Genocide during World War I (see also Assyrian Genocide and Pontic Greek Genocide). Lemkin then moved on to the University of Heidelberg in Germany to study philosophy, and returned to Lwow to study law in 1926, becoming a prosecutor in Warsaw at graduation.

Ever since 1929, Lemkin was the Public Prosecutor for the district court of Warsaw. In 1930 he was promoted to Deputy Prosecutor in a local court in Brzezany. While Public Prosecutor, Lemkin was also secretary of the Committee on Codification of the Laws of the Polish Republic, which codified the penal codes of Poland, and taught law at Tachkimoni College in Warsaw. Lemkin, working with Duke University law professor Malcolm McDermott, translated the Polish Penal Code of 1932 from Polish to English.[281]

Thus, in 1933 Lemkin was making a presentation to the Legal Council of the League of Nations conference on international criminal law, here in Madrid, for which he prepared an essay on the Crime of Barbarity as a crime against international law. As it was to be proven soon, his voice was of a single man, shouting in the dessert. The Council was so incapable of taking any measures and the Nazis were so keen in devising counter-measures that the world would have to bleed once again. After all, that is the evolutionary process of human learning: through repeated failures.

The League of Nations did little to bring any form of justice on the subject of Armenian, Greek and Syrian genocide by the Turks. As stated in the Council, the estimated deaths caused by the Turks between 1894 and 1922 were assessed as follows: 1.8 Million Armenians, 1.75 Million Greeks, and 100,000 Syrians.

This presentation and the inaction thereof of the League of Nations were noted by the leadership of the rising Nazi Party in Germany, as would soon the world find out.[282]

---

281 McDermott would later provide Lemkin with help in leaving Europe, when the Nazis were after him.
282 "I have given orders to my Death Units to exterminate without mercy or pity, men, women, and children belonging to the Polish speaking race. It is only in this manner we can acquire the vital territory, which we need. **After all, who remembers the extermination of the Armenians?"** - Adolph Hitler, 22 August 1939

Figure 24 Raphael Lemkin: The Heroic Man that Defined the Evils of Human Genocide

LICENSES (NEVROKOPI, 9ᵀᴴ OF MARCH 1934)

Early in 1934, we were searching for venues to sell goods to other villages besides Vathilakos. Drama was out of the question, since the city had no money, people were starving and competition among the starving peddlers was at its peak.

We decided to go to the area of Nevrokopi (the Lower one, since there is an Upper one in Bulgaria). Nevrokopi is a small town 40 kilometers NW of Drama. Our intent was to sell products from other areas of Greece, or to barter them in exchange with products from the villages around Nevrokopi. We had done a good job at Ochiron (Fort) a village 8 kilometers southwest of Nevrokopi in the past, and wanted to have some more successes.

On the evening of Friday, March 9, 1934, the holiday of Forty Martyrs we were traveling with a large cart towards Nevrokopi. The cart driver was Michael Sarantzalis and we were all dressed in winter garb and capable of traveling large distances. The cart was loaded with lots of general store products. In spite of the March timeframe, we had a heavy winter that year and Nevrokopi is known to be the coldest region in Greece.

We were coming to Nevrokopi from south in the dark, heading north near the village of Granites, 8 kilometers south of Nevrokopi, when our horse let us know that we had company. From the forest, on the left side of the road appeared a pack of wolves, surrounding the horse, ready to pounce on it. Michael got hold of the reigns, calming his animal, so that it does not stampede and throw our load and us in a ravine. We (my father and I) started yelling at the wolves, lighting with matches some paper and throwing it on the road. We then unwound some rope we had with us, with some noise-making cans, behind the cart. The wolves were howling, but kept their distance behind the cart, but not abandoning their chase. The horse behaved bravely, proudly pulling a ton of load forward.

The wolves followed us until we reached Ochiron (Fort) a village 3 kilometers off the main road, near Nevrokopi. There, near the church, we dismount and started looking for a shelter. We saw light in one house and started knocking at the door. We found there an old man that was called Demos (for Demosthenes) from Kerasus (Giresun) of Pontus. He opened his house to us, taking the cart inside his yard. We settled the sweaty horse inside the barn gave it food and water and slept in Demo's house. In the morning, Demos bought many things in exchange of beans, lentils, corn and potatoes, namely his crop. The area of Nevrokopi is famous for the tastiest beans and potatoes in Greece. He came along with us, as we started peddling our goods in the village of Ochiron, shouting our wares for everyone to hear. In a few hours, we sold everything we had. As we were wrapping things up, we see a police officer approaching.

"Please show me your license that allows you to practice selling in the Nevrokopi region."

Unfortunately, we had license to sell only in Drama.

"This is not a valid license," said the police officer when we showed it to him. "You need a license for this region."

Demos intervened.

"Can I speak with you young man?" He took him aside, where we could not hear. He was an old man with a great deal of respect in the village.

"It is to our interest to see people like them coming here. These people force our local storeowners to keep their prices down. Otherwise, the locals would scalp us with their high prices, which we will pay out of necessity. These people sell products at least 20% below our scalpers."

"Sorry Mr. Demos. " I just had complaints from the local storeowners. I had to put a stop on this, or they would escalate me to my superiors."

The police officer gave us a warning and asked us not to come again there without a license. Demos explained to us what he heard from the police officer. We realized that we could not sustain license fees in all regions. We managed though to earn 6000 Drachmas that day, splitting it three ways, 3000 to the driver and his horse and 1500 each to my father and me.[283]

KEMAL'S IMPACT ON TURKEY AND GREECE (APRIL, 1934)

Nineteen years had passed since that awful day in 1915, when the fatal landings occurred in Gallipoli. The first ANZAC veterans had now returned to Gallipoli to see where their buddies fell. On them, on behalf of the Turkish nation President Mustafa Kemal read the following message, as he dedicated a monument to the fallen:

"Those heroes who shed their blood and lost their lives... you are now lying in the soil of a friendly country. Therefore rest in peace. There is no difference between the Johnnies and the Mehmets to us when they lie side by side here in this country of ours... You, the mothers who sent their sons from far away countries, wipe away your tears. Your

---

283 A. Boinodiris, Book 1, p.202-203.

sons are now lying in our bosom and are in peace. After having lost their lives on this land, they have become our sons as well."

Kemal looked at the location where he and his troops were dug in on the 25 April 1915, when the Australian and New Zealand (ANZAC) forces were moving inland after landing at Anzac Cove. He was one of the several Turkish officers on the hills, facing the enemy forces. He remembered how his scared troops looked at him, after seeing all those ships disgorge enemy troops at the cove. He knew that fear is contagious and had to be stopped at once. So, he did the unexpected. He shouted to his troops:

"I don't order you to fight; I order you to die. In the time it takes us to die, other troops and commanders can come and take our places."

By nightfall the Anzacs had suffered 2,000 casualties and were fighting to stay on the beach. For the following two weeks the Allies remained on the beaches, losing one third of their force. Kemal, by holding off the Allied forces, earned the rank of Colonel. Now, as a politician he was dedicating a memorial to those that he helped kill.

After Gallipoli, Kemal had accomplished some surprising results since he took power. Since he was the primary person credited for saving Turkey from annihilation by the Greeks, he now had absolute power. After his initial changes, on August 11, 1930, Mustafa Kemal decided to try what the Greeks were trying to do for four hundred years, within the Ottoman Empire, namely a democratic, secular movement. He helped establish a new party, the Liberal Republican Party. But once again the opposition party became too strong, particularly in regard to the role of religion in public life. Finally, seeing the rising fundamentalist threat and being a staunch supporter of Kemal's reforms himself, its leader Ali Fethi Okyar abolished his own party and Mustafa Kemal never succeeded in establishing a long lasting multi-party parliamentary system. He sometimes dealt sternly with the opposition in pursuing his main goal of democratizing and modernizing the country.

There has been criticism of Mustafa Kemal, arguing that he did not promote democracy by dominating the country with his single party rule. In response to such criticisms, his biographer Andrew Mango wrote that: "between the two wars, democracy could not be sustained in many relatively richer and better-educated societies. Kemal's authoritarianism left a reasonable space for free private lives. More could not have been expected in his lifetime." Even though, sometimes he might not be a democrat in his actions, he has always supported the idea of eventually building a democratic state.

Mustafa Kemal also instigated economic policies not just to develop small and large-scale businesses, but also to create social strata that were virtually non-existent during the Ottoman Empire. However, the primary problem faced by the Kemalist state politics was the lag in the development of political institutions and social classes, which would steer such social and economic changes. After World War One, due to the lack of any real potential investors to open private sector factories and develop industrial production, Kemal's activities regarding the economy included the establishment of many state-owned factories throughout the country for agriculture, machinery, and textile industries, many of which grew into successful enterprises and became privatized during the latter half of 20th century.

Mustafa Kemal had a national vision in seeking state controlled economic polices. Kemal wanted to knit the country together, eliminate the foreign control of the economy, and improve communications. In 1930 he renamed Constantinople as Istanbul, a name also derived from Greek etymology.[284] Istanbul, a trading port with international foreign enterprises, was deliberately abandoned and resources were channeled to other, relatively less developed cities, in order to establish a more balanced development throughout the country. For Mustafa Kemal, as for his supporters, tobacco remained wedded to his policy in the pursuit of the economic independence. The second biggest industrial crop was cotton. Cotton planting during this period was promoted to furnish raw material for the new factory settlements in Turkey.

Mustafa Kemal also ordered the establishment of a railway network.[285] The road network was 13,885 km of ruined surface roads, and 4.450 km stabilized roads, and 94 bridges. In 1927 Kemal ordered the integration of road construction goals into development plans.

There was also a need for a truly national banking system that was capable of financing economic activities, managing funds accumulated

---

284 Istanbul is formalized from Stambul, a Turkish paraphrased version of "Is tin Poli," which in Greek means "to the City."
285 3,208 km of railroad was constructed during Kemal's lifetime and 370 km until 1950.

by savings. As a result, Kemal initiated the first Turkish Central bank in 1924. The Ottoman Bank's role during the initial years remained, until 1931, when Kemal established the Central Bank of the Republic of Turkey.

The Great Depression also hit Turkey. The young republic, like the rest of the world, found itself in a deep economic crisis: the country could not finance essential imports; its currency was shunned; and revenue officials seized the meager possessions of peasants who could not pay their taxes. Mustafa Kemal had to face the same problems, which all the countries faced: political upheaval. The establishment of a new party with a different economic perspective was needed. The Liberal Republican Party came out with a liberal program and proposed that state monopolies should be ended, foreign capital should be attracted, and that state investment should be curtailed. Mustafa Kemal supported the point of view that "it is impossible to attract foreign capital for essential development." A form of state capitalism took over. One of Mustafa Kemal's radical left-wing supporters, Yakup Kadri Karaosmanoglu claimed that Mustafa Kemal found a third way between capitalism and socialism in his Marxist journal.

Mustafa Kemal had to deal with the turbulent economic issues with a "high debt" which was known as Ottoman public debt. Turkish private business could not acquire-exchange credits and it was impossible to integrate Turkish economy without a solution. Kemal pursued a treaty signed in 1929 with the Ottoman Debt Council. While paying the Ottoman debt, Kemal's economic policies got recognition by the very first foreign borrowing from a private USA company amounting to 10 million dollars in 1930. This slowly followed with the replacement of previously isolated-economic policies to the integrated economic policies.

Kemal also built the first Turkish Aircraft Association. His famous quote, "the future lies in the skies", is embossed today on the Ankara airport facade. Kemal also supported the development of automobile industry that did not exist before. He did not just want to initiate an industry but an industry that would be a center to its region. The directive of Mustafa Kemal founded Turkish Aeronautical Association, in 1925. Kemal linked the educational reform to the liberation of the nation from the dogma, which he believed was even more important than the Turkish war of independence. He invited John Dewey in the summer of 1924 in order to receive advice that would provide ideas for reforms and recommendations benefiting the Turkish educational system, and to propel it towards a modern educational establishment. In order for citizens to assume roles in public life, it was recognized that they would need at least a basic level of literacy. Mustafa Kemal initiated his reforms on public education to enhance public literacy. Kemal wanted to have compulsory primary education for both girls and boys; since then, this effort has been an ongoing task for the Republic of Turkey. In order to promote social change from traditional to modern ways, Kemal assigned high importance to literacy. Literate citizens used the Ottoman Language written in Arabic script with the Arabic and Persian loan vocabulary, although this group comprised as few as 10% of the population. Dewey notes that roughly three years were necessary to learn to read and write in Arabic script on an elementary level with rather strenuous methods. At the initiative of Kemal, the Language Commission undertook the creation of the new Turkish alphabet as a variant of the Latin alphabet.

The Turkish alphabet was decreed on 24 May 1928, and by 15 December of that year the first of many Turkish newspapers was published with the use of the new alphabet. The fast adoption of the new alphabet was the result of the combined effect of opening the People's Houses throughout the country and the active encouragement of people by Kemal himself, who made many trips to the countryside in order to teach the new alphabet. The literacy reform was also supported by strengthening the private publishing sector with a new Law on Copyrights and congresses for discussing the issues of copyright, public education and scientific publishing.

Kemal also promoted the modern teaching methods in elementary education in which Dewey took a place of honor; as Dewey's "Report and Recommendation" for the Turkish educational system was a paradigmatic recommendation for an educational policy of developing societies moving towards modernity at the time. Besides general education, he was interested in forming a background (skill base) in the country through adult education. His adult education ideas found its way in People's Houses. Turkish women were taught childcare, dressmaking and household management, but also the tools that they could use to become part of general economy. He summarized the adult education as "to equip the new generations at all education levels with knowledge that shall make them efficient and successful in practical and especially economic life."

Public culture aimed that state schools had common curriculum, hence it became known as the "unification of education." The tremendous change realized by the "National Curriculum" was put into force on 3 March 1924. Unification of education law was inclusive; in its treatment of students, organized and operated to be a deliberate model of the civil community. The schools submit their curriculum to what was named as "Ministry of National Education" which was a government agency modeled after other Ministry of Educations. In 1933, Mustafa Kemal ordered the reorganization of the Istanbul University into a modern institution and later established the Ankara University in the capital city to make sure that the principles that are the expressions of a modern society, such as science and enlightenment, are held dear and protected.

Mustafa Kemal constantly discussed with his staff on issues like abolishing the veiling of women and integration of females to social life, and developed conclusions.[286] In November 1915, Mustafa Kemal wrote in his journal that "the social change can come by educating capable mothers who are knowledgeable about life; giving freedom to women; and, by changing men's morals, thoughts, and feelings by leading a common life with a woman."

Kemal with his adopted daughter, the world's first female combat pilot was to improve the status of Turkish women and integrate them thoroughly into the society. He saw secularism as an instrument to achieve this goal. Mustafa Kemal did not consider the gender as a factor in social organization. According to his view, society marched towards its goal with all its women and men together. It was scientifically impossible for him to achieve progress and to become civilized if the gender separation continued as in the Ottoman times. During a meeting in the early days of the newly proclaimed republic, addressing to the women, he declaimed: "Win for us the battle of education and you will do yet more for your country than we have been able to do. It is to

---

286 It is evident from his personal journal that Mustafa Kemal began to develop the concepts of his social revolution very early.

you that I appeal." To the men he said: "If henceforward the women do not share in the social life of the nation, we shall never attain to our full development. We shall remain irremediably backward, incapable of treating on equal terms with the civilizations of the West."

Opening the State Art and Sculpture Museum in Ankara, Mustafa Kemal believed in the supreme importance of culture; which he expressed with the phrase "culture is the foundation of the Turkish Republic." His view of culture included both his own nation's creative legacy and what he saw as the admirable values of global civilization, putting an emphasis on humanism above all. He once described modern Turkey's ideological thrust as "a creation of patriotism blended with a lofty humanist ideal." He emphasized the study of earlier civilizations, foremost of which being the Sumerians, and the Hittites, after whom he established, as well as other Anatolian civilizations such as the Phrygians and Lydians. The pre-Islamic culture of the Turks became the subject of extensive research, and particular emphasis was laid upon the fact that, long before the Seljuk and Ottoman civilizations, the Turks have had a rich culture. Remarkably absent among those civilizations was the most prominent civilization of Anatolia, namely the Greek civilization, whose evidence was omnipresent throughout Asia Minor. Kemal skillfully prohibited any relationship to the Greek civilization, in such a short time after a very bloody war with Greece.

There were many occasions that foreign tourists to Asia Minor heard Turkish guides talk in front of the Ephesus library, the Cappadocian caves, or any other Greek or Byzantine ruin as examples of "Early Turkish Civilization." Those that know a bit of history felt like laughing, but most of them had to control themselves for political reasons. The guides are simply following directives dictated since the time of Kemal. They simply cannot refer to it as "Greek."

Nevertheless, Mustafa Kemal passed a series of laws on dress code beginning from 1923, especially the Hat Law of 1925, which introduced the use of Western style hats instead of the fez. He regarded the fez as a symbol of oriental backwardness and banned it. He encouraged the Turks to wear modern European attire. After most of the relatively better educated civil servants adopted the hat with their own free will, in 1925 Mustafa Kemal wore his "Panama hat" during a public appearance In one of the most conservative towns in Anatolia, to explain that the hat was the headgear of civilized nations.

Even though he personally promoted modern dress on women, he never made specific reference to women's clothing in the law. In the social conditions of the 1920s and 1930s, he believed that women would adapt to the new way with their own will. He was frequently photographed on public business with his wife, who covered her head. He was also frequently photographed on public business with women wearing modern clothes.

Kemal effectively abolished the centuries-old traditions by means of reforms to which much of the population was unaccustomed but nevertheless willing to adopt. Kemal's strict religious reforms met with some opposition, and they continued to generate a considerable degree of social and political tension. But in Mustafa Kemal's world there was no dualism. He enforced his ideas to full extent. According to Mustafa Kemal, a progressive nation also was progressive in understanding its belief system. Mustafa Kemal commissioned the translation of the Koran into Turkish and he had it read in front of the public in 1932.

Notwithstanding the Islamic prohibition against the consumption of alcoholic beverages, he encouraged domestic production of alcohol and established a state-owned spirits industry. He was known to have an appreciation for the national beverage, the "rakı," and enjoyed it in vast quantities.[287] Also, tobacco production, a good that was banned twice during the Ottoman era, was monitored and encouraged by the state and the sector became one of the important suppliers of the USA cigarette industry.

Kemal's principal aim had been to save his people from humiliation and to transform Turkey into a modern, 20th-century nation. He pursued this aim with the total determination of a dictator, but with a political finesse of a patriot. Perhaps his most essential trait was his political realism; it enabled him to carry out his reforms without disastrous adventures and allowed Turkey to live in peace with its neighbors, probably because its neighbors liked what he did in Turkey. Ironically, among the greatest supporters of his actions were the Greeks; the same Greeks that he kicked out of Asia Minor, caused their slaughter

---

287 Kemal died on November 10, 1938, at the age of 57 from cirrhosis of the liver, probably caused by large alcohol consumption.

and whose traces of civilization he tried to erase from Turkey. They saw in his actions a change that they craved for centuries and struggled for many millennia to influence. What the Greeks hoped, and died for, for four centuries, Kemal did in less than two decades.

The Greek civilization that contributed so much to modern Turkey, since the days of Byzantium was now portrayed as a villain. All the contributions, from Gennadius, to Barbarossa, to all the Grand Viziers and millions of Greeks and other nationalities that lived in the Ottoman Empire, gradually trying to implement the Kemal changes were forgotten. Now, after a bloody war with the Greeks, anything Greek became villainous. Even the millions of Turks that know they are descendants of Greek ancestry, decided to turn their backs to their very unpopular heritage for practical reasons.

Yet, most Greeks in Greece and abroad felt some amount of retribution, after seeing the changes Kemal imposed on Turkey. They felt so, regardless of his dictatorial methods and the massacres of Greeks in Smyrna, Pontus and elsewhere; they liked these changes because they brought Turkey closer to a Western civilization and to a more tolerant society, which could work constructively with the rest of Europe. In some way, they felt that their forefather's struggle was not wasted, as long as Kemal's spirit of secular tolerance held.[288]

THE CAFÉ (MAKRIPLAGI, JANUARY, 1935)

In the fall of 1934, we started seeing some activity in tobacco purchasing. The drainage work was also still going on, but very slowly.

It was then that someone called Lazarus from Makriplagi encountered us. He was actually from Asia Minor and had immigrated to America. He was in his fifties and hard to adapt in the hardships of the New World. Therefore, he left America and returned to Greece, relatively broke. He settled in Makriplagi, where he built a café. Being relatively old now, he wanted his son Dimitris to take over the café. His son and his wife refused, since they were doing well in farming, by growing tobacco and tending a herd of goats and sheep. Lazarus asked us if we wanted to rent the café and three hectares of a field, on

---

288 Unfortunately, this was not to be either. Since the death of Kemal, at numerous times Turkey faced trying times that threatened the foundations he laid.

a plateau. We agreed to do that for 300 Drachmas per month. The café had some tables, chairs and a glass showcase.

We decided to plant potatoes on that field. One of the disadvantages of this deal was that the store and field did not have a good access road. A very old road was leading to the village, probably built during the Roman Empire days. It was covered with flat cobblestones that had deep grooves in them from cart use over the millennia. A horse cart could not climb up there, because the stones were too slippery. A weak mule or donkey would fall and be killed with any serious load. Traveling had to be made in broad daylight; otherwise any traveling animal or human had a good chance of slipping and falling off the deep ravine. It needed an expensive, strong mule, if we were to carry any load to or from that place. Therefore, carrying groceries up there was expensive, causing a great deal of damage, when things fell and broke. We lost olive oil, kerosene, vinegar, ouzo and other container goods, down the ravine of that road.

The 1934 ended with loss. The year of 1935 came, finding my father at that store selling, while I am struggling with the transportation of goods. My mother, with three children was at Vathilakos and Elisabeth started working at the tobacco factories. Irene was married at Komotini, as was Marianthi at Ptolemais in Western Macedonia.[289]

NEW REVOLT (DRAMA, MARCH 1935)

In February of 1935, we heard that the Popular Party of Kondylis, who was minister of defense, was planning to bring back the king. On this rumor, propagated by the press of the opposition, a revolt started. Many villagers took to the streets in opposition to the move. The immigrants had their own warlords, a leftover of their fight against the Turks. One of them, Stelios Kosmidis puts on his officer's uniform. Volunteers were mobilized from Evros, of the Turkish border to Thessaloniki; the volunteers waited to see how the Fourth Army Corps located in Drama, Kavala and West Thrace would react. If the Corps would join the revolt, the revolt could win.

I was then with the Democratic Party and for the revolution, joining the Makriplagi delegation that spoke against bringing back the King and supporting the revolt. Venizelos was in Crete; Plastiras was in

---

289 A. Boinodiris, Book 1, p.203-205 and Book 4, p.42-43.

Athens and the naval cruiser Elli was in Kavala. The Democratic Party revolt had as password: "democracy is in danger."

The commander of the third Army in Thessaloniki was Panayiotopoulos,[290] who betrayed the revolt. He first joined the revolt, on the side of the Fourth Army Corps and then switched sides and went with the Second Army Corps in Thessaly, which was on the side of Kondylis. In that coup, the leadership of the 4th Army Corps, located in Drama, Kavala and West Thrace was placed in jail. This Army was supported primarily by recruits and paid only 500 drachmas per month. They faced the well-trained professionals of Kondylis in Strymon River and lost the battle.[291]

Brotherly Greek blood turned the Strymon River red. Those soldiers that escaped did so by throwing away their uniforms and hiding in farmer clothes in the near-by villages. In that cold morning of March 1, 1935, many soldiers were exposed to the elements, cold, sneezing, and running in the fields without clothes. They were running in underwear from house to house, begging people to give them civilian clothes to hide in. People felt sorry for them, giving them whatever clothes they had. Some soldiers were dressed in women's clothes. The fortunate thing was that it was Mardi Grass time and could possibly excuse their outfits. The Kondylis soldiers chased them all over the fields.

Among them, a troop of soldiers from Nea Karvali ends up in my home. To escape capture, I gave them clothes and thus dressed for the Mardi Grass, they left for their houses.

Among the escapees were General Papoulias and Brigadier General Kimisis of Drama. A colonel, Colonel Volanis of the Calvary brigade from Serres was executed by the Royalists, in revenge for the executions of the six military men executed under Pangalos, after the military court found them responsible for the Asia Minor catastrophe. Volanis was the main force behind the building of a football stadium in Drama, to be used by a newly starting team of young refugees, called DOXA (GLORY). General Kamenos, of Kavala escaped to Bulgaria.

---

290 "Panayiotopoulos was a turncoat. First he was on the side of the Democratic Party. Later he sided with Kondilis." A Boinodiris Book 1, p.61.
291 A Boinodiris Book 1, p.61, 205.

Plastiras escaped in a barrel to the port of Marseilles, France. Kyriakos Venizelos, who was a boat captain, took the Venizelos family, consisting of Eleftherios and his son Sophocles to Paris.[292]

Koundouriotis was out, after finishing his term as Prime Minister and Kondylis from the ministry of Defense becomes Prime Minister, with the title of Viceroy, until the King returns.

The work to drain the swamps of Greece, which started under Venizelos, continued during the subsequent Tsaldaris regime during 1935. This regime got the leadership amidst great controversy on the legitimacy of the elections.[293]

ANGER IS SWEET, BUT ITS FRUITS ARE BITTER (DRAMA, MARCH 1935)

Drama was now under scrutiny by the Popular Party. PERITHALPSI was all with the Democratic Party, supporting Venizelos. Ninety per cent of the population of Drama consisted of Asia Minor immigrants, all of them on the side of Venizelos. The streets were now under control of local Macedonian police officers in their baggy pants. Some of these men were proven to have shaky alliances to Greece, since they were the first to change sides and work with the Bulgarians very soon in the occupational years, yet to come.

One of those March days of 1935, I went to Drama with my donkey for provisions. On my way, I see Tzoras (the scum that I talked about before) together with his brother. They were armed with rifles, not knowing how to use them and together with the local Macedonian policemen in their baggy pants were parading on the streets in support of the Popular Party. He saw me and I immediately knew that he was up to no good. I do not know to whom he talked and what he said against me, but at that same day, the police was in my house, in search for

---

292 The pro-royalist tendencies of the government led to an attempted military coup in March 1935, under the leadership of Venizelos and General Nikolaos Plastiras. After the coup's failure, Venizelos left Greece once more. After his departure, trials and executions of prominent Venizelos followers were carried out, and he himself sentenced to death in absentia. The severely weakened Second Hellenic Republic was abolished in October 1935 and George II returned to the throne, following a rigged referendum.
293 A Boinodiris Book 1, p. 61.

weapons, or a hidden soldier.[294] He was in front of the police, ordering them like a general. His harassment continued and I became enraged and for a short time, I wanted to kill him.

"I will get you, you Judas," I yelled at him, as the police officer intervened.

He was after me from village to village, badmouthing me and harassing me. I cooled down, thinking that I could not kill anyone. None has the right to take a life. I only had to get even with this person. Otherwise, my guts would eat me up. I was so enraged, that I could hurt myself if I did nothing. As I was passing his store that same night, I got a bottle of kerosene with which I doused it and set it on fire. After that, I went home and waited for the police. I knew that I must pay for what I did. This I had to do, in spite of the fact that I could have left for Makriplagi. There were no witnesses and I would have been in the clear. The police did not appear, so after an agonizing night I went to the police, where I confessed everything. I told them that my life was turned into hell by Tzoras and was not worth living that way. I must have a change in my life. I pleaded guilty, requesting that the police releases two other people arrested as suspects. It was then that I found out that Tzoras had done worse things to others, and he had threats and attempts on him from them. That prompted police to move against these people first during the night, as they were having fun in a tavern.

The local newspaper of the following day described the event as "Professional Jealousy."

Therefore, I was put in jail. Fortunately, I felt that I was in good company, among a bunch of political prisoners. There were 300 rebel officers, presidents of townships and village councils, newspaper publishers of "Tharos (Boldness)" and "Agon (Struggle)," the Mayor of Drama Stavros Kisagislis, correspondents like Pinatsis, Vezirtzoglou and Michael Karathanos. Among the officers were only two lower rank officers. There were few communists from Florina, Kastoria and Edessa.

---

294 A Boinodiris Book 1, p. 206.

They placed me in the first cell, to wait my trial. We hired a lawyer, old man Simigdalas. He was the father of the dentist Simigdalas and a fair lawyer.[295]

In my trial appeared sergeant Pitsikas, who took my side.

"The man had justification for his act, being continuously harassed by Mr. Tzoras, "he said.

"I had numerous complaints from him about Anthony. Frequently he brought unfounded accusations of stealing weight from his customers. Other times he brought similar accusations that Anthony's products were not pure. He also stopped the man from placing a stand, even though he did the same himself. On the other hand, Anthony never complained about him. He was just not behaving neighborly."

The district attorney Kolias asked Tzoras.

"Mr. Tzoras, can you please describe the accused in terms of his work habits? Is he lazy?"

Tzoras looked down at the floor, shaking his head. I felt that Kolias was also on my side.

"No, that is something I cannot accuse him of. He works very hard to make ends meet."

When it was time, old man Simigdalas defended me as follows:

"Anthony is a family man, trying to feed his family. It does not make sense for him to be driven to the point of putting Tzoras' store on fire, without justification. The whole community is taking Anthony's side, knowing that you Mr. Tzoras are a spiteful person, seeking backstabbing ways to harm your neighbor. Let us examine the accused. He has served in the Greek Army. He has clean civilian and military records. He has not received even a single day of punishment. He is a hard working and useful citizen. On the other hand, you have kept your Russian citizenship to avoid being drafted. You are both the same age, but he has spent two years of his life to serve Greece, a place where you seek protection. By serving for his country, he had to leave his business to his father, a person proven to be incapable of surviving in today's environment. Your honor, I ask that you treat this case with extreme leniency, so that the accused can be given a chance to rejoin the society as the useful citizen he was prior to this event."

---

295 A Boinodiris Book 1, p. 209.

The court issued me a four-year sentence for arson with an immediate right to appeal. The appeal was made the next day to the Appellate Court of Komotini, where I was sent in jail to wait for a decision.

I knew that place. It so happens that when I was soldier, my saddle workshop was right inside the yard of that Court. I had friends and relatives, who recommended I hire a lawyer, named Anastasiades. I did so. The lawyer took my written statement. The assistant district attorney that took the state's side happened to be good friends with Anastasiades.

During the court, Tzoras spoke first with all the witnesses of the prosecution.

Then the witnesses for the defense followed. I was advised by my attorney to disclose the truth, all about how I felt. How Tzoras has been harassing me continuously. I also told them about my move to turn myself in, instead of running away from the law.

"I could escape from the law," I said "but could not escape from the eyes of God. I did a crime in my anger, for which I had to pay. I regret doing what I did, asking that you forgive me for my rash act. "

The judge looked in my records and reduced my sentence to two years in prison. I was then sent to Drama to serve my sentence near my home.[296]

MY JAIL SENTENCE (DRAMA JAIL, MAY 1935– MAY 1937)

I was interned on May 15, 1935. The tiny jail in Drama had about 450 prisoners, from which 310 were political prisoners. Each one of the remaining was a common criminal. There was a jail for men and a separate jail for women, both ran by the same superintendent. The jail for women had separate female guards.

At that time, the country could not afford to feed prisoners. So, every prisoner depended on his family to be fed. The prison budget was very small, consisting of supervision wages and building maintenance. Poor prisoners depended on private donations for their food and clothing. Riots were commonplace from starving inmates, especially

---

296 A Boinodiris Book 1, p. 210.

when private donations ceased to flow in, during hard economic times.

At night, all cells were locked. The guards kept the keys in the guardhouse, where only one guard had night duty. All other guards left to go home for the night. Inside each cell was one can for urination with a lid on it, to be emptied every morning in the sewer.

The minute I entered the jail, I started thinking about going into business and making some money. I hated to wait idle for my family to send me spending money. I was placed in the fourth cell, with all the mild cases of criminals. They were desperate professionals that embezzled money, either as corrupt accountants, forestry agents, public officials and even priests.

One of them was Anthony Tzoraides, who was accused of being a bigamist. He refused to accept his previous marriage, left his wife and did not bother to go through the process of a legal divorce. While he was legally married to a woman elsewhere, he came to Drama, declaring himself as single. He was jailed for two years for falsifying his records.

A leather merchant, named Theoharis Tokatlis was serving four years for hitting his "stubborn" wife with a garden hoe. He was still alive in the late 1970's, residing in the Ionos Dragoumi Street.

While I was in jail in 1935, I discovered that my sister Irene (now Topalides) had a boy, to be named George.[297]

THE CONFESSION

Inside the jail we had a tiny church of St. Eleftherios (the saint of Freedom); a priest came every Sunday, offering confession services to the inmates.

One Sunday the priest came in and I went for my own confession. The priest responded:

"We are not Jews son. You followed the Law of Moses instead of that of Christ. Christ came in this world, not to tear down the Laws of Moses, but to amend these Laws of vengeance. By applying "an eye for an eye and a tooth for a tooth," the world would end up full of blind, toothless people. Christ told us to "turn the other cheek," showing your nemesis that you are of higher morals than he is, forcing him to rethink

---

297 A Boinodiris Book 1, p. 234 and Book 4, p. 51-55.

what he is doing. He may not improve a lot the first, the hundredth, or the millionth time, but you offer him the environment to improve."

After listening to him, I came to my senses. I asked forgiveness and vowed not to seek revenge on anyone, no matter what they did to me.[298]

THE CAFÉ

There was an old man, who was also the jail café owner. His name was John. He was serving five years for killing someone in self-defense. He was rather sick, and at the end of his sentence. He had a café inside the jail and was about to sell all his tools for 1500 Drachmas. I bought his business and became a café owner inside the jail. My rent was 300 Drachmas per month to the jail superintendent. Most of that money was going towards keeping the jail and the prisoners clean. They bought soap, brooms, mops and other items. My first jail superintendent, named Papasavas was a cold person who wanted me to spy on my inmates. I immediately refused. My customers were all the prisoners, the two guards Zisis and George Spanos and the jail superintendent. The guards were simply ex-army soldiers who needed a job.

One of my best customers was a 45-year old doctor from Prosotsani called Taoutis. He was drinking 40 to 50 cups of coffee per day. He is still alive in his 90's, because I saw him in the market last year.[299] Who said that coffee is not good for you?

I was also reading coffee cups for many of my customers, an extra treat, which my customers appreciated. Therefore, my sales climbed up and instead of asking my family to feed me, I managed to collect enough to send money and food home.

EXTORTION

Being successful in jail (or anywhere for that matter) makes you a target to those that have inferiority complex; and in jail, most inmates suffer from inferiority complex. One day, two bullies appeared.

"Nice café you keep."

"I try."

---

298 A Boinodiris Book 1, p. 212.
299 That must be during the late 1970s.

"We want you to treat us both three drinks per day from now on."

"I cannot afford it. I have to pay for these drinks."

"You cannot afford not to, wise guy. Not if you don't want this place to become splinters."

"I cannot afford that either. You are right. Let me think about that. What do you want to drink?"

"Two soda-pops…" I served them immediately.

When they left, I went to the supervisor, asking him to intervene. "I really cannot afford them superintendent."

"Send them away. Do not let them extort anything from you. If they start doing anything, you have my permission to beat them."

"How about legal repercussions…?"

"What repercussions. You are in jail. You will have no problem from me, or the law as long as you do not maim or kill anyone."

The next day, the same bullies appear. I was prepared by taking out two handles from two water cans. . The handles were about 5-7 centimeters in diameter and 40 centimeters in length.

"One coffee, heavy on the sugar please," said the first.

"A tea for me, with sugar and lemon," said the second.

"Your money first," said I.

"Are you serious?" said the first.

"Yes," said I, reaching for the handles under my counter. They smiled and winked at each other. Instantly they rushed to my counter, trying to tear it down, only to each receive a blow from a wooden handle across their shoulders. They backed off and I went after them. To avoid being hit they ran down the stairs, falling one on top of the other. From the whole commotion, the guards run in and grab them both. Upon the superintendent's instructions they were locked into the isolation cell, where the guards beat them some more.

We could all hear the guards saying repeatedly, "that is what we do to a bully;" a phrase, followed by a lashing sound and a painful scream from each one of the bullies.[300]

---

300 A Boinodiris Book 4, p. 56-57.

THE SUPERINTENDENTS AND GUARDS

The village secretary of Potamous, named Papasavas and brother of my first superintendent was convicted of embezzlement of the village funds. He was sentenced to 18 months in jail, serving next to his brother. His brother permitted him to sleep outside the cells, in the superintendent's office. This caused quite a scandal, especially since the numerous political prisoners in jail had a listening ear within the Greek press. The superintendent was forced to transfer his brother to another jail.[301]

This scandal also forced the Department of Justice under Taliadouros to change superintendents, taking out Papasavas. Dimitris Zosopoulos became my new superintendent.

Dimitris had Greek-Albanian background (Arvanitis), a straight, simple person who told you exactly his intentions. Even he had his problems. The family had a six-year old son. His wife, named Helen had tuberculosis. Helen's young sister was taking care of both, Helen and her son. The salary of the superintendent was not adequate to pay for renting a house, so he housed his family in empty cells of the jail for women.

Most of the guards were simple soldiers, mostly Military Policemen, who wanted to work after serving in the army. Among them was George Spanos, who married the only daughter of a local priest and was dipping in the priest's salary. He thought of himself as a big shot, treating all inmates like trash. I had to deal with this guard very carefully.

THE UNKNOWN CONNECTION

One day, the jail superintendent called me to his office. "Do you have a relative at the Appellate Court?"

"No superintendent."

"You seem to have some special supporter there. I have here a letter, addressed to me. It says:

'Mr. Supervisor, I warmly request to take good care of your prisoner, Anthony Boinodiris. He is a victim of a vicious man. Please place him with good company, so that he can return to his family. Respectfully...'

---

301 A Boinodiris Book 1, p. 217.

A signature and the seal of the Appellate Court followed the letter." He stared at me; "are you sure you do not have a relative in Komotini?"

"The only relative I have in Komotini is my uncle Charalambos who is a farmer. I do not know anyone in the Appellate Court."

"Never mind; the government plans to feed the prisoners by making a jail mess hall. We need to provide hot food and half a loaf of bread daily. The café shops will be abolished. How would you like to be a cook?"

He caught me by surprise. He continued.

"I am also trying to see if every day you work as a cook can count as two days in jail. If I can persuade my superiors, it means that your sentence may be completed in less time."

I smiled. "Thank you superintendent; of course, I want the job; thank you very much."

GEORGE ROUMANOS

One of the prisoners, named George Roumanos from Nevrokopi was a lifer by choice. He was in for misdemeanors, but every time he was released, he could not make it outside without getting into trouble again in a short time. As a result, he had been there for many years. He was used to clean the jail, helped the guards and was loaned regularly to do heavy labor work outside the jail, so that he can get some money for his ouzo and cigarettes. He was very well built and quite strong. He gambled avidly, pawning in my shop everything good he had, including watches, coats and other items.

When he won in gambling, he treated everyone. The game he was playing was called "parpouti."

When sober, he was quiet as a lamb, but when he had ouzo, he became drunk and foul mouthed, yelling and swearing against Holy Personages, keeping everybody awake with his loud voice. All prisoners avoided him then like a plague. George was a fanatic Royalist, supporting the Popular Party.

This prisoner was allowed to go outside often, where he managed to get ouzo, with which he was getting drunk. Every time he got drunk, we could not sleep. He raised hell in the prison, cursing God, and every saint and holy personage he could think of. This time he stayed out for quite a long time drinking. The police picked him up and brought him in late at night. We knew that we would not sleep that night.

The remaining nine prisoners of my cell agreed to a plan of mine, which would make him stop this habit. "Watch out. He is very strong," they warned me.

"That is fine," I said. "If you love the God, the same God that he is badmouthing, please stay neutral and out of my way. Now bring me some of those charcoal cans."

I took the handles off the charcoal cans using a hammer and I hid them under my pillow.

When George was led into our cell at midnight, the guards locked him up and left for the night to their homes, leaving the keys to an army sergeant with night duty.

George was very drunk. He immediately started with vulgar language towards Virgin Mary, followed by Christ and Anything Holy that came to his mind. Those that were asleep woke up. I sat on my mattress.

"That's enough vulgarity Mr. Roumanos. Stop, so that we and you can go to sleep."

He turned towards me, yelling louder vulgarities towards my Holy Personages.

I moved so fast, that he had no time to react. In less than half a second, my hand, holding a charcoal can handle was hitting his right arm, soon to be followed by a left arm hit. When I saw him incapacitated, I carefully hit him on the head, softly enough not to break skin but hard enough to put him out. He fell on his mattress and lay there without making any noise until morning. I checked him out; he was asleep. I pulled his legs up, but I left him uncovered. We went to sleep in peace that night.

George woke up the next morning, but went back to sleep. It took him two days to recover from his bruised hands. He found out what happened and started behaving. One guard approached me.

"How did you manage to tame this monster in your cell?"

I was hoping that my cellmates kept their mouths shut.

"I just had enough of the vulgarity he was dishing out on my God."

George stopped his vulgarity. Every time he was going out on a job, I advised him:

"Watch out your drinking and gambling George. If you become vulgar again, I will knock out your legs too."

Ironically, George became a good friend. He was willing to help me in jail and when I left the jail, he helped me in my business in exchange for some pocket money.[302]

From that day on, I was considered the local enforcer of the jail. If someone misbehaved, other prisoners came to me with their complaints, so that I could put them in place. Most of the time, I acted as a mediator. Soon, there were no bullies, or blasphemers in jail. I heard that these episodes were commonplace in all jails. In some jails, some inmates robbed and murdered each other for a few drachmas.

PICKPOCKETS AND BACK-STABBERS

Among the prisoners, we had some excellent pickpockets, with such fast fingers that they could be considered magicians. Their challenge was to frequently lift wallets from the innocent rookie guards. Soon, the guards learned not to enter the area without emptying their pockets outside the jail compounds.[303]

The café was quite busy now. I even had two helpers. One of them was Chris Vrakas, serving sentence for bigamy. He was from Epirus and was married there. He came over to Amygdaleon of Kavala and was married again to the daughter of the local priest. The second was Papaioanou, from Mikropolis of Drama. He was in for black market smuggling of cigarette papers. Cigarettes were a taxed item and untaxed cigarette paper allowed locals, who harvested tobacco to avoid paying taxes while consuming their own crop.[304]

Among the prisoners was a police officer, named Angelos. They called him "paplomatas," or "mattress man;" that is because while serving at Granites, he went inside a hotel there and stole a number of mattresses, which he peddled for profit. Angelos was Peloponnesian.

A few months after I got my café, Angelos requested to have a hearing with the district attorney Kolias. In that meeting, he complained

---

302 A Boinodiris Book 1, p. 215 and Book 4, p. 57-59.
303 A Boinodiris Book 1, p. 213.
304 A Boinodiris Book 1, p. 219.

of a biased behavior from the superintendent towards me, because he allowed me to have the café and offered me to take over the mess hall. The district attorney passed that information to the superintendent Dimitris Zosopoulos.

Dimitris was biased towards me, maybe because Angelos was single and relatively well to do and I was a family man. He also did not like a backstabbing police officer, which continuously complained. Dimitris approached me.

"Anthony. I know from the Department of Justice that in two months there will be no café stores in prison."

"How will the inmates drink coffee?"

"There will be no coffee. According to the Department of Justice, café shops tend to encourage laziness and mischief. They ordered that all café shops be eliminated. The only ones that will make coffee here are the superintendents in their office. The mess hall will offer food, but no coffee."

He saw me thinking about my investment and smiled.

"Don't worry. You will not lose your investment if you keep your mouth shut on the news I gave you. Angelos is making a fuss about being left out by me in doing some business here. Make a good deal with him and sell him the café at a good price. I know that this police officer has 100,000 Drachmas in the bank from extortion and theft. He is a bad cop. We know this, but we have no hard proof, to jail him for that. Make him pay as much as possible to you, and after he pays you come and talk to me."

"Thank you Sir."

I started negotiations with Angelos the next day.

My four-year old son John visited me in jail one day per week, playing in the courtyard with children of other prisoners. Unfortunately, that day he visited me on a no-visitor day, the same day that the District Attorney Kolias visited the jail. I had to hide my four-year old on a roof hideout. John kept quiet, as I instructed him. Kolias typically inspected the facilities and the café. He found everything in order and the café very clean and sanitary.[305]

"I understand that you are taking over the mess hall. Are you going to manage both facilities?"

---

305 A Boinodiris Book 1, p. 213.

"No Sir. I am going to undertake the mess hall, but I am negotiating to relinquish the café shop to Angelos."

He turned towards me and winked smiling. "Good."

I managed to get 3000 Drachmas from Angelos for the café shop.

THE MESS HALL

The decision by the Department of Justice under Taliadouros to organize a mess hall was welcomed by the inmates. The intent was to stop violence by the starving inmates. This expenditure was part of a bigger allocation, addressing shortages in the law-enforcement system. Wages were so small, that an honest police officer could not afford to support a family. A rookie police officer received only 900 Drachmas per month. A graduate of the academy was being paid 1200 Drachmas per month. Therefore, most police officers were corrupt. Some of them were even known to be thieves. The mess hall was for all inmates, guards and even the superintendent's family, who lived inside the jail.

Having no background as a cook, I placed a professional prisoner cook to do the job, while I helped him and learned the trade. The cook's name was Parpenides, an old man from Malakopi of Cappadocia, working as a cook in Constantinople before migrating in Drama. He was in for two months for a misdemeanor, enough time for me to learn how to become a reasonably good cook.

My service as a cook of the jail was one of the most memorable ones. I had to serve food to over 120 prisoners with all sorts of personal problems and weird habits.[306]

When the mess hall opened, I was allowed to shop freely in the market. As I was passing by the jail for women, I stopped by to see my superintendent Zosopoulos, who was eating in the mess hall there.

"I sold my shop Sir. I received 3000 Drachmas. Knowing very well how many expenses you have, I like to donate 2000 Drachmas to alleviate your problems."

I handed him the money. He smiled and took it.

"Thank you Anthony..."

After a pause, he continued.

"I was reading your case papers. I understood immediately that you were a victim of a bad man. Do not worry, because I believe that you

306 A Boinodiris Book 1, p. 218.

will be out soon. I had applied before to make every day you work count for two, but the people in the higher echelons rejected it. Next month I plan to do it again, since we had some changes in the government."

I nodded. The King came back in 1936. Until he returned, Kondylis was the real power, instead of President Tsaldaris. When King George II came, Kondylis came to Piraeus to greet him and give up his role of a Viceroy. When he invited the King to join him in his car, the King refused. Instead, he joined Metaxas, who had very little power then. Kondylis was furious. He is to have said to his group: "I can send him back, as fast as I brought him." However, before he could make another coup he died. The rumor has it that the Royal Family poisoned him and made him "look at dandelions from their roots." The Royal Family always had to face the accusation of his death.

When Kondylis went out of the government, many of his followers had to go also. In 1936, the Royal Family decided to give amnesty to all political prisoners, except the communists. The communists started complaining and pleading for their release, but the King rejected their pleas. The communists in the jail of Drama were about 25 rough men, primarily from Western Macedonia regions, like Kastoria, Florina, Edessa and Kozani.

THE HUNGER STRIKE

When the communists heard that their plea was rejected and they, as a group were isolated from amnesty, they went into hunger strike for a month. The same day, the district attorney appeared in jail: "Anthony. I am ordering you to continue to serve them daily. Hot tea with the daily breakfast, lunch and dinner, regardless of whether they eat it or not."

I was serving them as ordered, but they refused to eat. In one month, the 25 men became like skeletons. They were only drinking water. I had to throw all food in the garbage cans, but saved all bread to send it home to my family. My mother Evanthia, or my mother-in-law Makrina, who visited me often, brought my laundry and took the leftover bread home. Every Sunday, my wife Elisabeth and the now five-year old John visited me. He played with the children of my superintendent and the guard (George Spanos). Many times, I went to the market and from there I veered to the house of Kyriaki Zoumboulides, my sister-in-law. I bought a lot of food (meat, fish, and vegetables) for the jail from Costas Hourmouziades, who had a store on the Alexander the Great Street.

Meanwhile, the communist propaganda was working hard inside and outside the jail. This started to worry the District Attorney. Twenty days passed and the district attorney found out that the communists were not eating their food, and the food was thrown away. The communists also managed to increase their support within the jail through their propaganda. A prisoner's mind can be brainwashed by other prisoners faster than when he is a free man. The District Attorney reported the incidents, waiting for orders.

He came over and looked at their skeleton-like faces:

"I have asked again the Minister of Justice for your pardon. I suggest that you start eating. Anthony has made chicken soup with egg-lemon sauce, which is extremely tasty."

"Forget it Mister. We do not eat until we are treated the same, as any other political prisoner. You can tell the Minister to take his soup and use it as enema."[307]

"Your choice; if you want to go to hell, I am not going to stand in your way."

The 25 men started yelling. Their leader raised his hands and stopped them:

"Mr. Kolias, you think like the Pharisees, who crucified Christ because he spoke the truth. You will go to hell. We will not die, because we are the only true workers and humanity needs us".

The hunger strike lasted a month. After that, they were taken to the hospital and then to Makronisos, a prison island near Attica.[308]

---

307 A Boinodiris Book 1, p. 220.
308 A Boinodiris Book 1, p. 221.

RECOVERY

THE BEGINNING OF RECOVERY (1936-1937)

Ever since 1932, the increasingly strong royalist faction, led by Panagiotis Tsaldaris, and the Venizelos followers struggled for control of the government. A large part of the army, strongly republican, revolted in 1935 against the rising current of royal support. Kondylis, the leader of the rival military faction, quelled the rebellion. Royalist military leaders forced the resignation of Prime Minister Tsaldaris who, although a royalist, had promised to defend the republic. Kondylis then assumed dictatorial powers for the second time and influenced the parliament to vote for a restoration of the monarchy. A plebiscite, organized and directed by the Kondylis government, sustained the vote. The republican constitution of 1927 was set aside, and a revised version of the monarchical constitution framed in 1911 was declared in force. George II was restored to the throne in late 1935.

Venizelos died in Paris in 1936;[309] Tsaldaris resigned in 1936; this increased the social unrest and a growing Communist labor movement marked the political scene, complicated by the deaths of Kondylis, Venizelos, and Tsaldaris during that same period. Disliking

309 Venizelos died in 1936 while staying at the Hotel Ritz, of Paris. A crowd of supporters from the local Greek community in Paris accompanied his body to the railway station prior to its departure for Greece.
The naval destroyer "Kountouriotis" took his body to Chania, avoiding Athens so as not to cause unrest. He was subsequently buried in Akrotiri in Crete with much ceremony.

the Communists and fearing a coup, on 13 April 1936 King George II appointed Metaxas, who was then minister of war, to be interim prime minister; the appointment was confirmed by the Greek parliament. General Metaxas, who led the Free Opinion Party and had the support of the army, took over. By a coup in August, he made himself dictator and proclaimed a state of martial law.

The same year of 1936, the farmers of Drama and the distributors were retooled for planting and distributing new agricultural products other than tobacco. By now, we started eating our own wheat and corn, while in the past we were dependent on American and Canadian grains, paying for it 300-350 drachmas for a 50 Oka sack (64 kilos).

The villagers started planting filberts and chestnuts, adding to their income. The government moved into the sugar production, using beets, so the beet production went up. A new factory was built for that purpose, saving us from having to pay money for foreign sugar. It took some time for people to become wise and start planting wheat, rice, cotton, fruit, olive trees, lemon trees, vegetables and other produce. The people started harvesting forests, making lumber and pulp for paper.[310]

The Metaxas dictatorship imposed rigid press censorship, abolished political parties, cracked down on the labor movement, and countenanced no opposition. Metaxas outlawed communism and set up Nationalist Youth groups, called "Phalangites," similar to the fascist model of that time, instead of Boy Scouts. The Communists in Russia were furious with the news in Greece, regarding the open government prosecution of communists. In revenge, Stalin ordered all Greeks, living around their ports (Georgia, Caucasus, Crimea and especially Odessa) to be exiled deep into Siberia.

From what I heard, Metaxas treated the communists harshly; this was not unlike Stalin, who sent all his opposition, including all Greeks to Siberia. Some reports around us included tortures with forced feeding of castor oil, beating and placed naked on blocks of ice. The more such news came to the simple people, the more these simple people became communist sympathizers. The communist propaganda was working through their martyrdom. The peasants were now comparing communist plight to that of St. George and St. Demetrius. Metaxas

---

310 A Boinodiris Book 4, p. 21-22.

and the King were compared to such Emperors as Diocletian and Caligula.[311]

Metaxas was less a fighting general, than an organizer. This was because he learned how to organize and supply, as part of his training as a Chief of Staff. He was beneficial, in view of the threat of an upcoming War, because he organized the Army and its supply depots and routes. Bomb shelters were built and ammunition was distributed and hidden underground, to evade air raids. Communists, who opposed his regime, were sent to remote island jails. They would stay in jail until the start of World War II. "[312]

Metaxas was not harsh only against the communists. He prosecuted corrupt businesses, especially those that cheated customers by selling unhealthy or diluted products at high prices. Therefore, instead of feeding the communists, I now had to feed new inmates, some of them my ex-colleagues.

From Perithalpsi, the jail received Nikos Nikiforos, the brother-in-law of Costas Tolios for peddling smuggled cigarette papers. Two police officers, both from Epirus were now also inmates; they were convicted for taking a bribe; one of them was a sergeant and the other a police officer in the village of Xiropotamos. I knew them way back from my Vathilakos business.

In January of 1937, the café shops were abolished. When the ex-policeman Angelos found out, he went bonkers. He came to me, requesting his money back.

"I have no money to give you Angelos."

He immediately went to the superintendent and to the district attorney. Kolias told him:

"You came to me begging me to help you take over this business. You took your chances and purchased it. Anyway, why are you bellyaching? Things could be worse. You have 100,000 Drachmas of extortion money in the bank. Use the interest from it to survive."

Angelos lowered his head and slammed the door as he exited the superintendent's office.

---

311 A Boinodiris Book 1, p.221.
312 A Boinodiris Book 1, p.61.

PANAGIOTIS PAPADOPOULOS (DRAMA, MARCH 1937)

While I was in jail, my father was still running the store at Vathilakos. We did reasonably well in Vathilakos from 1933 to 1936, because we did not charge much to the villagers. We got our transport expenses and a small profit out of the general store. Our clients were farmers, cattle, sheep and goat herders, most of them from a local tribe, called Saracatsanei. We filled the house with wool and hides from their animals, which we sold for cash.

In 1936, again, when Panagiotis Papadopoulos saw that our business was doing well, he notified us to leave after three years, so that he can take over.[313] Since he could not break his contract, he took over the additional room, where we had housed our family. I was in jail and could not communicate and reason with him. Consequently, after we vacated it, he wanted the remaining store and back room. He started threatening us to the point that my father decided to leave after 36 months. Again, the villagers were disappointed that we were leaving and started calling Panagiotis a barbarous peasant. We left, not having collected all the debt that the villagers owed us. Panagiotis took over the store, while we went back and operated from our store in PERITHALPSI, in Drama. Every Sunday my father traveled to the winter huts of Saracatsanei near Vathilakos; the huts were located about one kilometer away from the road, 1.5 kilometer before you reach the village, to the left.

I heard the following story from Theodoros Papadopoulos, brother of Panagiotis, a few days after the event happened, while I was shopping for supplies, as required for the jail stores.

When Panagiotis found out that my father was still dealing with the Saracatsanei herders, he decided to set an ambush on him, hurt him and make him abandon his sales route. Before he does it, he goes to his brother Theodoros and his brother-in-law Efthimis who were plowing in a field and asks them for help to beat up my 56-year old father. The two started advising him.

---

313 A. Boinodiris, Book 1, p. 195.

"Panagioti, you better behave and not act like a jealous brat. These people have worked hard. George was the one that brought us food at the fields when we were busy."

"So what...? Are you, or aren't you my family?"

"When it comes to your stupidity and greed, we are not related. These people have families to feed. You have lumber, farming and animals. Now you want no competition for your store. Not only that, but George comes only on Sundays, something that does not affect you that much. "

"If you don't come with me, I will go and beat the daylights out of that old man. I don't want him in my territory and he should know it."

"You are crazy. How can you go to beat up a man that did nothing to you? We are ashamed of you and have nothing to do with your nonsense. Anyway, George does not look like the person that will let you beat him up."

"You will see."

Panagiotis goes and hides behind a bush on the road, waiting to bushwhack my father. He waited for about two hours there, before my father showed up, chanting religious hymns, as he usually did when he traveled.

He had one donkey with him, loaded with cheese and wool. He also had a can on his shoulders, full of eggs, cushioned with wool. Panagiotis attacked with a large stone, about 3 kilos, tossing it against my father. My father ducked and the stone whizzed by his head. He was trying to save the eggs. Panagiotis hurled a second stone. This stone hit him on the buttocks, but fortunately it did not break a bone. My father then threw the can of eggs on the ground and went on the attack, before Panagiotis could go for a third stone. He hits Panagiotis below his left chest with such force that Panagiotis, who was a tall man, buckled in two. He used his fist, but in a method which he picked up in Russia, sinking the knuckles under the ribs of his opponent. My father stared at the buckled heap on the ground.

"Your greedy eyes are starving and they will always starve for more, no matter how many times you set an ambush for me and whatever beating you get." From what he saw, Panagiotis had tough time breathing. "From what it looks like, I do not need to hit you twice, do I?"

He picked up the can with many eggs broken, lifted it on his shoulder and resumed his walk to Drama. It took some time for Panagiotis to get to his feet. When his brother asked him what happened, he told him, blaming his relatives for not joining him in his fight.

That night, George showed us his buttocks, which had a large black bruise. My mother applied mashed raisins and onions on a fresh goatskin, which he had just purchased from the Saracatsanei. We also used a paste, made out of ground linen seeds and yeast. The bruise disappeared very slowly.

On Monday, I waited in front of the inn, where Panagiotis frequented. I saw Panagiotis with Apostolis Papadopoulos. I grabbed him by the collar.

"You are scum, Panagiotis. I am on my way to sue you. My father will be in bed for three months, because of the stone you threw; you will pay for all his expenses for him and his family, or you will end up in jail. "

Panagiotis was filled with fear. He became softer in his attitude.

"Please Anthony. I promise never to harm anyone again. I went to beat him up, but instead he beat me. I had a tough time yesterday reaching my village."

We decided not to press charges after all, in spite of all that he had done to us. We detest courts and lawyers. My family had scrambled eggs with potatoes for a few evenings from the broken eggs my father brought that Sunday. I visited Theodoros Papadopoulos who gave me details of that event several days later.

CHRISTOS FROM FARSALA (DRAMA, 1937)

I was released from jail early in 1937 and began to sell goods in the open market. One day, a one-eyed man arrived from Farsala, Thessaly; his name was Christos. He started watching my operation near the water pump. I heard later that he went to a relative of his, a police officer and managed to get a license for selling goods. The police officer asked him for the location and he responded that he wanted to be next to the water pump. One Monday morning I go with my wares to my shed that was anchored on a steel post next to the pump and see the anchor broken, my shed moved and his new shed placed where mine was. I immediately removed his and placed mine back in place. A few minutes later, he arrived with his cart loaded with merchandise and started yelling and pushing me away.

"What right do you have to remove my stand?"

"I was here first, for over two months."

People gathered. One of them said:

"Stop it. We know Anthony. He was here for quite a long time."

The rest of them joined in supporting me.

"Yes, but does he have a license for this location?" said Christos, showing them the permit with the location on it.

"This place belongs to the city and I was here first with my permit," I said. "I am not moving."

He immediately brought two police officers that checked the situation. One of them looked at him: "Listen mister, the police commissioner probably did not realize that this place was already taken when he gave you this permit. We know this person. He has been here for a long time. What are the people going to say? Should we allow you to toss this person out and take his spot because you are from Thessaly and have the police commissioner as a relative? There are plenty of locations on the other side for you to place your stand. You can gain customers by competing with him in price and quality. "

He moved across from me and started buying better products and selling them below cost. He did that for two months, so that I go out of business. I was selling oranges one per drachma and he sold eight for five drachmas. After some initial trying times, he failed because of his personality. During that Christmas, many people still were coming and buying from me. He was now getting extremely frustrated and started insulting my customers. The more he insulted them, the more of his own customers he lost.

"Look at that idiot over there. Instead of getting eight oranges, he wastes his five drachmas and gets only five ones from that no-good peddler," he was yelling aloud, making obscene gestures with his hands and nose.

One of my customers got very upset. I immediately went and gave him a strong slap in the face. "Stop insulting people," I told him; "we can no longer take your crap."

"I will take you in to the police," he started yelling. "You will lose everything you own."

The customer intervened. "And I will be a witness against you," he said. Several others, that had enough of him came and formed a circle. "So will we," said another of the bystanders.

The customer continued:

"You may be missing an eye fellow, but we are not blind. We see what you sell and why. If you continue with your jealousy, you may lose the only other eye you have."

A few days later, he stopped selling. Instead, he bought a handcart and started carrying products for peddlers.

I decided to normalize my relations with him and upon occasion to give him some business, in spite of his belligerent nature.[314] My approach to life is to eliminate long-term animosities, by disarming people through good deeds.

THE EX-GUARD (DRAMA, SUMMER 1937)

George Spanos, my ex-jail guard was a fellow from Old Greece (that is the name used for the Greek mainland below Thessaly). He came as a young man and was married in Drama, to the sole daughter of a priest. The priest endowed his daughter with a home on the hill, approaching the military hospital to the NE of the city. He had a boy and a girl and he had a job as a guard in the jail. His children were often visiting the jail and played with the children of the inmates. George always looked to the inmates as trashy varmints and his arrogant behavior was passed through and became even more evident through his children.

"Give me that toy this instant," would say the boy, "or I will tell my father. Guess what is going to happen to you and your father if you don't do what I tell you." It is strange how fast children absorb prejudices from their parents.

One day I saw my guard George Spanos in the market, where I was selling dry goods.

"What are you doing here Anthony; are you running around like a mongrel again?"

I looked at him and controlled my anger.

---

314 A. Boinodiris, Book 4, p. 69-71.

"Why George...? Did you miss me? I hope to see you around sometime."

I turned my back at him and he left. The next time that I would see him would be around 1942 and he would not be as arrogant. He would be on the receiving end of life's surprises.[315]

SERGEANT MAJOR BASIL DIMITRIADES (DRAMA, JANUARY 1938)

One wintry Sunday of January 1938, I visited a warehouse across the hotel "New Life." I was preparing my merchandise that I planned to sell in the bazaar on Monday. There, Basil Dimitriades walks in. Basil was an ex-sergeant-major in the army and had two little girls and one lovely boy. He was married to Marika Giorouzoglou from Ambelokipous of Drama. He was wearing a brand new sports coat.

"Anthony. Can you please loan me 100 Drachmas?" I looked at him, as he started taking his coat off. "Don't worry. I am going to leave with you my coat as a pawn item. It is new. I will pay you back."

I handed him 100 Drachmas for his coat, which I could really use, since I did not have a coat.

I see him walk to the hotel across the street. A minute later he walks back bringing with him a scale with its weights.

"Anthony, I will trade 100 Drachmas for this scale and weights."

"Enough Basil; I will not give you the 100 Drachmas."

"Why? You don't think that these items are worth 100 drachmas."

"It is worth a lot more than that, but I am not in the pawn-shop business. I also advise you to keep your tools. Aren't you ashamed? How can you wager all you have on a card game, without consideration to your family? I am ashamed on your behalf. Tomorrow is Monday and you will need your scale in the bazaar, to make a living. How are you going to feed your family?"

He looked at me, and then sat in a chair near by. He started talking to himself in a low voice.

"Here is a man who gives me the right advice. I have all sorts of friends who get me in trouble, but one who can tell me to my face how stupidly I behave, even if it is to his benefit to look the other way."

---

315 A. Boinodiris, Book 1, p. 225 and Book 4, p. 66-67.

Then he got up and faced me. "I want you to become my partner."

I was stunned. "Are you nuts? Who can stand a gambler like you as a partner?"

"I swear on the life of my children, here and now that I will never play cards. I will only play backgammon." He paused. "Let me tell you what I can bring on the table. I have many more connections than you do and I am a better salesman than you and you know it. Think it out."

Indeed, he was right on both counts. If he were not a gambler, he would have been the most successful peddler in the market. After thinking it out, I took a chance and became partner with Basil Dimitriades. This trust paid its dividends. He was a faithful and good partner, until 1940, when Italy declared war against Greece.[316]

I rented a small grocery store around 1937 with him. The store was on a property between the city garden and the St. Barbara ponds of Drama. When the war broke out on October 28 1940, we left the store to our wives and both of us went to the front. "[317] Both, Basil and his wife Marika were from the Cappadocian town of Bor. Basil had three brothers, George, Climes and Nikos.[318]

As mentioned earlier, prior to the depression, I often purchased goods from a Jewish merchant named Abraham Cohen. After going bankrupt during the depression, I owed him 2500 drachmas that I could not repay. I was so ashamed, that every time I saw him I changed direction, so that I would not have to face him as he asked for his money.

One day Abraham happened to bump onto me. He looked at my face, which evidently showed my embarrassment.

"Anthony, my boy," Abraham said smiling. "I know you as an honest person and I hate to lose you as a customer. I realize that you do not come to my store because you feel ashamed for what you owed me five years ago. I want you to forget about the past. Come and shop in my place, anything you want. Credit is available to you. What we went through was a bad storm that went away. "

---

316 A. Boinodiris, Book 1, p. 230-231.
317 A. Boinodiris, Book 1, p. 89.
318 A. Boinodiris, Book 4, p. 71-74.

"Thank you Abraham."

"How is your business?"

"It is better now. I have now a new partner; you know Basil; Basil Dimitriades."

"Oh! No!" said Abraham. "Not him. How did you manage to partner with him? He is a crazy loudmouth of a man who gambles everything he has. I hope that you two don't kill each other."

"Mr. Cohen, he swore to me on his three children that he would not gamble again. I felt sorry for his children and his wife, who begged me to help rehabilitate him."

"I am worried about you Anthony," said Abraham leaving. "Best of luck...."[319]

THE MAFIA FROM PONTUS (MAY, 1938)

One dealer of animals, named Constantine Vamvakidis, together with his partner George Baltoghlou became the local bullies with their activities in the market. These people were issued gun licenses, to protect themselves and their herds because they dealt with horses and other animals.

This legal ownership of guns seems to have gone to their heads as power over others in the form of extortion. Every time they needed to move merchandise, they saved money by "borrowing" our handcarts without asking. They used the carts to carry grain and hay for their animals, in spite of the fact that there were many carriers with handcarts that they would hire. Not only they took our carts, but also they did not return them to their place. We decided therefore to put our cart under lock and chain. One day we find our chain cut and the cart moved and placed inside their stable.

Basil and I went and complained.

"Constantine, this is not a way to behave," said Basil. "You must stop this practice immediately."

Constantine went for the throat.

"Who are you to tell me what I must do? Get out of my face before I flatten you. Do you know who I am?"

I backed off. I was still on probation from my jail sentence and could not afford to get into a fight.

---

319 A. Boinodiris, Book 4, p. 74-75.

We went back and replaced the chain, with a heavier one on the empty handcart while the other was loaded with merchandise. Again, after "borrowing" a heavy sledgehammer from an ironsmith, he broke our heavier chain and again we find our cart near his stable.

These were men from the mountains of Pontus, who managed to survive Turkish occupation and barbarity by being more barbarous than the Turks. They were always carrying weapons, had no respect for laws and found it normal behavior to "borrow" from others, to survive. They were known not to hesitate killing someone that insulted them by calling them thieves even though that is exactly what they were. Not all people of Pontus were like them, but the ones I encountered happened to be from there. Unfortunately, people like them were dispersed throughout Macedonia among all the refugees that came from Asia Minor.

When Constantine was passing in front of our stand, Basil tried to talk to him again.

Constantine immediately started to attack him. Basil turns around and sees a case of orange and lemonade sodas. He grabs the case and breaks several bottles on Constantine's head and hands. He immediately takes off through the restaurant of Mr. Iliades and disappears from the rear door, leaving Constantine with a head and hands full of blood from his cuts. He was taken to the hospital, where they stitched his cuts. I then heard that instead of cooling off, he put his partner to seek vengeance from Basil, armed with his handgun. Scared for Basil's life, I suggested that he leaves for Piraeus, where my cousin Justinian's partner was a friend of his. He stayed there for three months.

Meanwhile, Basil's brother-in-laws tried to talk some sense into Constantine and George.

"Alright guys, suppose you kill Basil. He has a wife and four children. Are you prepared to pay for raising them? Because, that is exactly what you will have to do after we start the lawsuits against you to the District Attorney."

Finally, after several attempts the Pontian mafia members promised not to harm Basil. By then, Greece was preparing for war against Italy and the Pontian mafia had bigger problems to worry about.[320]

---

320 A. Boinodiris, Book 4, p. 75-77.

The story on the mafia from Pontus was not over. They will surface again in the next few years.[321]

HOME BUILDING (DRAMA, JUNE 1938)

After Easter time of 1937, we had collected enough money for Elisabeth and me to dream for a house. By the time we found a lot, we had collected 16,000 Drachmas. We preferred to purchase a lot in the Central Subdivision, west of the high school of Drama. Elisabeth was justifiably distressed, having to raise a family together with her father-in-law's family in a two-room house for seven years. She had enough of expensive rentals and cruel proprietors. She wanted a shack or a tent, which she could call her own.

The lot we found cost 7000 Drachmas; the person that sold me the lot, someone called Basil Takforides was an ironsmith in trade. He had purchased the lot from a landowner, named Costas David, but he changed his mind, after inheriting a lot from his wife. Takforides was a partner of Kyriakos Peloponides, my neighbor-to-be, who also bought a lot next to Takforides. Both, Kyriakos and Basil were ironsmiths from Paphlagonia, a region of Asia Minor between Bithynia and Pontus on the Black Sea. This area produced some of the best ironsmiths of the Ottoman Empire.[322]

I started planting vegetables in my new lot. My mother was coming often to pick fresh onions. I discovered that from May of 1938, we were going to be forced to tear down our stores in Perithalpsi, by city ordinance. Not knowing the laws, I went and bought four truckloads of stones, one truckload of sand, 4000 bricks and about two tons of limestone and placed them on the lot.

I went to Drama's City Hall to get a license for building in my lot. They refused me because the lot was out of city plan. The lot was only 250 square meters and building permits required 750 square meters. I started crying in front of the employee in the city hall.

"I bought this land from someone who told me that I can build a house on it. How am I supposed to know all the rules and regulations you are imposing on us? I have spent my money on the material for

---

321 The Vamvakidis and Baltoghlou saga ends in 1945, during the Greek Civil War with their execution by ELAS. See "Andros Odyssey – The Return."
322 A. Boinodiris, Book 4, p. 61-63.

building the house. What am I supposed to do with all that? I am a poor man and have difficulties making it, even without all these losses that your rules say that I must sustain."

The employee looked at me; then he took me on the side, away from everyone else.

"You are a victim of an unscrupulous land owner, Anthony. He sold it to you by violating laws of sale on city lots. He could only sell this lot to adjacent owners, for the purpose of expansion. I suggest though that you go ahead and build it, but build it on the sly. However, for the name of God do not tell anyone that I told you this. I am a family man and I will lose my job."

I took his advice. I found a good builder near by; he was an old man named Peter, living next to the lot with his granddaughter Katina. He advised me on how to use my shed to build a home. I planned the foundations without using an engineer.[323]

We set up a strong foundation for placing my shed on the new location. We laid there the shed with the help of Jordan Zoumboulides as a temporary structure, which does not need a license. That shed was relatively sturdy and was made out of thick wood. In the entrance, it had an overhang. The add-on section, which caused so much commotion with Tzoras, we moved and placed it behind my father's house, to be used as a kitchen and toilet area.[324]

After setting the skeleton in the foundations of my new lot, Peter went to work silently inside the shed. He raised the foundations to 1.5 meters. He added a new roof, supported by posts and placed new European tiles[325] on the roof. He slowly started laying brick, braced with wood beams. I had to supply him with material at night, so that none could report our activities to the police. Soon, we managed to build one room and one living room. The living room was placed on the overhang, which was initially boarded.

323 A. Boinodiris, Book 4, p. 61-63.
324 A. Boinodiris, Book 4, p. 61-63.
325 European tiles were larger and flat, rather than the curved ones, which were called Eastern.

Figure 25 High School of Drama, Greece, Built in the 1930's Using Immigrant Labor.

EVANTHIA'S DEATH (DRAMA, JULY 1938)

A great event was planned for Drama in July of 1938. King George and John Metaxas were to be present and kick off the Pan-Thracian Athletic Games. A new stadium was built next to the Drama High School and was to be inaugurated. About 200,000 visitors flooded Drama, making resources, from drinks to food very scarce. Many vendors went into the streets, selling food and drinks.

Basil Dimitriades and I were selling soft drinks, near the stadium.

One Friday in July, it was very hot. Ice was scarce and lots of the food was turning bad, even though the aroma of the grease and cumin was enticing. Not only electric refrigerators did not exist, but also iceboxes were scarce. My mother was left alone at the house and craved for some of the sausage that the vendors sold in the streets. She asked the ten-year old Paul to buy her ten such sausages, wrapped in pita bread.

If Elisabeth or I were there, we would have advised her not to eat that stuff. The sausages were bad, soon causing severe intestinal pains. Who knows how that hamburger was contaminated?

Besides food and drink, the flood of 200,000 people in a town of 35,000 people caused hospital shortage. People were dropping like flies, from heat, exhaustion, dehydration and food poisoning.

It so happened that day we had a major additional incident. The crowds were so large and the bleachers so full, that many people were standing, leaning against the supporting walls of the stadium. In one crowd push, one of the walls ruptured and fell on top of people below, injuring a good number of spectators. The single, small hospital of Drama was overwhelmed from the arriving wounded.

By the time my mother made it to the hospital, she was in bad shape. Elisabeth, Paul and Georgia followed her there. The seven-year old Georgia was terrified. She saw her mother, white as a sheet and dragged Elisabeth's skirt, refusing to enter the hospital.

"Let's go home Elisabeth. I am afraid of this place."

"I must see your mother sweetheart. We cannot leave her alone in there." Elisabeth knew that the nursing staff was overwhelmed and without her support, her mother-in-law would be certainly left neglected.

Georgia started bawling at the top of her voice.

"I want to go home."

Elisabeth was forced to take the children home, leave them with a neighbor and rush back to the hospital alone. I joined her later that night, after work with my father. The ten-year old Paul was so drawn out in playing soccer with his friends he did not show any interest on the condition of his mother. Paul was a peculiar child. He cared about nothing except soccer. He played soccer all the time and because of that he needed new shoes every month.

Elisabeth visited Evanthia again on Saturday alone. I worked that day and visited her that night with my father. On Sunday morning Elisabeth, John and I went to see her, only to be stopped by the nurse in front of a steel door railing. I knew the nurse.

"Why don't you let us in and you let everyone else?"

"No, Anthony. I am sorry, but your mother is dying."

My head started spinning. I immediately lurched over the railing. To stop me cold, the nurse immediately revealed that she was lying. "Anthony. You will not find her alive. She died through the night. I am very sorry to see such a woman leave her two young children. "

I was devastated. My blood pressure went up and instantly my nose started bleeding. The doctors took me in and started working on me, trying to stop my bleeding. The whole neighborhood of Perithalpsi and most of Nea Karvali appeared next day in Drama. They took her from the hospital and buried her. I was still in the hospital during her funeral. The doctors refused to discharge me, afraid of further hemorrhage. In the 40-day memorial, we had Makrina Zopoglou from Nea Karvali and Irene (my sister) helping us.

In a few months after that memorial, Makrina Zopoglou, daughter of Basil Zopoglou married Anestis Zoumboulides.

My mother, after all this adventure from Asia Minor to Greece managed to see us get a house and escape from rentals, but did not enjoy our recovery. She died unexpectedly overnight in such a weird act of fate.[326] To her last days, she was extremely frustrated with my crazy father, who paid more attention to his friends than care for his family. As for his infidelity in Russia, and his bigamy, I never heard her say anything about it. Yet, I know somehow that she was hurt.

I always blamed my father for her death at that early age of 49. I told him many times ever since then that it was better if he never came back from Russia. The only benefit we had from him was the lives of my brother Paul and my sister Georgia. Other than that, he was extremely harmful.[327]

THE ORPHANS (DRAMA, AUGUST, 1938)

When my father became a widower, Elisabeth and I had to make a major decision about my brother and sister. It did not take long to decide to take them in our home. My father's callousness rendered him incapable of raising a family. I asked him to pay some amount for the children's support, but he refused. We had no choice. We undertook their support on our own. We brought them home and decided to raise them until they became adults.

326 A. Boinodiris, Book 1, p. 232-233.
327 A. Boinodiris, Book 1, p. 183.

I now had a job and a store with Basil Dimitriades, selling nuts, fruit and a number of other merchandise. Basil got a small lot also and built his own house at Ambelokipous, behind the railroad station of Drama. My father had an animal with which he peddled merchandise in villages. Every Monday he was coming to the store and was helping us for a small salary, so that we can attend and sell merchandize in the weekly Drama bazaar. Together we managed to sell one ton of dried raisins and one ton of dried figs in every Monday's bazaar.[328]

At that time, an opportunity arose to buy another, much bigger lot and close to mine. It was selling for only 5500 Drachmas. I advised my father to get the lot, so that he can be next to us. He refused to listen to me. I went to Kyriaki Zoumboulidou, giving her the tip. That same night, Jordan Zoumboulides met with his brother Anestis, who bought the lot for his family. Anestis and Makrina Zoumboulidou would later build a house there and become our neighbors.

Ever since 1938, my brother and sister stayed with us, being raised with their nephew John as brothers and sister, until they became adults and started working.[329] My father did not help even a little with their expenses. He was investing all his money in copper utensils, which he liked. He was saving his money in a lamp with a stand, with a removable bottom. He would unscrew the bottom and place all his money there.

I went to Komotini in 1938 and found out that the third son of Despina Papadopoulos, named Dimitris Papadopoulos, who was a fanatic communist, went insane. His grandfather Kalinikos was now 95 years old. His grandson shaved his beard and went into the Reverend's private room, which was used as a chapel and grabbed all his icons, which he took to the yard and burned them. Then, he took all his books and burned them too. Communists like him, were the cause for some of the radical actions that Metaxas had to take.

Dimitris had lived in Constantinople. He migrated to the United States and brought over the younger, fourth son Abraham Papadopoulos there, before returning to Greece. Abraham, contrary to his brother was a fanatic right wing man. Abraham married a German woman in the United States and as I heard from my Uncle Pandel Mayo, did

---

328 A. Boinodiris, Book 1, p. 240.
329 They remained in Anthony's custody until 1950.

extremely well in business. He used to have a restaurant on Ellis Island in New York. The family adopted the name Papadopoulos (meaning son of a priest) because of Father Kalinikos.[330]

THE DREAM HOME (DRAMA, SEPTEMBER 1938)

During 1937, in the middle of our home construction, a police officer dropped by.

"Do you know where Marika Karamanina lives?"

"I am sorry; I am new too in the area; I do not know her."

He looked at our dirty clothes.

"What are you doing here? I see you building something in there. Show me your permit."

"Sorry officer; I asked for a permit, but it was refused."

"You and the builder and worker come with me downtown."

Peter, the builder was full of limestone.

"I have to go in and wash," he said.

When the worker heard what the police officer said, he jumped the fence and disappeared behind the house through the tobacco fields. I took a deep breath, prayed to God and approached the officer.

"Listen son. For you to become a police officer you must come from a poor family. I am a victim, rather than a violator. They told me I could build, but I found out otherwise. I spent all my hard-earned money on materials, before I discovered from the city what happened. I plead with you do not prevent me from building, because I have a family with three children and they would be left in the cold." I told him that because at that time, besides my son, we also were now raising my brother and sister. "We simply cannot afford renting a place. If you let it go, I will eternally be in your debt. If you take me in, I will eternally be cursing you."

He looked at me and smiled. "My name is Michael. I have not seen anything, but watch out so that you are not caught. You cannot do what you are doing. First, you brought too much material, all at once. You must bring material, but very little at a time, so that it is not so obvious. I am going to let it go now, but be on your guard. If you are caught, the penalty is 3000 drachmas and jail up to a month for the

330 A. Boinodiris, Book 1, p. 284-285.

builder. After you are done and place your family in, come to the New Life hotel and ask Panagiotis, the café manager about me. After I finish my duty rounds, I will come and see you so that we can inaugurate your new home with a drink or two. "

He left, rotating his baton in his hand. The construction time became very slow and very secret. It lasted through all of 1937 and half of 1938 to be completed. Around June of 1938, the building was completed. At inauguration, the external lumber was torn out, revealing the illegally built structure. The police could stop us from building further, but had no authority of tearing up a brick structure. The external lumber was used to construct an attached shed, used for kitchen. My mother came and congratulated us. We moved in; besides Elisabeth, John and me, we had my sister Georgia and my brother Paul. The house consisted of one bedroom, a small hall and the shack, used as a kitchen and utility room combined. We thought we were in a palace. To anyone reading this now it may be trivial; but for us, and most of the immigrant refugees at that time it was an immense accomplishment.

In September of 1938, I met the police officer that helped me by looking the other way; he was at the hotel New Life. We had some drinks together, but when I offered to pay for them, he refused.

I had to wait until 1941 to repay him. When the Greek government was been disbanded and the Germans rounded up all the policemen, he appeared in front of my home asking for help. I provided him with civilian clothes to return home without being captured. I never felt so good about repaying someone as that day.

While I was working near the hotel New Life selling dried goods, George Roumanos from Nevrokopi came out of jail and sought me out. Having being in jail, I knew the difficulties this man faced, having a background as a drunk, thief and obsessive gambler. I gave him some money and advised him to return to Nevrokopi.

"You must go and work from now on, instead of depending on gambling," I said to him. "You are still young and strong and you should not despair. It is never too late. In Nevrokopi, there are fertile fields and lots of other work. It is not worth it for you to steal and end up rotting in jail. "

"I had been influenced by bad company," he replied. "They dared me to gamble and steal. My family disowned me. "

"I want you to go back to your family and ask their forgiveness," I said. "Go straight to the priest of your church and ask to be forgiven." Then I remembered my favorite author, Victor Hugo in Les Miserables. I told him briefly the story. "Like John Val John of Les Miserables, you can turn to be the best citizen. You are very strong and hard working. "

"Thank you Anthony. All I can give you is my solemn oath that I will try to follow your instructions."

I have not seen him since and do not know what became of him. I hope that he turned things around in his life. Regardless of what happened to him, I helped him because I wanted to help myself. When someone like me has a low morale because of the years I lost in jail, it pays to help others that are less fortunate. Helping George, a person with more serious problems, helped me probably more than him.[331]

---

331 A. Boinodiris, Book 4, p. 60-61.

EPILOGUE

PRELUDE TO WAR (1939-1940) (A. BOINODIRIS, WRITTEN IN 1980)

My explanation for World War II is simple: greed on all sides. After winning World War I, the allies left Germany poor and humiliated. This was a big mistake. They took all the colonies from her and did not help her when the economic crisis hit. It did not take long for the six million Germans out of work to find a crazy man that can promise them a better future. After he organized them, as he wanted, he armed them and got ready to take on the rest of the world. He walked over Austria, after assassinating President Souznik. He requested elections in Alsace and Lorraine in France. To make sure the elections run his way, he invaded the region. After the elections, the region became part of Germany. He now had more resources, but he needed money. He wanted German financiers to dedicate their capital to his cause. The Jewish financiers opposed him, realizing his end goal. He proceeds to persecute them. Their persecution leads to a mass exit of people and funds to the West. His propaganda makes Jews look like criminals. In 1938, he attacks Czechoslovakia, who happened to have 3.5 million German speaking Sudite residents. "[332] As he goes about conquering his German speaking neighbors, he has a co-conspirator, called Mussolini in Italy.

In 1935, Italy attacks Ethiopia. They had colonies in Somalia and Eritrea, which they wanted to expand in competition with other

---

332 A. Boinodiris, Book 1, p. 65.

colonial powers. The Ethiopian King Haile Selasie fought hard to defend his country with old weapons, including spears but could not do anything against tanks, aircraft and poisonous gas warfare. General Patolio becomes Viceroy of Ethiopia.

In 1936 starts the Spanish Civil War. The Leftist president Miacha faces a rebellion from General Franco, supported by Mussolini and Hitler. Spain sees a great deal of destruction, not unlike the destruction, which followed up in Greece after World War II.[333]

In 1938, Mussolini makes a pact with Hitler. Soon, Japan joins the pact. In spite of questions from the West on his intentions, Hitler gets a loan from the West. Stalin, not understanding the purpose of the loan and thinking that it was targeted to help Germany fight Russia, jumps the gun and sends his representative to make his own peace pact with Hitler.

In 1939, Finland and Russia go to war over the peninsula of Karelia. It lasts for eight months and Finland gets help from Germany. Greek immigrants from Russia started coming to Greece. Drama was filled with new refugees, which had to be accommodated.

The same year Hitler attacks Poland, to be united with East Prussia. His reasoning: uniting East Prussia by opening a path through Poland's only Port of Dansig. Of course, the Poles resist and in a few days, tanks, aircraft and a massive invasion overwhelm them. The Polish Army retreats to the East, only to face a new attack from the Russians. The Russians capture many Polish officers. They collect them all in the Catin forest, hands tied up with wire and they shoot them. This was one of the great acts of man's inhumanity to man of the Second World War. Many Poles escape to England to fight with the allies. Poland was split between Germany and Russia. France and England, who had a treaty with Poland, declared war against Germany, in spite of the fact that they were unprepared. The British Army (about 200,000) landed in Belgium. Yet, at that time England and France combined did not have as many planes as Italy and Italy had fewer planes than Germany. Hitler managed to trick the allies. He received a loan to oppose communism from the West, got prepared and hit first the West and then turned and

---

333 A. Boinodiris, Book 1, p. 49.

hit Russia. One beautiful morning on May 10 1940, German troops attack Belgium, Holland and Luxembourg.[334]

That was the time that nations were beefing up their defensive lines. These lines were fortifications based on knowledge from previous wars and monuments to the stupidity of man. France had the Maginot line. Germany had the Siegfried Line. Finland had the Mannerheim line. At that time, Metaxas ordered the construction of a Metaxa line with the Bulgarian frontier. The Germans avoid the Maginot line and in two days Belgium, Holland and Luxembourg are in their hands. Many allied troops are trapped at Dunkirk.

For some reason, Hitler did not attack them fast enough. There are some speculations that Hitler intended to strike a treaty with England against France. Through a heroic move, English ships from small motorboats to battleships were mobilized and saved most of the trapped army. Hitler immediately turned against France. The Germans managed to always be a step ahead of the French. The French army found no reason to be slaughtered and retreated from the Marne River. Soon, Paris surrendered. At that time, Italy declares war against France, requesting Corsica and Tunisia. General Peten signs in Versailles the surrender of France to the Axis powers. France installs the puppet government of Vichy, which is to pay heavy taxation and the French Navy is to be annexed to the German Navy. Most of the French Navy was in Oran, Algeria at that time, waiting any time to be taken over by the Germans. A young French officer called De Gaulle, who refused to obey the surrender terms of France, declared his troops as the seed of the Free French forces. As the Germans sent their people to take over the ships, the British Navy surrounds it and with the help of the Free French forces sinks most of it.

After dealing with France, Hitler turns against England, starting a continuous air bombardment, causing many casualties. Several attempts of invasion failed. If England were not an island, it would have been invaded. At that time, the words of Winston Churchill managed to encourage the beleaguered English. Having failed, Hitler tried to strike a treaty by sending hi emissary to England. Churchill refused. Spain and Portugal stayed neutral during the War. They pleaded with Hitler

---

334 A. Boinodiris, Book 1, p. 69.

not to pressure them for help, for they were already destroyed by their Civil War.

Denmark fell without a fight. After their occupation, Hitler ordered that Jews wear the Star of David on their lapels. The Danes made a decision, in absence of their King who was in exile in England to wear the Star of David also. The Germans had a tough time separating Jews from non-Jews, saving the lives of lots of people.

Sweden stayed neutral. Norway joined the Allies and soon was invaded in a few days. Hitler's troops boarded in merchant ships land overnight in key ports and after neutralizing any resistance a full invasion wipes out all opposition. All members of the Norwegian government, including the King escape to England. Many Norwegians, like others in occupied countries become partisans.

The war at sea began when the British trying to bring in supplies by sea, while the Germans were trying to sink their ships by submarines or by "pocket" battleships. One such battleship, called Graf Spee escaped in the Atlantic and started sinking many ships. It was finally located and cornered in front of Montevideo, Uruguay, in a neutral country's port. Surrounded by more ships, Von Spee was scuttled by its crew, instead of fighting out to the death.

News during those times, primarily from newspapers and newsreels of the cinema was rare and precious. A person had to be careful in discriminating news from propaganda. Radios were almost non-existent and only in the hands of extremely rich people and key government services. I do not know if and who had any radio in Drama. Television was not even known to us until the 1960s.[335]

In the beginning of 1939, the Italian navy attacks Albania and captures its ports after bombardment. Albania's King, Ahmet Zogou escapes to Greece, seeking political asylum. In two days, all Albania is in Italian hands. The Greek army calls all draft-eligible soldiers to rejoin the army for one month's training in new weapons. Metaxas and the King started inspecting the Greek fortifications. Air alert sirens were installed in buildings. Shelters were constructed. Aircraft practiced night attacks, testing antiaircraft batteries. This signaled imminent war.
[336]

---

335 A. Boinodiris, Book 1, p. 71-74.
336 A. Boinodiris, Book 1, p. 236-237.

I received orders to appear in secrecy at certain locations and be retrained in new weapons. My partner, Basil Dimitriades also received similar orders, to organize his platoon. Everything was done secretly, so that the fascists are not aware of our mobilization.[337]

One month after the Italian invasion of Albania, Mussolini started accusing Greece, invading Greek territory from Albania. They provoked continuous border disputes until August 15, 1940. It was on that day that the leaders of the Greek government, including King George and President Metaxas went on a pilgrimage to the island of Tinos, in memory of the celebration of Holy Mary. After they left from the destroyer Elli, a submarine torpedoed and sunk Elli in the port of Tinos.

Even though the government knew that the destroyer was Italian, they kept silent. This did not stop foreign press, like the Russian Press from spilling the beans. After declaring war against France, Italy attacked English Somalia. The English send some help to Ethiopia and a guerilla war started there.

At that time, Egypt was an English colony, controlled by them since the Turks left it in World War I. Syria, Lebanon and the territory of Cilicia was in the French hands after the War. The French evacuated Cilicia and gave it to Turkey in 1922 in support of the Kemal regime. Palestine, Jordan, Arabia and Iraq were under English control. England controlled key locations, like Suez, Gibraltar, Aden and Singapore. Italy was holding Libya and the Dodecanese islands, which they had captured from the Turks in 1911. The Italians and the British started fighting in North Africa, between Libya and Egypt, in a dessert war battlefield that went back and forth.[338]

In the first months of 1940, we, the two partners managed to gather some money, after selling all sorts of nuts and dried fruit. Work was scarce, so Basil was in the café, playing backgammon most of the time. He was not paying much attention to the international events, but his wife Marika was.

One day, Marika, Basil's wife asks me: "Are we going to a war Anthony?"

---

337 A. Boinodiris, Book 4, p. 77.
338 A. Boinodiris, Book 1, p. 75.

"I believe so. The Italians sank our ship in Tinos and they are ready to invade us from Albania. I do not want to keep cash any more. I am about to purchase durable food."

"Anthony, what is going to happen to us? What would happen to my four children if you two go to war?"

"Don't worry Marika. As I am concerned for my household, I am concerned of your household too. You are my extended family. Next week we are going to get supplies for both households. That includes wood, charcoal, flour, tea, soap, sugar, pasta, beans, rice, kerosene and olive oil. "

I loaded the supplies and distributed them to both households. When Basil came home and saw all the supplies lined up in his living room, he was surprised.

"What are all these stuff? "

"I talked to Anthony and he brought all this stuff for our own survival, in case something happens."

"How is it that I do not know anything about this?"

"If you manage to take your head out of your backgammon game, you would. You do not even read newspapers to find out what is going on around you. I am only happy that you have Anthony as your partner and bookkeeper to take care of your family. "

The next day, Basil comes to the shop early and waits for me.

"Good morning sergeant major," I greeted him in a military manner jokingly. He turned abruptly.

"Tell me partner, who told you to purchase for my house all those supplies?" His face seemed angry. He was much bigger in stature than I, and his angry face towered menacingly over me as he walked forward, his nose over my forehead.

I became somewhat concerned. "Why? I thought I was helping you Basil. If you don't want the stuff, I will buy it back from you."

Before I could react, Basil grabs me angrily around my waist and lifts me up, my face, buried in his chest as he turned me around with my feet flying horizontally. Then, to my surprise, I feel a kiss on my head and Basil lets my feet touch the ground.

His face was now smiling warmly.

"I must be a genius to have joined up with a man like you. You are a gem to have thought and acted on your own; you really care about my house, just as much as you care about yours."

"Honestly Basil," I said in a solemn way, trying to recover my composure. "It is about time we clear our books, so that there is absolutely no doubt where our money is spent. I have been trying to get your attention off the backgammon to clear our books for some time now." I tried to bring him down from his burst of excitement.

"You always think like a bookkeeper. Alright, let's do it now."

Sergeant Major Dimitriades was a unique person that I could trust and work with as a partner. If it were not for the war that fell upon us, I would probably have worked with him until my retirement. He was impulsive and was weak at temptations, but he knew how to judge a person. He also knew and managed my shortcomings, as I knew and managed his.

So, all our profits and expenses, which I kept books for, were reviewed and all remaining cash was distributed equally. The store had few items and we kept little cash to run it. We agreed to prepare it so that if tomorrow we were both drafted, our wives could take over. Our partnership also geared for war.

I passed all my earnings to Elisabeth, so that she and the children can use them to survive.

Elisabeth stacked in our home raisins, 120 boxes of 22 kilos each. That year we had a bumper crop of black raisin from Corinth. It sold for 10 Drs per kilo, but we bought it for seven. This food can last a long time; it was nutritious, filling and would be very valuable. When sugar becomes scarce, honey and raisins become very valuable.

At that time, Greece did not produce sugar from beets, as it now does. Sugar was imported from Czechoslovakia, in exchange for tobacco. We had two large meat grinders with which we ground the raisins into a paste to make petmezi and retseli. Both of these products are placed into jars and last for a long time. We also bought a cart full of pumpkins with which retseli was made. Elisabeth started making these products immediately, helped by my neighbor Thanasis Peloponides. This process went on through the war. We filed some barrels with the paste, together with water. We added a type of clay in the barrel, which makes the skins of the raisins go to the bottom. We skim off the grape juice, filter it with cheesecloth in a clean pot and boil the grape juice.

As the Italians started bombing everything they considered a target in Greece, Elisabeth and Thanasis started using fire during daylight hours only, so that their fires would not be seeing by the Italian planes at night. We all braced for this new war, knowing that it could only bring pain and suffering.

APPENDIX

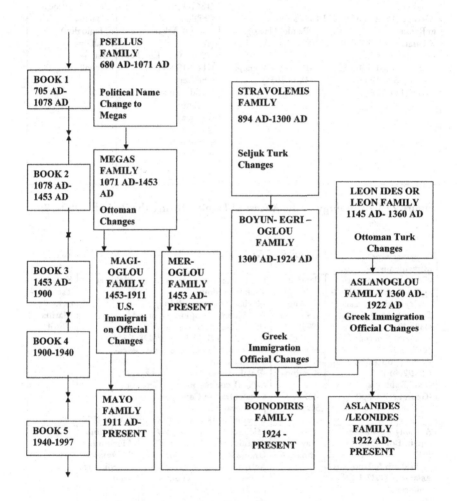

Figure 26 Families from 680AD to Present

Boyun-egri-oglu (Stravolemis-Boinodiris	Magioglou	Aslanoglou	Tsekmezoglou
Paul Boyun-egri-oglu (1849-1926) – potter / Katina Makisoglou (daughter of Anthony Makisoglou) Children: -George (1882-1967?) died in Russia -Charalambos (1890-1953?) --farmer --Katina (1881-1963?) -Orsia (1880-1965?) -Irene (1892-1910)	Haji-John Magioglou (1845-1919) – Director of the Railroads /Makrina Suzanoglou Children: -Pandel Magioglou-Mayo (15 Aug 1893-Oct 1984) -Evanthia Magioglou (1888-1936)	Christos Aslanoglou (1856-1919) Merchant, Church Leader -/1st Wife: Kyriaki (1861-1891) Child: -John Aslanoglou (1875-1926) -/2nd Wife: Elisabeth (1862-1920) Children: -Prodromos -George -Marika -Jordan -Despina -Calliope	Basil Tsekmez-oglou (1851-1920)/ Maria Zopoglou. Children: -Makrina (1880-1953)(Aslanides) -Martha (Magioglou) -Calliope -Stavros -Kyriakos

Figure 27 Chronology of the Ancestral Family during the Period: 1900-1997

Boyun-egri-oglu (Stravolemis-Boinodiris	Magioglou	Aslanoglou			Tsekmez-oglou
-George Boyun- egri-oglou (Bointaris) (1882-1967?) died in Russia/-Evanthia Magioglou (1888-1936) -Anthony Boinodiris (1905-1997) -Irene (Topalidis) (1912-2001) -Paul Bointaris -Georgia (Kasapi)	Pandelis Magioglou (15 Aug 1893- Oct 1984) - Pandel Mayo/ Katina Kominos -John Mayo	John Aslanoglou (Aslanides)/ Makrina Tsekmezoglou -Kyriaki (Zoumboulidou) -Michael Aslanoglou – Aslanides -Elisabeth (Aslanoglou -Aslanides-Boinodiris) (1912-10 May, 1986) -Marianthi (Aslanoglou-Aslanides-Tsavdarides) -Basil Aslanoglou-Leonides (WW II correspondent, German Concentration Camp survivor, photographer.) -Fevronia (Aslanides-Rousakis), born 1922			Kyriakos Tsekmez-oglou/ Martha -Basil -Basiliki
Anthony Boyun- egri-oglou -Boinodiris (1905-1997) /Elisabeth Aslanoglou -Aslanides (1912-1986) Children: -John -Stavros	-John Mayo/ Christina	Michael Aslanides/ Urania/ Katina -John -Charalambos -Christos -Michael	Lazarus/ Marianthi Tsavdarides -Elisabeth -Thomas	Aristodimos / Fevronia Rousakis -Theoklitos -Jordan	

Figure 28 Chronology of the Ancestral Family during the Period: 1900-1997 (cont.)

REFERENCES

1. **"Ten Notebooks,"** by Anthony Boinodiris, Drama, Greece, 1975-1995 (Greek);

2. "U.S. Merchant Marine, U.S. Maritime Service, Army Transport Service, Military Sea Transportation Service, and Military Sea Lift Command; **"www.usmm.org**

3. "Reducing Seasonality in Dairy Production," by Richard N. Weldon, Andrew A. Washington, and Richard L. Kilmer, Choices, The Magazine of Food, Farm and Resource Issues, 4th Quarter, 2003.

4. "Salonica, City of Ghosts, Christians, Muslims and Jews – 1430-1950," by Mark Mazower, Vintage Books, New York, 2006.

5. "The Mechanism of Catastrophe," by Speros Vryonis, Jr., GreekWorks.com, New York, 2005

6. Dominik J. Schaller and Jurgen Zimmerer: Raphael Lemkin: the "Founder of the United Nation's Genocide Convention" as a historian of mass violence, Journal of Genocide Research (2005), 7(4), December, 447–452

7. Raphael Lemkin and the Invention of 'Genocide', James J. Martin, The Journal of Historical Review, Spring 1981 (Vol. 2, No. 1), pages 19-34.

8. "Land of Exodus and Beauty," A documentary DVD by Bahar Çınarlı on the personal stories of the 1923 Population Exchange between Turkey and Greece, baharimajproductions@gmail.com

INDEX

S

Saracen xxii
Sargos 201, 202, 234
Schinias xv
Selefkia 10, 21, 72, 73, 74, 75, 126,
    127, 134, 144, 185
Seljuk xxiv
Seljuk Turks xxiv
Serb 2, 59
Serbia 46, 57, 58, 60, 61, 74, 79, 104,
    113, 201
Serres 59, 93, 103, 135, 202, 257
Shenyang 10
Skilitsi 239
Smyrna 10, 21, 106, 109, 113, 115,
    116, 119, 121, 124, 127, 129,
    131, 134, 136, 137, 138, 139,
    140, 142, 143, 148, 149, 151,
    178, 183, 195, 205, 207, 211,
    255
Stefan Dousan 2
St. Elias 237
St. Gregory 10, 20, 73, 90, 100, 174
St. Petersburg 10, 189
Syria xxii

T

Talaat Pasha 80, 81, 87, 243
Tamerland xxv
Tarsus 10, 160
Taurus Mountains 39, 74, 75
Taxiarchis 225, 226, 230, 232, 233,
    234, 235, 237, 238
Tenedos 56, 116
Theophanes xv
Thessaloniki 2, 29, 30, 46, 55, 58, 59,
    60, 61, 62, 78, 104, 108, 113,
    118, 129, 165, 166, 167, 168,
    169, 175, 176, 177, 202, 256,
    257

Treaty of Alexandrpol 56
Treaty of Bucharest 61
Treaty of Lausanne 143, 146, 147, 151,
    176
Treaty of Portsmouth 10, 117
Treaty of San Stefano 4, 28
Tselembi 3
Tsimiskis xxii
Tsolakoglou 6, 7, 8, 9, 10, 11, 12, 22,
    37, 54, 63

U

United States xiii

V

Varosi 3
Vathilakos 236, 237, 238, 245, 256,
    275, 276
Venetian xiii, xiv, xxiv, xxv
Venizelos 56, 57, 60, 61, 62, 63, 104,
    105, 111, 112, 113, 114, 116,
    118, 119, 120, 121, 124, 127,
    132, 146, 147, 153, 154, 163,
    164, 166, 169, 171, 176, 178,
    179, 192, 200, 201, 202, 221,
    223, 229, 239, 240, 241, 256,
    258, 273
Vladivostok 117

W

War of the Stray Dog 177
Warsaw 243
Wright xvi, xix

Z

Zoful 77, 89